Choosing
& Using
Hand Tools *

Choosing & Using Hand Tools

Andy Rae

LARK BOOKS
A Division of Sterling Publishing Co., Inc.
New York

Art Director: **KATHLEEN HOLMES**
Cover Design: **BARBARA ZARETSKY**
Lead Photography: **EVAN BRACKEN**
How-to Photography: **ANDY RAE & SIMON CRONLEY**
Illustrations: **ORRIN LUNDGREN**
Assistant Art Director: **HANNES CHAREN**
Assistant Editor: **VERONIKA ALICE GUNTER**
Editorial Assistance: **RAIN NEWCOMB**
Art Intern: **SHANNON YOKELEY**
Proofreading: **DIANE WIENER**

Library of Congress Cataloging-in-Publication Data
Rae, Andy
    Choosing & using hand tools / by Andy Rae
      p. cm.
    ISBN 1-57990-294-4 (pbk.)
    1. Woodworking tools. I. Title: Choosing and using hand tools. II. Title.
  TT186.R34 2002
  684'.082—dc21   2001038724

10 9 8 7 6 5 4 3 2 1

First Edition

Published by Lark Books, a division of Sterling Publishing Co., Inc.
387 Park Avenue South, New York, N.Y. 10016

© 2002, Lark Books

Distributed in Canada by Sterling Publishing, c/o Canadian Manda Group,
One Atlantic Ave., Suite 105, Toronto, Ontario, Canada M6K 3E7

Distributed in the U.K. by: Guild of Master Craftsman Publications Ltd., Castle
Place, 166 High Street, Lewes, East Sussex. England BN7 1XU Tel: (+ 44) 1273
477374 Fax: (+ 44) 1273 478606 Email: pubs@thegmcgroup.com Web:
www.gmcpublications.com

Distributed in Australia by Capricorn Link (Australia) Pty Ltd., P.O. Box 704,
Windsor, NSW 2756 Australia

If you have questions or comments about this book, please contact:
Lark Books
67 Broadway
Asheville, NC 28801
(828) 236-9730

Printed in Hong Kong

ISBN 1-57990-294-4

Acknowledgments

Writing a comprehensive book on woodworking hand tools and their use isn't a job for the lone woodworker. It's a collaborative event.

First, my appreciation to the talented art and editorial staff at Lark Books—from publishers to proofreaders—for their expert help and support. The drawings, executed by illustrator Orrin Lundgren, are clear, concise, and show the tricky stuff. Thanks, Orrin.

The numerous photos in this book tell the real story. For photographic insights and impromptu lessons, I credit my original shutterbug mentor, John Hamel, who knows the fine art of shooting swift but sure. The how-to photos I shot for this book are in large part thanks to his example. For style and grace, many thanks to Evan Bracken, who took the beautiful lead photos that pepper the chapters. And for unexpected photography while visiting the States, praise goes to my British school chum and studio photographer, Simon Cronley. Ta, mate.

I would be remiss not to recognize some of my many woodworking pals who helped in large and small ways to shape this book. The wisdom gained from this talented pool of hand-tool enthusiasts, specialists, and teachers is boundless. Special mention goes to woodworkers Michael Callihan, Patrick Edwards, Yeung Chan, Paul Anthony, Frank Klausz, Mario Rodriguez, Simon Watts, Toshio Odate, Steve Metz, Drew Langsner, Jim Krenov, Larry Williams, Ellis Walentine, Pat Curci, and Graham Blackburn. Equally important are the tool manufacturers and suppliers that allow us to pursue the craft, not only by selling us their tools, but by backing up their sales with their own curiously infectious love of tools. Thanks to Leonard Lee, President, and Wally Wilson of Lee Valley Tools, Fred Damsen of The Japan Woodworker, Tom Lie-Nielsen of Lie-Nielsen Toolworks, Mark Wirthlin of Woodcraft, Zack Ethridge of Highland Hardware, and Osamu Hiroyama of Hida Tool. These guys really know their stuff.

Last, my deep gratitude to Lee, Zy, and Shade for their complete support—if not their total understanding—for my passion to work wood. Those late nights in the shop are for ya'll.

Andy Rae
Asheville, NC

Contents

Introduction

Flip through any woodworking tool catalog and you'll come across a dizzying array of hand tools. There are thousands to choose from. Seeing all those exquisite tools—and their lofty price tags—can be delightful, but mystifying. Which tools do you really need? Of those, which ones are good, and which are better? And how do you use them with great results?

This book answers those questions, and more. The good news is that you need only a relatively small selection of hand tools to work wood, especially if you're a beginner. When I was just starting out, my tools were limited, but they sufficed for making furniture—and lots of it. Looking back, if I had to pick an essential hand-tool kit for the beginner, it would consist of fewer than 50 tools all told. Chances are you already own some. (Hint: my "survival kit" includes a pair of safety glasses.)

Of course, you'll need more hand tools as your woodworking repertoire expands. After more than two decades of working the craft, I now own thousands of hand tools. This overgrown collection is the result of a lifelong passion for woodworking, combined with a somewhat uncontrollable knack for gathering tools simply because I fall in love with them.

First, let's get something straight. While I have a deep affinity for hand tools, I'm no purist. If a machine can do it better, I'm quick to plug it in. Nevertheless, I've found in many instances that hand tools—old, antique, or new—are more efficient, quicker, and offer better results than power tools. And hand tools often work in tandem with power tools to get a job done quickly, efficiently, and without fuss. I also favor hand tools for their beauty and feel, and their overall quietness. The tools you'll find in this book are here because they get used on a daily basis in my shop and in the shops of serious woodworkers everywhere. That's why I've written this book. Consider it a guide to outfitting your basic collection, a collection that's sure to grow (sometimes alarmingly) as mine has over these past 20-plus years.

Another goal of the book is to tell you *where and how* to use the tools you'll see in the following pages. There's even a section on buying new and used tools. Some tools you can easily make yourself, as I'll show. Just as important, you'll also learn how to tune and maintain your tools, and how to keep them sharp. And because hand tools require skill to master, you'll find detailed explanations, including photographs and drawings, to help you work with these tools successfully.

After that, it's up to you. Just remember that hand tool skills are not born overnight: It takes practice—and more practice—with each tool. But having the right tools can make the journey fun rather than frustrating.

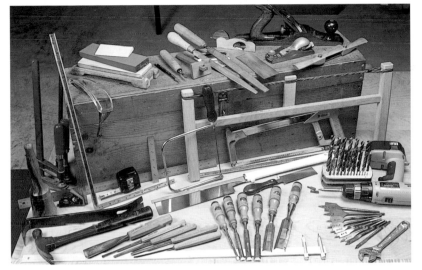

Survival kit. The author's essential hand tools are safety glasses; medium and fine benchstones; slipstone; quick clamps; mechanical pencil; marking knife; tape measure; 6-inch and 24-inch rules; marking gauge; trammel heads and stick; 6-inch combination square; 20-inch framing square; claw hammer; wood mallet; pry bar; cordless drill with assorted driver bits; set of twist bits and spade bits; adjustable wrench; patternmaker's rasp; large mill file; card scraper; set of bevel-edge chisels; set of carving gouges; flat-bottom spokeshave; low-angle block plane; jack plane; small rabbet plane; Japanese backsaw; flush-cut saw; coping saw; bowsaw; and a metal-cutting hacksaw (you will cut metal sometime).

So go ahead, dig in and read the book. You'll find tools grouped by the tasks they perform, from clamping and layout work to striking, pulling, and drilling chores, as well as scraping tools and cutting tools, such as chisels, planes, and saws. You can read methodically page-by-page, or, if you're like me, thumb through the photos of stuff that looks interesting. Either way, you'll find a complete list of hand tools to better your woodworking projects. What you *won't* find are tools I judge spurious at best, and downright silly at worst. This book sorts out the junk from the jewels.

A word about safety. Hand tools, with their quiet simplicity, can lull you into a false sense of security. Yet some of the worst accidents I've seen have come from improper use of hand tools—not power machinery.

I count myself an example. Years ago, while cutting dovetails, my saw slipped mid-stroke and caught two fingers. I was lucky the damage wasn't severe. Even luckier, I knew exactly why the accident happened. It was the combination of a dull saw, which encouraged me to push too hard, and a rushed attitude. The lesson? Keep your tools sharp—*razor sharp*. A sharp tool is safer because it affords greater control. Also, learn to work at the pace your tools demand—not the other way around. A sharp attitude will ensure years of productive, enjoyable, and ultimately safe woodworking.

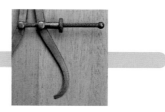

Acquiring Tools...and Taking Care of Them

Every tool collection I've ever come across is a work in progress. This is good news for the beginning woodworker, since you'll have a lifetime to acquire and look after your tools. Buying tools over time results in greater satisfaction than buying them all at once, since you'll get the tools you really need as your woodworking skills expand. And knowing what to look for when buying tools is key to successful woodworking. This chapter is aimed at steering you in the right direction.

Once you start to amass a decent collection of hand tools, you'll want to think about storing your gear in an efficient and organized manner. There are many options shown in the pages ahead. Thoughtful tool care also involves keeping your tools clean and well sharpened, ready to use.

Which are better—old tools or new? Should you choose an old tool made at the turn of the century, or a brand-new tool manufactured using modern machinery, with nary a hint of rust? Ultimately, the answer is one of personal preference. A new tool is guaranteed to include all its working parts, and will need minimal tune-up to get into working condition. (See Tool Maintenance, page 22.) Older tools may need more work, but often consist of beefier castings, thicker parts, and solid handles made from select woods such as hickory, oak, walnut, and rosewood.

And many older tools in good condition have an undeniable visual attraction. Both new and old tools can perform identically. But an old tool has a certain vintage appeal, like an old car that's been garage-kept and cared for over the years. (See photo, below.) Another way to look at the old-versus-new debate is to invest in the future. Go ahead and buy a new tool. With care, your shiny new tool will one day become an old favorite.

Buying New and Used Tools

Buying hand tools demands a huge investment of your time and your money, and because of this you'll want to buy the right tools. My advice is to invest in the highest-quality tools your budget will allow, and to buy them as you need them. This way, you'll be acquiring tools as your proficiency increases, and you can make more informed decisions about which tools you really need and when you really need them.

So how do you know which tools to buy? And where should you look? To answer these questions, we'll need to examine the issue of new versus old tools. You can pick up a shiny, brand-new tool at a hardware store or through a woodworking catalog. Hopefully, some of your tools will come handed down through friends or family, or picked up at yard sales or auctions. Whether old or new, it pays to know what to look for when acquiring a hand tool. Used tools especially demand careful attention to see that they're in good working condition. But you might be surprised at the possible pitfalls of buying a new tool.

As you begin your tool search, you'll undoubtedly come across many old tools. This begs the question:

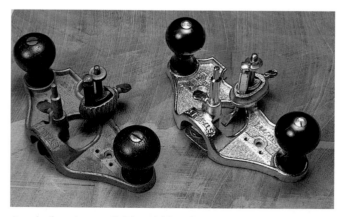

Age before beauty? The old Stanley No. 71 router plane (left), with its rosewood handles and dark patina, looks and feels sweeter as time goes by. A brand-new No. 71 (right) takes shavings just as competently, but it's missing that comfortable lived-in look only time and use can give.

New tools. Buying a new tool often involves extensive research and price-comparison. A good way to become informed about a particular tool is to talk with fellow woodworkers familiar with the tool you're considering. Fair warning: Get a woodworker started on tools, and you better put on a pot of coffee. You'll be awhile. But the more you know about a tool, the better the odds that you'll get what you need. After you've researched a particular tool, you'll need to do a little hands-on investigative work before you shell out the dough.

Before you buy a brand-new tool, you should make sure the parts fit well and move as they should. Look for tight-fitting handles, easy-to-turn locking knobs, smooth-sliding fences, and the like. You can sand or file rough corners or stubborn parts. But certain tools require more investigation.

Hand planes are some of the more complicated pieces of gear, and it pays to confirm that they're in decent shape before you commit to owning one. Verify that parts intended to be straight, flat, or square are indeed straight, flat, and square. Use a square to check for square, such as the side-to-sole of a shoulder plane. And use a small straightedge to test that the sole of a new plane is indeed straight and flat. (See photo, below.) When you're ready to buy, new tools are easy to find. Just head to the hardware store, flip through a tool catalog, browse a website, or check out the sources on page 206.

Once you've acquired a new tool, please don't expect to put it straight to use. Many brand-new

tools need some attention first. (See Tool Maintenance, page 22.) However, the good news is that new tools generally need less tune-up work than older tools.

Old tools. Whether used or so old they can be considered antiques, old tools offer a gold mine of value. But before you rush out and pick up a box load of used tools, it's best to educate yourself first. Read up on old tools by picking up books on the subject, and talk to tool dealers and collectors. Keep in mind that the condition and rarity of a tool will often determine its selling price. This is often good news to woodworkers. Collectors typically turn up their noses at minor

Big mouth. The chip around the mouth of this block plane is irreparable, and results in a plane that performs poorly.

defects such as dings, surface rust, or a worn or chipped Japan finish. These small blemishes can be a boon to the user, making a tool less expensive but perfectly usable.

When considering an old tool, make the same inspection as you would a new one. Is the sole of a plane flat? Do parts move smoothly, and are square surfaces actually square? Are handles firmly held to the body or working part of the tool, be it an old square or an ancient axe? After this initial scrutiny, used tools need closer inspection.

Stay away from bent or broken tools unless you can fix them. Bent or kinked saw blades won't cut straight. And certain tools are prone to chipping. For example, the thin areas on the castings of some hand planes, especially around the mouth, can become chipped and result in poor performance. If you come across a tool in this condition, walk away. (See photo, above.)

Flat check. Use a small straightedge to check that the sole on your new plane is indeed flat.

Years ago a buddy steered me to an old, run-down barn where I found a beautiful antique adz, hidden among a questionable pile of equally old tools. The thrill of that discovery never left me. Finding old tools certainly takes more work than plunking down your cash for a new tool does, but searching is part of the fun. The good news is that there are many places to look for old or antique tools.

Talk to woodworkers. Like the barnful of tools I found years ago demonstrates, it pays to ask your woodworking friends (and other tool hounds) where to find old tools in your area. For longer-distance tool searching, get in touch with tool collectors around the country. There's a vast network of woodworkers who collect, sell, and trade old tools. You can find them by contacting the antique tool associations listed in the sources on page 206.

Search the Internet. Old tools are available in abundance electronically, listed on newsgroups, pictured on websites, and available at auction sites. Be sure to get a complete description of the tool (including a photograph) before buying. See the sources on page 206 for some of my favorite websites.

Stop at flea markets and yard sales. You can find real deals here. But be prepared to know about the tool in question; the seller probably won't. Missing parts are common, so check the tool thoroughly before buying.

Attend tool auctions. Some genuine gems are found at auction, often for a bargain. But be sure to eat a good meal and take a nap before attending one of these fast-paced events—you'll need all the calmness and attentiveness you can muster. It's important to know your limits; prices can skyrocket at an incredible pace, sweeping you up in the buying frenzy. Expect to acquire "box lots" of tools to get the tool you want. Check your local newspaper for tool auctions in your area, and be sure to sign the auctioneer's mailing list when you show up. The same auction house will often stage several auctions in different areas, and you'll get advance notice by mail. Lucky you.

Visit old tool dealers. Buying from antique or old-tool dealers can be a truly rewarding experience, and it's one of my favorite methods of acquiring old tools in excellent working condition. Dealers are knowledgeable about the tools they stock, including antique tools (expect to pay more) as well as old, or used tools. This is the place to shop for hard-to-find tools or complete lots, such as an entire set of wooden molding planes or a full box of bench chisels. You can find local dealers by checking the newspaper or asking around. Better yet, get acquainted with some of the better-known used tool dealers listed opposite.

In addition to the obvious signs, look for cracks, repairs, and loose or missing parts. Often an empty, threaded hole is a clue to a lost part or accessory. Welded repairs can be fine, but check around the weld for straight and square; the heat from welding can distort a tool beyond usability. Carry a rag to wipe away grime; it can conceal cracks or flaws.

Don't let a dirty tool turn you away, however. Grease, grime, and surface rust can easily be removed to restore a tool to working condition. (See Tool Maintenance, page 22.) Heavy rust, however, can permanently bind parts or show up as deep pitting, ruining a tool, especially its cutting edges, or its registration surfaces, such as a fence or sole. Oftentimes a "bargain" tool turns out to be a lemon when you realize there's no practical way to get it into working shape, as shown in the photo, below.

Finding old tools takes some diligence. What you won't find are store shelves stocked with rows upon rows of identical chisels, planes, and saws. Instead, you'll have to go hunting, which is part of the fun and appeal of acquiring old tools. (See Where to Find Old Tools, opposite.)

Collectors only. This beautiful but rusty antique compass plane is deeply pitted on its sole, making it a lively conversation piece but worthless to a user.

USED TOOL DEALERS

Clarence Blanchard
Antique & Collectible Tools
27 Fickett Rd.
Pownal, ME 04069

Hans Brunner
70 Chermside Rd.
Newtown, Queensland, Australia 4305

Martin Donnelly Antique Tools
31 Rumsey St., Box 281
Bath, NY 14810

Bob Kaune Antique and Used Tools
511 W. 11th St.
Port Angeles, WA 98362

Tony Murland
78 High St.
Needham Market
Suffolk, England IP6 8AW

Pete Niederberger
Box 887
Larkspur, CA 94977

Douglas Orr
671 Cooper St.
Ottawa, Ontario, Canada K1R 5J3

Bill Phillips
4555 Golden Key Road
New Tripoli, PA 18066

Andy Stevens
Inchmartine House
Inchture, Perthshire, Scotland PH14 9QQ

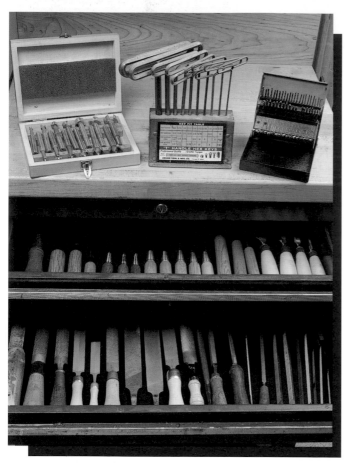

Easy to see. Arranging tools on shelves housed in a cabinet keeps them clean and makes them easy to grab.

Storing Tools

If you can't find it, you probably won't use it. That's ample motivation for finding creative storage solutions for your hand tools. Other reasons include protecting your tools from mishandling, dirt, grime, and—the worst culprit of all—moisture, which promotes oxidation and rust. Kept in a clean area, a properly stored hand tool should be easy to get to, and it should be just as easy for you to notice *when it's missing*. After all, what good is a tool if you can't find it easily? Luckily, several strategies fill the bill.

Shelves, hanging racks, drawers, and toolboxes are all likely candidates for harboring your tools. But before you commit tools to specific spaces, first gather them into functional groups, such as all your saws, and your entire hand plane collection. Then try to find an appropriate space where your tool grouping can reside. This will organize your collection, making it easier to find specific tools without hunting all over your shop. Equally important is to store all those tools close to your workbench, where you'll be using them.

Shelves are probably the easiest solution to tool storage. Keep in mind that tools on open shelves are easy to see, but also attract dust. Shelves housed in a cabinet stay cleaner, as shown in the photo, above. Open cubbyholes are another option, and they're even easier to organize than they are to build. (See fig. 1.)

Hanging racks can come in many forms. Most of us are familiar with pegboard, a sheet of thin hardboard with a series of small holes perforating its surface. Metal wires fit into the holes and hold tools. Use ¼-inch-thick pegboard,

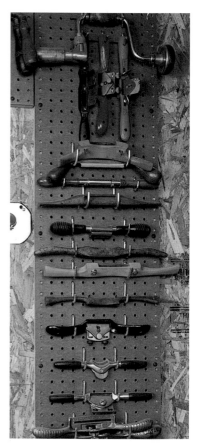

Pegged in order. Pegboard and metal hooks are a snap to put on a wall, and will hold a wide variety of tools or your entire spokeshave collection.

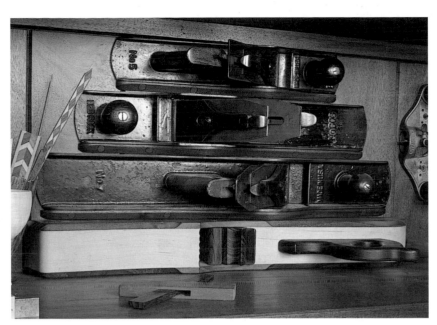

Plane ledges. The author stores larger planes on narrow ledges screwed into the back of a cabinet. Each shelf is sculpted to the outline of the plane it holds.

Flexible dividers. Custom-fit dividers can hold chisels or other tools. Using sliding dovetails—with no glue—allows you to remove a divider and add a new one as your tool collection evolves.

not the thinner version, so that wires stay put and the panel stays flat when loaded with tools. (See bottom photo, opposite page.)

More elaborate hanging systems include custom-fitted racks and narrow shelves for specific tools. Planes and other bulky tools can be housed on ledges, as shown in the top photo, left. Horizontal dividers and wooden hooks attached to a box-type door are another option. The dividers fit into dry dovetail sockets in the door frame, allowing you install a new divider as your tool collection grows or changes. (See top photo, right.)

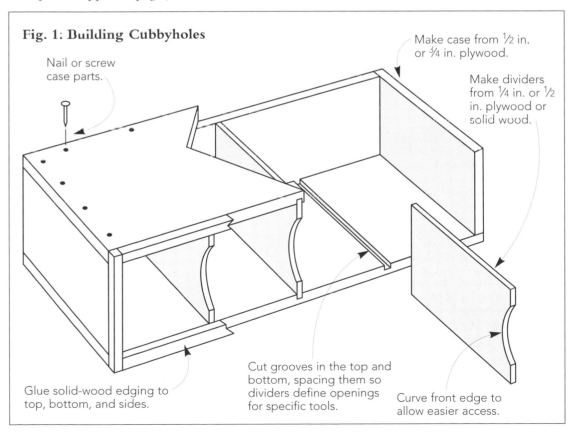

Fig. 1: Building Cubbyholes

Nail or screw case parts.

Make case from ½ in. or ¾ in. plywood.

Make dividers from ¼ in. or ½ in. plywood or solid wood.

Glue solid-wood edging to top, bottom, and sides.

Cut grooves in the top and bottom, spacing them so dividers define openings for specific tools.

Curve front edge to allow easier access.

Fig. 2: Dividing a Drawer

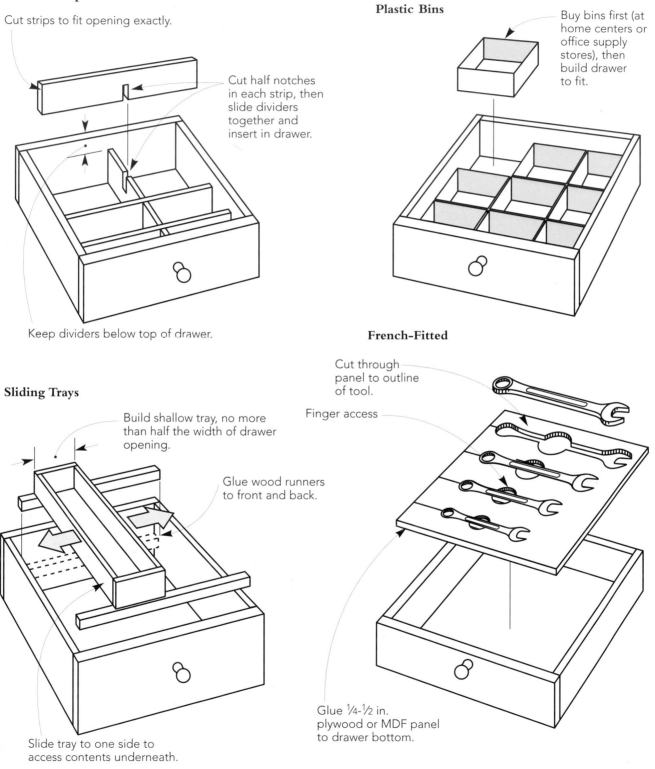

Divider Strips

Cut strips to fit opening exactly.

Cut half notches in each strip, then slide dividers together and insert in drawer.

Keep dividers below top of drawer.

Plastic Bins

Buy bins first (at home centers or office supply stores), then build drawer to fit.

Sliding Trays

Build shallow tray, no more than half the width of drawer opening.

Glue wood runners to front and back.

Slide tray to one side to access contents underneath.

French-Fitted

Cut through panel to outline of tool.

Finger access

Glue ¼-½ in. plywood or MDF panel to drawer bottom.

Drawers are my perennial favorites for storing tools, especially for small gear. Drawers are easy to access, keep your tools clean, and can be efficiently organized with the use of dividers, as shown in figure 2.

Generally, shallow drawers and trays work best. They keep clutter to a minimum by preventing you from stacking tools on top of each other, and they can be brought to the bench so you can pick through them. (See photo, below.) For bigger or bulkier items, deeper drawers with commercial metal slides will hold up to the demands of the workshop. Full-extension slides let you reach to the very back of a drawer, as shown in the photo below, bottom.

One solution that pays big dividends is to build French-fitted drawers, in which the drawer is divided to cradle specific tools. (See photos, below.) With your tools organized in this manner, finding a particular tool is child's play, and you'll notice right away when a specific tool is in use (or missing!) by the empty pocket or slot it leaves. You can custom-fit any type of drawer by first laying out your tools on a sheet of

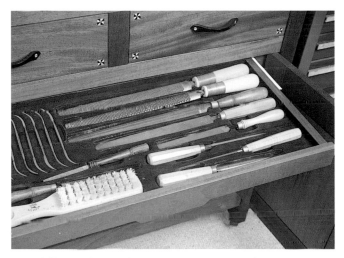

Fitted files and wrenches. Organizing your tools into custom pockets inside a drawer, called French-fitting, makes them easy to get to and, from files (above) to wrenches (below).

Shallow service. These slim drawers hold a single layer of small tools, preventing you from stacking tools and creating a mess. And they are easy to transport to the bench.

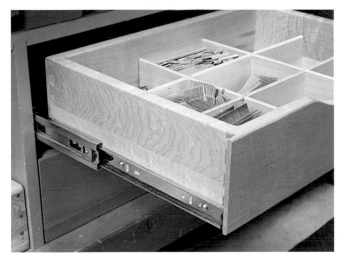

Full reach. Get to the back of a drawer by equipping it with full extension metal drawer slides.

Tool tradition. This six-board chest (above) is just one of furniture maker Patrick Edwards' collection of antique joiner's chests. Jam-packed with hand tools, a chest can hold treasures in lift-out trays or even on the inside of the lid (left).

plywood or MDF, then cutting the sheet on the band saw or with a jigsaw, and gluing the sheet into the drawer. (See fig. 3.)

Toolboxes and cabinets date back to the earliest woodworkers, and are the ultimate tool-storing devices. Toolboxes can employ all of the storage ideas already mentioned, keeping your hand tools in one convenient spot. Besides, making your own toolbox is a long-standing tradition among woodworkers, and you'll be left with something you'll be proud to call your own. The sky is the limit when it comes to tool-box design, and there are many good books and articles on the subject to help you get started.

A portable toolbox, or tote, can hold lots of small tools in an organized manner, and allows you to take

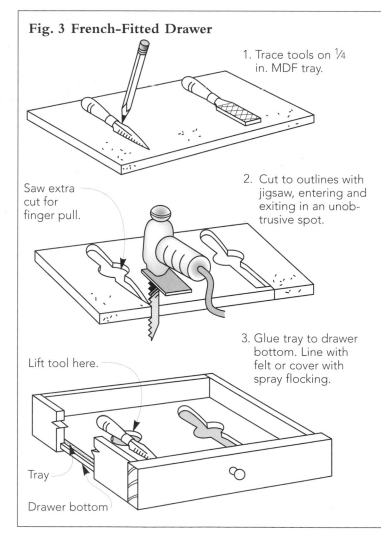

Fig. 3 French-Fitted Drawer

1. Trace tools on ¼ in. MDF tray.

Saw extra cut for finger pull.

2. Cut to outlines with jigsaw, entering and exiting in an unobtrusive spot.

3. Glue tray to drawer bottom. Line with felt or cover with spray flocking.

Lift tool here.

Tray

Drawer bottom

Curvacious tool transport. This exquisite curved-top tool tote (above, top), built by woodworker Pat Curci, has ample room for tools on the go. A locking handle keeps tools safe during transport. When you open the curved lids (above), you access small drawers at both ends. A deep tool till beneath the lids accepts bigger cargo.

them with you. If you take the time to build a showcase box, it can be your calling card to potential customers. (See bottom photos, opposite page.) Larger collections require bigger boxes. A traditional six-board tool chest fits the bill, and was a common sight in eighteenth-century shops. Fitted with lift-out drawers and trays, a chest will hold lots of tools yet lets you sort through the contents easily. And a hinged lid keeps out dirt and dust. (See top photos, opposite page.)

Tool cabinets can be built in (attached to walls or floors) or freestanding, and can range from base units with worktops to large, tall cases that store the bulk of your tools. A low cabinet, similar to kitchen cabinet-type construction, stores tools very efficiently with its pull-out drawers and trays. It also provides a heavy-duty worksurface, as shown in the photo, below.

More elaborate tall cases with drawers and hinged doors can hold a surprising number of tools. My own tool cabinet has every square inch maximized for tool storage, keeping my most-used tools visible and immediately accessible, as shown in the photo, right.

Tools at a glance. Favorite tools in the author's freestanding tool cabinet are stored in plain sight on the doors, perched atop narrow ledges, and inside cubbyholes. A bank of narrow drawers holds small tools and accessories. Less frequently used tools are stored below behind doors.

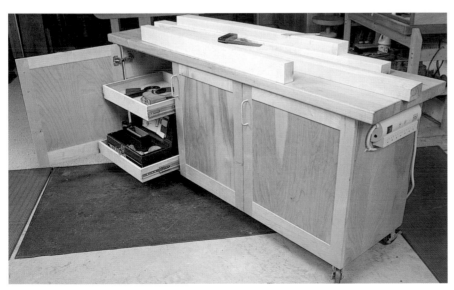

Movable access. Made from plywood with frame-and-panel doors, a heavy maple top, and built-in electrical service, this roll-around cabinet can be moved to any convenient spot in the shop. Shallow pull-out drawers behind the doors make tool access a cinch.

Wax job. A generous coat of paste wax rubbed on your tools, then vigorously rubbed off, will repel moisture and ward off rust.

Tool Maintenance

A well-maintained tool will provide years of service and joyful use, while a dirt and rust-encrusted tool will frustrate you no end. Even worse is a dull tool, which not only will defeat your woodworking aims, but poses a real safety hazard. Keeping these three maintenance goals in mind—preventing rust, cleaning, and sharpening—will keep your tools in tip-top shape.

For regular rust prevention, it's a good idea to oil or wax your tools. A light machine oil works fine when lightly wiped on metal surfaces and buffed with a clean cloth. Another option is to use paste wax, rubbing it into the surface and then buffing away any excess, as shown in the photo, above.

If you keep a lot of tools in drawers, throw a few packets of silica, a desiccant, in with your collection. The packets absorb moisture from the air, keeping your tools dry. Be sure to keep your packets fresh by popping them in the oven on a regular basis to dry collected moisture.

For continually damp workspaces, it pays to invest in a dehumidifier, which pulls excess moisture from the

Combating Rust

Excessive moisture is a genuine problem for almost all hand tools because of the materials from which they're made: Cast iron, steel, and brass react to moisture, resulting in rust or oxidation. Couple this with the fact that many of us work in drafty garages and damp basements, and you have a recipe for disaster.

air. Place the dehumidifier in a central location, such as under your bench, as shown in the photo, right. Some dehumidifiers need to be emptied on a daily basis; other units can be hooked up to a drain hose that runs outdoors or to a drainage sink.

Keeping air and tools dry. A dehumidifier positioned centrally in your shop will remove excess moisture from the air, keeping tools dry and free from rust.

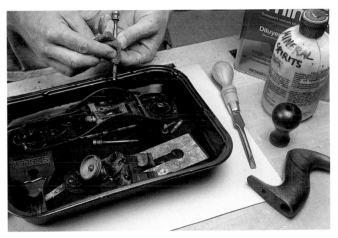

Mineral bath. Loosen difficult grime by soaking metal parts in a shallow tray filled with mineral spirits.

Cleaning

Keeping your tools clean will help promote their accuracy and make them more enjoyable to use. Old tools picked up at flea markets or auctions, coated with grease or packed shavings and dust, are likely candidates for a thorough cleaning. Sometimes new tools are culprits, too, because manufacturers often coat them with lacquer, heavy oil, or other protective coatings for safe shipment overseas. This gunk needs to be removed before you can use the tool.

First a word about old tools: Some vintage tools are collector's items, and overzealous cleaning can diminish their value. Collectors look for original finishes, and often praise oxidized surfaces or those with a heavy patina. Intense scrubbing can often remove these sought-after surface qualities.

Oil, grease, and grime can be removed by wiping with a soft rag dampened in mineral spirits, a solvent that won't harm finishes, paint, or Japanning. For stubborn debris, try using a brass-bristle brush or a fine-grit, nylon abrasive pad soaked in mineral spirits to scrub away dirt. Use lacquer thinner to remove lacquer, but be careful not to get any thinner on paint or other finish coatings as it quickly removes them. The best approach is to use a rag dampened in lacquer thinner to control the application.

Really tenacious gunk requires soaking before you can remove it. First disassemble the tool into individual parts and remove any wooden handles or knobs. Place the metal parts in a shallow tray filled with mineral spirits, and let them sit for 10 to 15 minutes. (See photo, above.) After soaking, scrub the parts with a brass brush or nylon pad, then wipe them with a clean cloth or blow them dry with compressed air. To retard rust, finish up by wiping your tools with a light oil or paste wax as mentioned above.

If you scrub wooden parts, you risk removing the finish. If a wooden surface looks dry or thirsty after cleaning, wipe on a few coats of shellac or varnish. (See photo, below.) A protective coat or two will retard dirt and grime. Over time, the natural oils from your hands will color the wood and the finish to produce an attractive, mellow patina.

One last step is to break any sharp edges with 220-grit sandpaper, especially on new tools. Rounding over these areas makes the tool more comfortable to use. Just be sure to avoid sanding on or near cutting edges or reference surfaces such as teeth, backs, soles, or any other critical areas that affect the performance of the tool.

Handle shine. A couple of coats of 1-lb.-cut shellac, wiped on with a cloth, restores the luster and protects handles and knobs.

Sharpening

Mastering your hand tools begins with a successful sharpening regimen. While chisels, planes, saws, even drill bits require skilled hands to use and operate, this facility is greatly enhanced if your tools are sharp—and stay that way. A dull tool will skip or chatter over the cutting surface and requires undue force, making it dangerous in your hands. A sharp tool is much safer. It cuts quickly and cleanly with a light touch, allowing you more control over the process because you don't have to pull or push as hard.

Surprisingly, sharpening is often thought of as a form of magician's art, or at least dauntingly difficult. Nothing could be further from the truth.

Correct sharpening is simple. The goal is to get you back to work as quickly as possible. While there's an amazing amount of sharpening techniques and sharpening systems available, you can pare down your investment into three basic types of gear for all your sharpening needs. You'll want some files, a bench grinder, and a few benchstones. Each of these sharpening aids will leave a different finish, from coarse to fine, so you'll need to choose the right one for the particular tool you need to sharpen. Let's take a look at the basic tools involved. (You'll find specific sharpening techniques for individual tools under their tool categories in the book.)

Files (see page 134) are good for sharpening coarse-edged tools such as axes, adzes, and other chopping tools; but fine files also work well for finer-cutting tools such as drill bits and saws. A 10-inch or longer mill file is

Grinder and rests. A 6-inch bench grinder equipped with a 120-grit white wheel will quickly dress dull blades and edges, remove nicks, and shape profiles. Sturdy toolrests—such as the aftermarket rests shown here—are essential.

Dressed for success. Keep your grinding wheel free of particle build-up and true its edge with a wheel dresser. Pointed or flat-tip diamond dressers (left) are impregnated with industrial grade diamonds and quickly clean glazing and debris. Carborrundum sticks (right) cut slower and do a good job of smoothing and truing.

a good, general-purpose sharpening aid for coarse edges, such as for axes. Finer files with pointed tips work well for touching up drill bits, and triangular saw files make quick work for sharpening saw teeth.

For dressing a new cutting edge to shape or removing nicks from dull edges, you'll need a **bench grinder**, which spins an abrasive wheel for grinding the edges of tools. (See top photo, above.) A wheel diameter of 6 to 8 inches is sufficient, and a 120-grit white or ruby wheel will leave a suitable finish for most of your tools. Look for a slow-speed (1,700 rpm) grinder, which grinds quickly without overheating the tool edge and ruining its temper. If your grinder came with a flimsy toolrest, or none at all, there are plenty of sturdy aftermarket rests available that allow you to grind comfortably and in a controlled manner. Use the guard that comes with the tool, and always wear eye protection when grinding. Sparks, small bits of metal, wheel swarth, and other flying debris can quickly ruin your day if it comes into contact with your eyes.

To keep your grinding wheel in top shape, you'll need a **wheel dresser** or two, which you rub against the wheel to remove glazing and for truing the edge. I prefer a **diamond dresser** for quickly removing heavy build-up. Pointed-tip dressers are particularly handy for shaping wheels to custom profiles. After cleaning, I like to follow up with a **carborrundum stick dresser** for smoothing and flattening the edge. (See middle photo, opposite page.)

A ground edge is not sufficiently sharp for fine cutting tools such as planes, chisels, and knives. And sharpening profiles such as drill bits can be impossible to do on a grinder. The answer is to hone your edges by hand on **benchstones**. The goal for knife-like tools is to produce an edge that's razor sharp.

You can choose from a bewildering array of honing devices, from oilstones and natural or synthetic (manmade) waterstones, to ceramic and diamond plates and files. I've sharpened with all of these systems—I've even used sheets of sandpaper adhered to plate glass—and they all work great. Over the years, I've managed to pare down my sharpening kit to a few basic pieces of gear: a diamond plate, two waterstones, various slipstones, and a diamond file, as shown in the photo below.

With a basic honing system like mine you can tackle almost all your honing chores. While it's expensive, a diamond plate is handy to keep on hand for quickly flattening surfaces, since it cuts extremely fast and wears a long time. Flat benchstones get the most use, and are good for flat cutters, such as plane irons and chisels. To fill in the gaps, an assortment of shaped slipstones and a diamond file let you hone all sorts of hard-to-reach areas and curved edges such as drill bits and carving gouges.

Choosing the right benchstones is ultimately a matter of personal preference. The important thing to remember is to choose the correct grit for the task at hand, and for that you'll need a minimum of two stones. Generally, a medium-grit stone (800 to 1,200 grit) is sufficient to hone a ground edge smooth, followed by a fine stone (4,000 to 8,000 grit) to produce a mirror polish. I favor waterstones for their speed in cutting, and their overall cleanliness (although you *will* splash water, so don't wear your best clothes). I find that having two stones, a 1,000- and a 6,000-grit stone, covers the majority of my honing needs.

One important note: To hone successfully, your benchstones must be flat. Repeated sharpening often produces a dip in the middle of a stone. There are two ways to correct this. The first is to concentrate on using the entire surface of the stone as you hone. The second, more practical approach, is to periodically re-flatten your stones. You can do this by simply rubbing two stones together, regardless of their grit, until both mating surfaces are dead flat. For stones that are seriously out of flat, rub them on a sheet of 320-grit wet-dry sandpaper taped to a flat surface, such as a piece of melamine-coated particleboard. Use plenty of water as a lubricant.

Honing medley. The author's favorite benchstones and plates, from left to right: two-sided (coarse and fine) diamond plate, 1,000 and 6,000-grit synthetic waterstones, medium and fine slipstones in various shapes, and a two-sided diamond file.

Once you've settled on the sharpening gear you need, it's wise to set up a dedicated sharpening area. While sharpening with a file can be done on your workbench or with clamps and vises, grinding and honing require more sophisticated spaces. Ideally, your set-up should include two work surfaces at differing heights, one high surface for grinding and a lower spot for honing. A relatively high surface (about 44 in.) is perfect for grinding, since it places your arms and hands at a natural angle and promotes control over the work. (See photo, left.)

Honing is best if done near lots of natural light (or decent task lights), and on a low bench. To find the right height, measure from your wrists to the floor, then set up your stones so their top surfaces correspond to that measurement. This lower surface allows your arms to work at a relaxed angle, and lets you place great pressure over the tool with your upper body while powering the stroke. (See bottom photo, left.)

Grind high. For optimum control, set up your grinder so the toolrest is level with your elbows when your forearms are bent at 90 degrees, or about 44 inches from the floor.

Hone low. For the most control, hone on a surface about 36 inches high, or the height of your wrists. At this height you can work comfortably, extending your arms and your upper body over the work for more control.

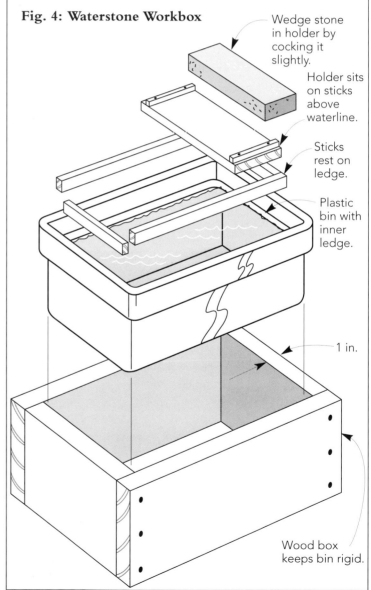

Fig. 4: Waterstone Workbox

Wedge stone in holder by cocking it slightly.

Holder sits on sticks above waterline.

Sticks rest on ledge.

Plastic bin with inner ledge.

1 in.

Wood box keeps bin rigid.

Because I favor waterstones, I fashioned a container that houses my stones in water, keeping them well-saturated and ready for use. At the top of the box is a platform for holding the stones above water while I hone. It's a simple affair based around a plastic box bought at a home-supply store and some scrap wood, as shown in figure 4. If you don't want to build your own waterbox, there are some excellent commercial versions available from woodworking tool suppliers.

Grinding

The grinding process is fast and simple. To grind a beveled edge, first set your toolrest at the correct bevel angle, which for most tools is the angle that came with the tool. For plane irons and chisels, you may want to re-grind an angle for specific tasks, but generally a bevel of 25 degrees is a good all-purpose angle that covers most woodworking applications. (See fig. 5.)

Once you've set the toolrest, begin grinding by keeping the tool firmly on the rest while moving it side to side. Never let the tool remain stationary, or you'll overheat the edge. Use light pressure as you push the tool into the wheel, and keep a steady hand to ensure

Keep it moving. As you grind an edge, move the tool side to side in order to prevent burning and to keep the grind straight and square.

the edge remains straight and square to the wheel. (See photo, below.) If in doubt, stop and check the edge often with a small square, as shown in the photo, right. If you notice any out-of-squareness or dips and curves, note where they are in your mind's eye and try to correct them as you grind. Then check again with the square.

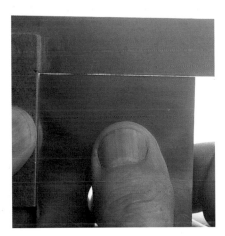

Check for straight and square. When hold in front of a strong light, a small machinist's square lets you read the cutting edge. Look for a straight edge that's square to the sides of the blade.

Grinding square is a knack, and takes practice. To help you get there sooner, you can buy a jig designed to work with a grooved toolrest to guide the tool dead-square to the wheel. Or you can make

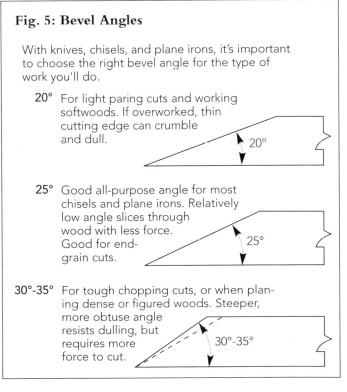

Fig. 5: Bevel Angles

With knives, chisels, and plane irons, it's important to choose the right bevel angle for the type of work you'll do.

20° For light paring cuts and working softwoods. If overworked, thin cutting edge can crumble and dull.

25° Good all-purpose angle for most chisels and plane irons. Relatively low angle slices through wood with less force. Good for end-grain cuts.

30°-35° For tough chopping cuts, or when planing dense or figured woods. Steeper, more obtuse angle resists dulling, but requires more force to cut.

Pivoting a curve. You can grind a gentle curved edge by free-handing the blade on the toolrest, pivoting it in a small, controlled arc.

one yourself from some leftover scraps of wood and plywood. (See fig. 6.)

If during the grinding process you do manage to overheat and burn the blade (relax; I'm speaking from experience here), you'll immediately notice a dark bluish-colored spot in the steel. Bluing is a sign that the steel has softened and lost its temper. While you can sharpen the tool just fine, it won't hold an edge worth a plugged penny. The only fix is to grind past the spot. To overcome excessive heat, some woodworkers like to quench the blade periodically in water. This is a bad idea. Quenching in this manner introduces microscopic cracks in the thin metal at the cutting edge, resulting in a blade that crumbles and dulls very quickly in use. A better solution is to keep an eye (or a finger) on how hot the blade is getting. If your

blade gets too hot to touch, it's a sure sign you're overdoing it, and getting close to overheating. Ease off on the amount of forward pressure, and don't try to grind the edge in one pass. Instead, make a few passes, then stop and cool the blade by holding it near the airflow of the spinning wheel, and grind again.

Curved blades, such as a scrub-plane iron, require pivoting the blade on the toolrest by hand. It takes some practice to pivot the blade as you grind, but the process is not particularly difficult and you can get great results the first time. (See photo, left.)

Honing

After successfully grinding the bevel, it's time to hone the blade. You have three options here. You can hone the entire bevel; hone just the back and front, or leading edge, of the bevel; or create a special secondary bevel, called a microbevel. (For more on microbevels, see Sharpening a Plane Iron, page 178.)

For a standard bevel, start by placing the tool bevel-side down on your medium stone, with the bevel making full contact. You can feel this with your hands, especially if your stones are dead flat. Because the tool was ground on a wheel, the resulting hollow-ground bevel will make contact only at the front and back of the bevel, which greatly eases the honing process. Concentrate on holding the tool in this position, and rub back and forth until the grind marks at the front and back of the bevel have disappeared, using firm pressure. (See photo, right.) Some tools fare better if the full face of the bevel is fully honed, such as heavy-duty striking tools like mortising chisels. To hone

Hand honing. Rub the bevel over the stone to remove grind marks and smooth the cutting edge. Keep the bevel in full contact with the stone as you move the tool.

Fig. 6: Jig for Grinding a Square Edge

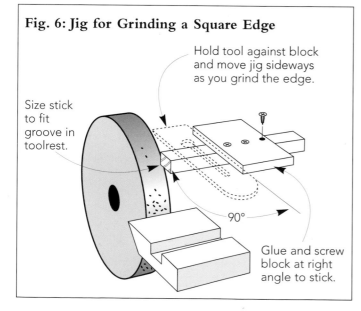

Hold tool against block and move jig sideways as you grind the edge.

Size stick to fit groove in toolrest.

90°

Glue and screw block at right angle to stick.

Honing help. When in doubt, use a commercial honing guide to hold the bevel at the correct angle.

the entire bevel, simply keep honing until the whole surface is an even sheen.

After working the bevel, hone the opposite bevel if it's a double-bevel edge, using the same honing technique, or work the flat side with the tool flat on the stone. When honing the flat side, make sure never to lift the tool— not even a little bit. Then alternate between both faces, this time letting up on the pressure. End with a few light strokes on the flat, or back, side of the tool. Now repeat the same procedure on your fine stone, honing both sides, slowly decreasing the pressure until you've produced a polished, mirror-bright surface.

If honing a bevel by hand intimidates you, try a **honing guide**, which is designed to hold chisels, plane irons, and other blades at a precise angle during honing. (See photo, above.) Keep in mind that using a honing guide will slow down the overall sharpening process, but it's a very accurate and satisfying device for beginners. As your sharpening skills progress, you'll probably gravitate toward free-hand honing for its speed and convenience. The entire process from grinding to honing should take only 10 minutes or so; and less than a minute if you're only touching up a worn edge.

So how can you tell when your tool is sharp?
One test is to slice a piece of paper in half. Another

Beautifully sharp. This polished end grain on pine, shaved with a low-angle plane, shows what a truly sharp blade can do.

method is to place the back of the cutting edge flat on your fingernail, then slowly tilt the tool upward until it's perpendicular to your nail. If the cutting edge remains in place without sliding

or skipping off (it should make a small nick), it's sharp. But the best test is where the rubber meets the road: Try shaving some end grain, preferably in a soft wood. If you see any track marks or trace lines in the grain, the tool isn't sharp. A truly sharp edge produces an even, polished surface on the work … and leaves an irrepressible smile on your face. (See photo, below.)

WHY HONE A TOOL?

Take a brand-new plane iron or chisel—or any bevel-edge tool—out of its box or wrapper and examine the bevel and the back closely. You're likely to notice machined grind marks or a regular scratch pattern in the steel. Although the tool may feel sharp to your fingers, under magnification you'd see that these scratches or grooves create a series of peaks and valleys right at the cutting edge. (See fig. 7.) While a ground edge can take a shaving, the sharp, pointed peaks crumble and fracture easily during use, quickly dulling the edge. Honing on a hard stone or other fine abrading tool reduces the depth of the grooves, refining these jagged mountains and leveling them to a less pitted appearance. The result is a sharper, more durable cutting edge.

Fig. 7: A Honed Edge is Superior

Ground Edge	**Honed Edge**
Under magnification, a ground edge has a pattern of deep grooves that create a series of peaks and valleys at the cutting edge.	Honing the surface reduces the grooves for a finer, longer-lasting edge.

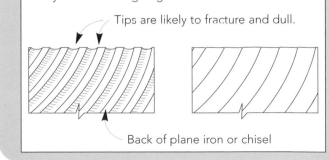

Tips are likely to fracture and dull.

Back of plane iron or chisel

Holding Your Work

Gripping your work is fundamental to good woodworking. While standard woodworking clamps are essential for gluing wood joints and assembling furniture, these same clamps and other grasping devices—homemade or commercially-available—are important tools for holding and supporting your work. In addition, there are specialty clamps and vises for carving, picture-framing, chairmaking, and other specialized aspects of the craft.

Although these days you can buy a decent workbench, most woodworkers prefer to build their own, saving money in the bargain. There are many great workbench designs that have been published in books and magazines; check your local library. Good wood choices for benches are hard maple and beech, both dense and heavy woods that are relatively stable. You can pick up most of the necessary bench hardware at a hardware store; specialty hardware such as vise screws and handles are available from woodworking stores and catalogs. In addition to a thick top and stout legs, the key to a solid bench is in the lower rails: make these thick and wide enough, and your bench won't rack. (See fig. 1.)

My favorite bench is a traditional European-style joiner's bench, as shown in the photo, below. At roughly 2 feet wide by 7 feet long, it's plenty big enough for all my handwork. Don't overlook the height of your bench—it's a key factor in using your tools effectively. Too high, and you'll have a hard time pushing or pulling a tool, such as when face planing. Too low, and you won't be able to see the

Working Surfaces

One tool that stands above all else as the primary holding and supporting device for any woodworking endeavor is a **workbench**. If you're just beginning to acquire tools, there's no better place to start than with a quality bench.

A good workbench should be solid and heavy, free from racking (cocking side to side or front to back), have a variety of built-in clamping or gripping devices, and possess a dead-flat top. The heavier the bench, the better. A weighty bench absorbs the pushing, pulling, prying, and pounding that goes hand in hand with our tools, and transmits this energy to the floor—not into the work or back to the tool. Solid, heavy parts resist racking, and a flat top surface allows you to use your bench as a reference plate for activities where flatness counts, such as hand-planing or cutting joints.

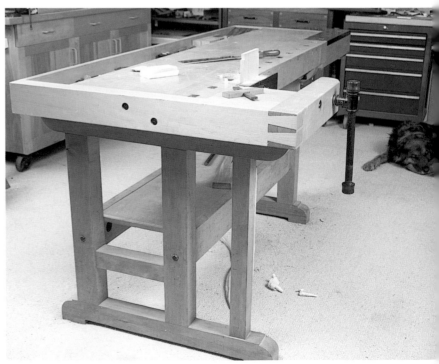

Faithful and dependable. The author's European-style maple workbench has a massive, flat top and a stout undercarriage that resists racking.

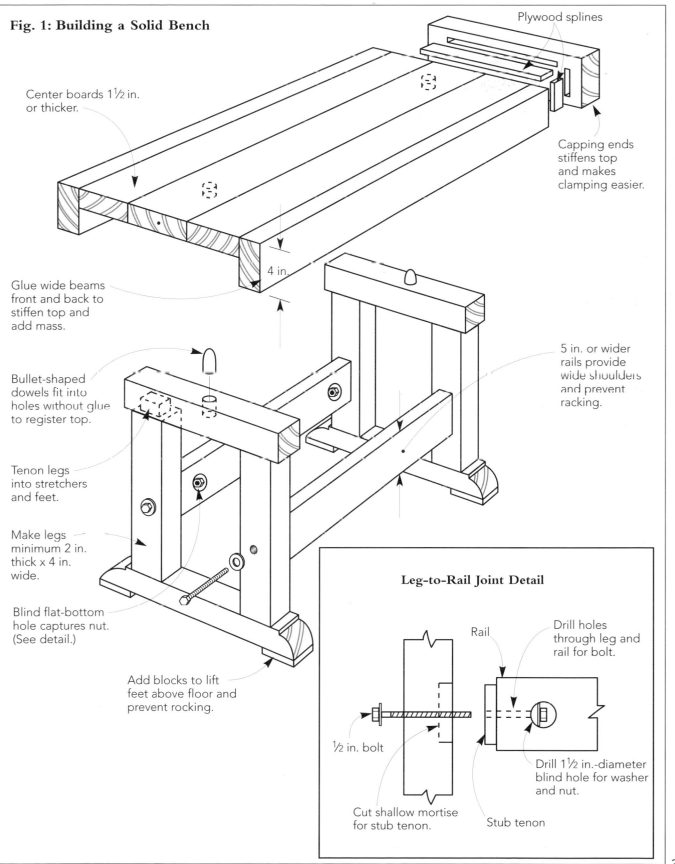

Fig. 1: Building a Solid Bench

Plywood splines

Center boards 1½ in. or thicker.

Capping ends stiffens top and makes clamping easier.

4 in.

Glue wide beams front and back to stiffen top and add mass.

5 in. or wider rails provide wide shoulders and prevent racking.

Bullet-shaped dowels fit into holes without glue to register top.

Tenon legs into stretchers and feet.

Make legs minimum 2 in. thick x 4 in. wide.

Blind flat-bottom hole captures nut. (See detail.)

Add blocks to lift feet above floor and prevent rocking.

Leg-to-Rail Joint Detail

Rail

Drill holes through leg and rail for bolt.

½ in. bolt

Drill 1½ in.-diameter blind hole for washer and nut.

Cut shallow mortise for stub tenon.

Stub tenon

action without stooping over your work, an important consideration when it comes to joinery work. The right height gives you maximum control over your tools, and lets you work for hours at the bench without fatigue.

The optimum height of a bench is a personal matter, yet it's always a compromise. I've settled on a bench height of 36 inches for my work. It's low enough for comfortable hand planing, yet high enough for laying out and cutting joints without getting a sore back. But don't take my word for it; adjust the height of your bench to suit your own particular needs and your physical stature. Try working at various heights on other people's benches, or set up temporary surfaces to get a feel for a height that's best for you. One good rule of thumb for

Horse work. Trestle-style sawhorses are lightweight, yet stable and strong, and can be made in any height you choose. The trestle design allows you to nest horses together, making it easy to carry two in one hand and store them out of the way.

determining bench height is to stand with your arms resting by your sides and your hands bent at 90 degrees, then measure from your palms to the floor, as shown in figure 2.

Sawhorses shouldn't be overlooked as convenient tools for supporting and holding work. With a sheet of plywood on top, a pair of sawhorses can quickly become a useful workstation or staging platform. You can pick up sturdy sawhorses at home centers, or you can build your own at a height that suits your work. For example, low horses (18 inches or so—I call 'em "ponies") are great for assembly tasks on the floor or purchased high on a table, while higher horses (34 inches or higher) are well suited for joinery and layout chores.

The traditional carpenter's sawhorse incorporates compound-angled legs, which flare outward for stability. This kind of sawhorse is very stable, but can be tedious

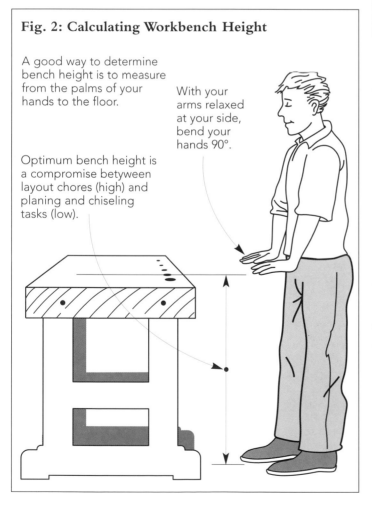

Fig. 2: Calculating Workbench Height

A good way to determine bench height is to measure from the palms of your hands to the floor.

With your arms relaxed at your side, bend your hands 90°.

Optimum bench height is a compromise betyween layout chores (high) and planing and chiseling tasks (low).

to build because of its complex joinery. And I've seen many a carpenter's horse wobble like crazy after a couple week's hard work when the joints start to loosen. I prefer **trestle-style sawhorses** for their superior strength, as shown in the photo, opposite page.

If you build your own horses, be sure to use a strong hardwood. Species such as maple, oak, cherry, or mahogany are all suitable choices. Avoid softwoods. They don't have the necessary beam strength to safely carry heavy loads. (See fig. 3.)

Fig. 3: Trestle-Style Sawhorse

This svelte sawhorse is lightweight, knocks down, and handles a big load. Build the height and length to suit your needs. Make all the main parts from ¾ in. thick by 3 in. wide stock, except for the feet, which are 1 in. thick.

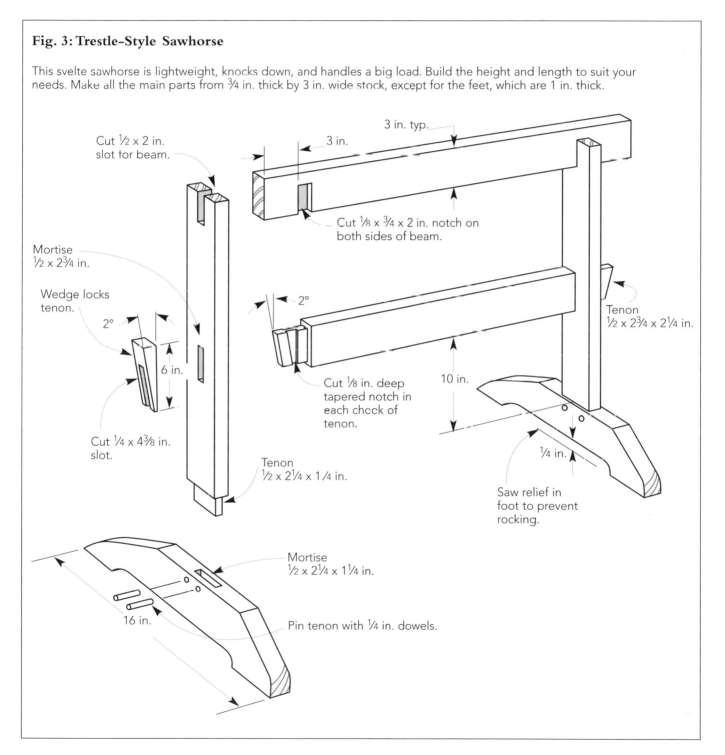

Cut ½ x 2 in. slot for beam.

3 in.

3 in. typ.

Cut ⅛ x ¾ x 2 in. notch on both sides of beam.

Mortise ½ x 2¾ in.

Wedge locks tenon.

2°

6 in.

Tenon ½ x 2¾ x 2¼ in.

2°

Cut ⅛ in. deep tapered notch in each check of tenon.

10 in.

¼ in.

Saw relief in foot to prevent rocking.

Cut ¼ x 4⅜ in. slot.

Tenon ½ x 2¼ x 1/4 in.

Mortise ½ x 2¼ x 1¼ in.

16 in.

Pin tenon with ¼ in. dowels.

Bench Vises

A dedicated clamp such as a bench vise works in tandem with your bench to increase the amount of control you have over your work. Grasping your work firmly at the bench not only supports the work, but also supports the tool with less vibration, resulting in cleaner and more effortless cuts. While your arms and hands—even feet—can often provide purchase, a bench vise fills this need with aplomb.

Economical clamper. The tried-and-true edge vise is a work-horse found on most benches. This quick-action model lets you open or close the jaws without having to turn the handle for faster clamping action.

Traditional holding devices for a workbench are plentiful and versatile, as shown in figure 4. Most of these clamping mechanisms can be adapted to fit any style of bench, and provide numerous ways for clamping all types of work. You can make some of these holding contraptions yourself; others are commercially available and can be fitted to existing benches.

The standard on many benches is an **edge vise**. A movable steel jaw opens and closes via a threaded rod, or vise screw, and two sturdy steel rails guide the movable jaw in and out. The fixed jaw bolts to the underside of the bench, making installation easy. (See photo below, left.)

You can mount an edge vise anywhere along a bench's edge, but typical installation involves screwing or bolting the vise to the front of the bench at the far left or far right, flush with the top of the bench. Right-handers usually find that the left-side mount is preferable for gripping long boards on edge. The opposite is true for southpaws, where a right-mounted vise is more convenient. The most useful style of edge vise is one

Working at the end. An end vise has massive jaws that effectively clamp wide work at the end of the bench.

with a quick-release mechanism. This feature lets you position or release the work quickly before having to turn the vise handle.

Like the edge visc, an **end vise** has a fixed jaw and a movable jaw, with accompanying guide rails between the jaws. This is a massive vise that mounts on the end of the bench, and usually spans its entire width. Like the edge vise, rails between the jaws can keep work from being clamped securely. But with its longer jaws, this vise shines when it comes to gripping wide or long work, as shown in the bottom right photo, opposite page.

Most end vises and larger edge vises suffer from one nagging flaw: When you clamp work in one side of the vise, the jaws rack out of parallel, and the work

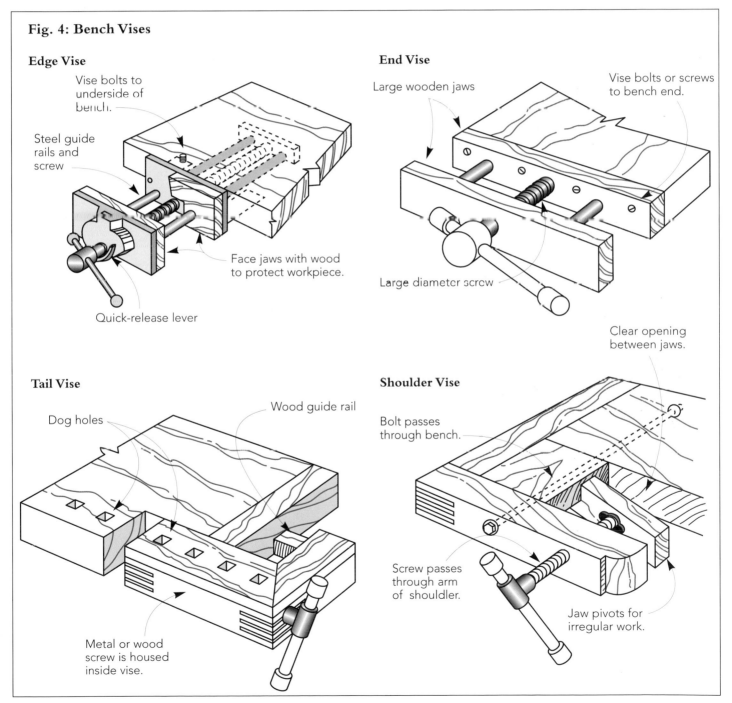

Fig. 4: Bench Vises

Edge Vise

Vise bolts to underside of bench.

Steel guide rails and screw

Quick-release lever

Face jaws with wood to protect workpiece.

End Vise

Large wooden jaws

Vise bolts or screws to bench end.

Large diameter screw

Clear opening between jaws.

Tail Vise

Dog holes

Wood guide rail

Metal or wood screw is housed inside vise.

Shoulder Vise

Bolt passes through bench.

Screw passes through arm of shouldler.

Jaw pivots for irregular work.

slips. You have a couple of options to deal with this. The first is to drop a spacer into the jaws at the opposite end. (See Preventing Jaw Twist, below.) A second more convenient, but pricier, alternative is to mount a **twin-screw end vise** onto your bench. A twin-screw vise employs two vise screws spaced at the ends of the vise, linked by a chain drive. With this type of mechanism, you can clamp anything anywhere in the vise, and the jaws remain parallel. Problem solved. (See photo, right.)

Often touted as the king of all bench vises and revered by woodworkers, the **Emmert pattern-maker's vise** swivels, tilts, locks in any position, and clamps odd shapes with pivoting jaws. Its unique

clamping capabilities served the needs of patternmakers who had to hold odd-shaped wooden patterns for casting metals. While these vises are incredibly

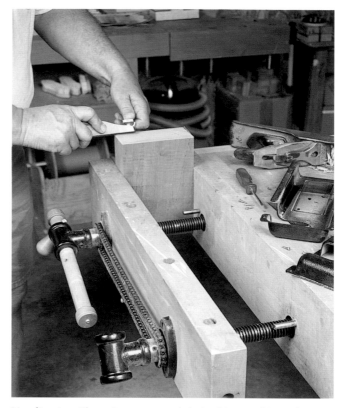

No-slip vise. The twin screws and chain drive on this end vise allow you to grip small work to one side without racking the jaws. Turning a single handle opens or closes the vise.

PREVENTING JAW TWIST

One annoying drawback to most end vises and larger edge vises happens when you're clamping work in only one side of the vise, a common task for any woodworker. In this type of clamping situation, the jaws can rack out of parallel, and the workpiece slips when you put pressure upon it. To ensure a positive grip on the workpiece, place a scrap piece of the same thickness as the work in the opposite side of the vise. If you cap the top of the spacer with a block, the spacer won't fall through the vise when you're positioning the workpiece.

Clamping without twist. A T-shaped scrap spacer at the opposite end of a long vise prevents racking, keeping the jaws parallel and the workpiece firmly planted.

Versatility, at a price. This amazingly agile Emmert pattern-maker's vise rotates, swivels, and pivots. But it's pricey, and older vises are often chipped or missing parts like the handle.

versatile, they are expensive. In addition, the brittle cast iron is prone to cracking and chipping, and lost parts are common, as shown in the bottom right photo, opposite page. So why would you need any other vise? Perhaps the answer lies somewhere in the acquisition of such a device: If you can even *find* an Emmert vise (they're no longer made), you'll pay a small fortune for it. My best advice is to look in the classified ads in woodworking magazines, and be prepared to dig deep into your pocket.

If you can't locate an Emmert, you can do just as well or better with a modern version, called the **Tucker vise**, made by a reputable tool company. This vise has all the features of the Emmert, and then some. (See bottom photo, left.) Similar in versatility (and price!) to the Emmert, the Tucker is made from a lighter, less-brittle alloy than the cast iron found in the Emmert. In addition, the Tucker sports a quick-release feature, and has a free-floating front jaw that conforms to odd profiles automatically. Emmerts require a manual adjustment. If you've got the dough, this is a vise worth looking into.

Found on traditional European workbenches, a **tail vise** is a complicated assembly that requires a large investment of your time and skill to build. But the result is a solid vise with lots of versatility. Located on the right end of the bench toward the front, this L-shaped assembly incorporates a truncated end of the benchtop itself as its fixed jaw, and has a large movable jaw that rides on thick wooden beams or rails. The entire assembly operates via a large metal screw. Traditional tail vises worked on a large, 2-inch diameter wooden screw, and were known for their sensitive action and feel. This is a massive vise with lots of solidity and gripping power. And due to its design, a tail vise can grip a variety of work between its unobstructed jaws. (See photo, below.)

While the tail vise excels at clamping work between its jaws, its primary function is to help grasp work atop the bench when used in conjunction with a pair of dowels or rectangular pegs, called *bench dogs*. One dog slips into one of a series of dog holes located in the vise itself; the second dog fits into one of a series

Better than Emmert? The modern Tucker vise has all the features of the Emmert, plus the ability to pivot its front jaw automatically to conform to irregular-shaped work.

Clear clamping. Work placed between the jaws of a tail vise isn't obstructed by any hardware, letting you clamp long pieces with solid support.

of holes along the front of the bench and in line with the vise holes. Each dog hole is canted forward about 2 degrees, such that the angles oppose each other. By placing your workpiece between the dogs and closing the vise, then tapping down on the work, you can grip boards tight to the benchtop. This pulling action lets you flatten slightly curved or bowed work (assuming your bench is flat, of course), and it's is a real boon for holding boards for hand planing or other tasks where you don't want clamps projecting above the work. (See photo, below.)

Take note: Building a tail vise isn't for the faint of heart. You should plan on taking several days to build one, install it, and tune its action to get it working just right. The important thing to remember when building this type of vise is to make sure you assemble the various parts dead square to each other. This attention to detail will make a big difference in how smoothly the vise opens and closes. The necessary hardware is commercially available (you can even buy those wonderful 2-inch wooden screws), and there are several good plans available in woodworking magazines and books to get you started. The good news is that many existing benches can be retrofitted to accept this style of vise.

A **shoulder vise** is another European woodworking tradition. It juts out from the left front side of the bench, using the edge of the bench itself as one of its jaws. Truly the most versatile and handiest of all bench-built vises, a shoulder vise can grip large or small work, and isn't fettered by rails or other hardware between the jaws. This feature lets you clamp workpieces clear through to the floor and centered over the jaw opening, allowing you to securely grip tall and wide work. The movable jaw also pivots, allowing you to clamp odd-shaped or angled work. (See photo, below.)

One compromise you'll make with a shoulder vise is the somewhat awkward space it consumes. Instead of a rectangular benchtop, you'll end up with an L-shaped top, or shoulder, which can impede workflow around the bench. On the flip side, I've found this shouldered area to be a useful worksurface for all sorts of small trimming and layout tasks. One tip learned from painful experience: Leaving the vise screw extended is a nasty hip banger. To maintain your sanity and prevent bruises, make it a habit to fully close the vise when you're not using it.

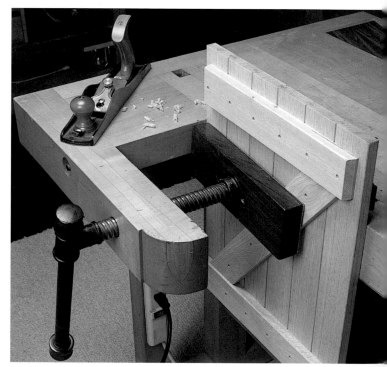

Dogged clamping. Used with a tail vise, bench dogs grip the workpiece at both ends, giving you full access to the work without having any clamps in the way.

Shoulder clamping. Arguably the most versatile of all shop-made vises, a shoulder vise can clamp small, big, tall, or wide work between its unimpeded jaws. The movable jaw angles slightly to accommodate tapered or irregular work.

Capturing carvings. This carver's vise has a deep-threaded lag screw that pierces the bottom of the work, then threads to a clamping knob through a hole in the benchtop. This set-up gives you free access to the sides and top of the work.

Like the tail vise, you can buy the requisite hardware for a shoulder vise and build it yourself. Construction is simple and straightforward. The only caveat is that this vise in not particularly well-suited for adaption to existing benches, since the clamping strength of the vise in large part depends on a threaded rod that runs through the width of the benchtop. (See fig 4, page 37.) The hole for the rod is best drilled in stages before gluing up your benchtop, so this vise makes more sense if you're building a bench from scratch.

Specialty vises are useful if carving, toymaking, chairmaking, or other specialized aspects of the craft are on your woodworking agenda. Three-dimensional, or "in-the-round" carvings, need access from all sides. One solution is to support the work with a **carver's screw**, as shown in the photo, left. A couple steps up in versatility is a **carver's vise** that swivels and rotates side to side, front to back, and adjusts up and down in height. The vise can be bolted to the bench, or you can attach a clamping block to the vise and grasp the tool in a bench vise. (See photo, below.)

Carving any angle. For the ultimate in accessibility, this upscale carver's vise rotates, swivels, and locks at any angle for comfortable, in-the-round carving. Bolting the base to a T-block lets you grip the vise in your bench vise for quick mounting.

PROTECT YOUR WORK WITH LEATHER

Metal and even wood vise jaws can quickly mar a freshly planed or finished piece of work, so it pays to line your jaws with an appropriate padding material. Top-grain cowhide is an excellent choice.

On metal-jawed vises, you'll need to first cover the jaws with 1/4 inch or thicker wooden blanks to give the leather the necessary padding. Wood jaws can usually be attached from behind using the screw holes machined in the vise.

Cut the leather pads a little oversized for each wooden jaw.

Then brush a sealer coat of diluted white or yellow glue (75 percent glue to water is a good ratio) on the inner, rough surface of the leather. Wait about five minutes, and with the leather still damp, brush some full-strength glue onto the face of the jaws. Position the leather pads onto the jaws, insert a scrap board between the jaws, and clamp. Once the glue has dried, use a razor-sharp knife to trim the excess leather to the outline of the jaws.

Protective padding. A single layer of leather glued to each jaw of a vise protects your work from dings and scratches.

Most woodworkers are called upon to make the occasional picture frame, and one of the best ways to hold miters together for gluing and nailing the joint is to use a **picture framer's vise**. (See photo, below.) This relatively low-cost vise is designed to hold picture-frame material (which usually has a rabbet on its back side) while leaving enough room for hitting nails or driving screws into the joint.

Picture this. This low-cost picture framer's vise holds miters together and provides room for nailing the joint as it's clamped.

Chairmakers typically shave and shape chair parts such as rungs and spindles using drawknives and spokeshaves. This kind of work calls for a clamping arrangement that lets you quickly clamp, release, and clamp again as you reposition the work. One specialty clamping tool that accommodates this changing grip is the **shaving horse**. (See photo, below.) The traditional shaving horse has a movable clamping head, called a *dumb head* (don't ask) that pivots to hold the work as you press on a wooden treadle with your foot. This keeps both hands free to work with the tool.

A shaving horse is an uncomplicated piece of gear to make, requiring little in the way of tools or supplies—practically any type of wood will suffice, although hardwood is preferable for the clamping surfaces. Plans for shop-made shaving horses are available in woodworking catalogs and on the Internet (see sources, page 206). Interestingly, there are chairmakers and other woodworkers who sell their own shaving horse designs, either in kit form or the whole kit and caboodle.

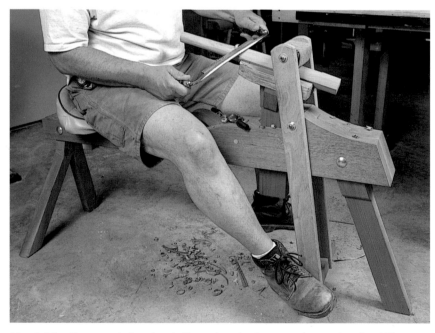

Horsin' in the round. For drawknife and spokeshave work, woodworker Mike Callihan sits on a homemade shaving horse to work spindles and other chair parts. The clamping head is actuated by foot pressure, leaving hands free to control the cutting tool.

Off the beaten woodworking path are clamps for metalworking. While metalworking is a vast trade unto itself, the fact is as woodworkers we invariably need to grind, saw, file or otherwise work small bits of metal. Such things as filing and making small adjustments to metal hardware, cutting bits of metal to length, plus a myriad of other small metalworking jobs all cry out for a decent clamping arrangement. A woodworking vise is usually insufficient for these tasks, and clamping unforgiving metal in many of these devices can permanently damage them. The best tool for these jobs is a **metalworking vise**, as shown in the photo, below. Look for a vise with a swiveling base, which lets you rotate the vise head for the optimum angle of attack.

To protect your work from hard metal jaws, you can line them with strips of wood. If you glue magnets to the back of the blocks, they'll stick in place when you need them, as shown in the photo, bottom.

Metalwork in the woodshop. You can buy large or small metalworking vises. These heavy-duty vises will grasp metal parts securely without damage to the vise itself, and they have sufficient mass to dampen the significant vibrations that working metal produces.

Instant wood jaws. These strips of wood protect the work from metal jaws. Magnets epoxied to the back of the strips let you attach them quickly and painlessly.

Bench Stops

To complement your standard bench vises and to make your wood-holding power more versatile, bench stops and bench hooks shine as invaluable aids. As testimony to their usefulness, many of these holding devices preceded the common screw-based woodworking vise, and were sometimes the only bench-clamping contraption to be found in our forebears' shops. One of the more appealing aspects of these tools for me is an admireable trait: these mechanisms are stone simple. Most of them can be made in the shop using leftover scrap and a few hours of your time.

Most bench stops and bench hooks can be cobbled together in a matter of minutes, and serve to register or stop the work from moving or sliding around as you push or pull against it. The wonderful thing about most bench hooks is that they don't require any clamping action to use them. Instead, they utilize the edge or end of your bench to register their hooked ends. There are a variety of designs for specific tasks,

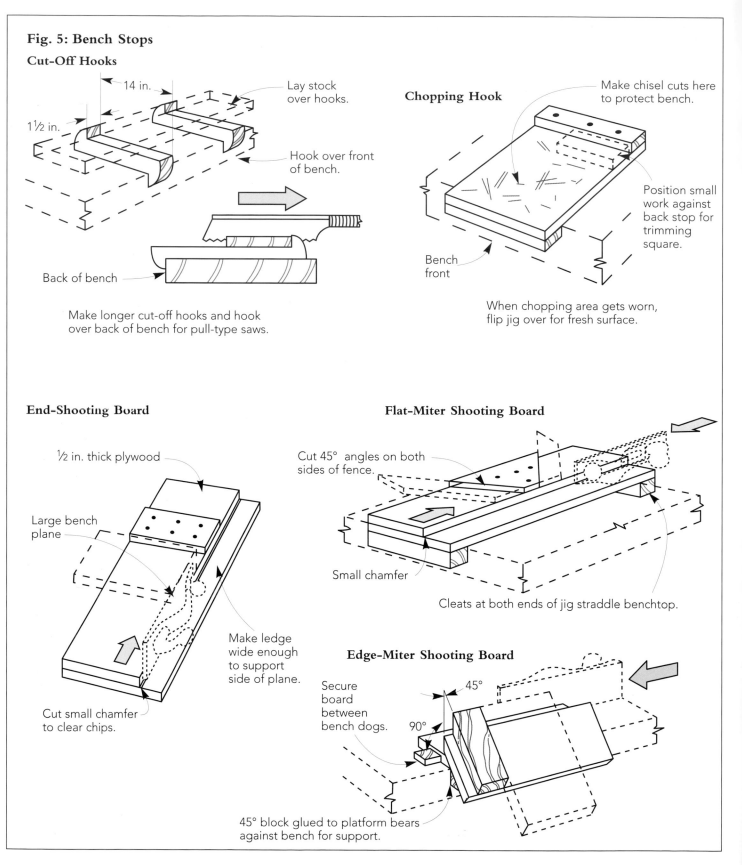

Fig. 5: Bench Stops

Cut-Off Hooks

14 in.

1½ in.

Lay stock over hooks.

Hook over front of bench.

Back of bench

Make longer cut-off hooks and hook over back of bench for pull-type saws.

Chopping Hook

Make chisel cuts here to protect bench.

Position small work against back stop for trimming square.

Bench front

When chopping area gets worn, flip jig over for fresh surface.

End-Shooting Board

½ in. thick plywood

Large bench plane

Make ledge wide enough to support side of plane.

Cut small chamfer to clear chips.

Flat-Miter Shooting Board

Cut 45° angles on both sides of fence.

Small chamfer

Cleats at both ends of jig straddle benchtop.

Edge-Miter Shooting Board

Secure board between bench dogs.

45°

90°

45° block glued to platform bears against bench for support.

from sawing and chopping to miter work and shooting square edges, as shown in figure 5.

One of the simplest and most useful types of bench stop is a **bird's mouth**, which consists of a board with a tapered notch cut in one end. By clamping the device to the benchtop, you can hold thick or thin work on edge, as shown in the photo, below. This particular holding device is really handy when you need to work the edge on several workpieces, since there's no need to clamp the stock, letting you move quickly from piece to piece. Generally, 1-inch thick stock is perfect for this stop (use thicker stock if you need to hold really tall work), and

No-clamp edge work. The tapered opening of a bird's mouth vise lets you hold thick or thin stock for working on its edge.

Cut-off work. These cut-off bench hooks protect your bench during crosscut work, lifting the work above the bench and holding it firmly as you push with a saw.

the notch is easily cut on the band saw or by hand. Make the opening large enough to accept your thickest boards, or make several stops in different sizes.

Pairs of **cut-off hooks** serve to lift boards off the work surface for crosscutting and other through cuts, and can be made from leftover 2x4 scrap. (See photo below, left.) Traditional cut-off hooks work with standard push-cutting saws; if you're using a pull-style saw, such as a Japanese dozuki (see page 196), you can make longer hooks and reverse them so they engage the back of the bench, as shown in figure 5.

A **chopping hook** can serve dual purposes. The raised back makes a positive stop for trimming small work with a plane or saw, and the flat surface is perfect for making chopping cuts with chisels or other knife-edge tools. (See photo, below.) While the rear fence works well for small trim cuts, I prefer to think of this device as a welcome mat for my chopping tools and small saws. Instead of marring the benchtop, I hook this jig over the edge of my bench whenever I need to make chopping through cuts in small pieces, such as trimming the ends of delicate work. When the chopping surface starts to resemble the work of a beaver on steroids, simply flip the board over and use the opposite side with its fresh work surface and fence.

Trimming and chopping. Protect your benchtop by using this chopping bench hook's broad surface for chisel and knife work, or place work against the back edge of the bench hook when trimming or planing.

A more specialized type of bench hook, the **shooting board**, is used for trimming ends and miters when used with bench planes. Some shooting boards incorporate a cleat at one end for hooking over the edge of a bench; others can be clamped in a bench vise or between bench dogs. Probably the most useful variety is an **end-shooting board**, which works well for trimming the ends of work, especially end-grain surfaces. I reach for this shooting board when I need an exact fit, or when I want to trim a slight out-of-square cut made with a power tool. (See photo, below.)

The best approach to using shooting boards is to choose the longest or heaviest bench plane in your arsenal, checking that the plane's sides are square to the sole. If you're cutting end grain, choose a plane with a low angle. Set the iron for a very light cut, and lay the plane on its side on the jig. Make an initial rough cut on your workpiece using a saw, then position the sawn end a hair past the work stop on the jig. Register the plane's sole against the jig's long fence, and use firm, swift movements to push the plane past the workpiece.

The heavy mass of a big plane helps to power the cut, and a sharp iron leaves a glassy-smooth surface that's precisely square in two planes. With a properly set plane, you should be able to take full-length shavings, even in end grain. (See photo below, left) Try to avoid planing into the work stop. If the stop *does* get chewed up, pop it off and add a new one. Waxing or applying a light coat of finish to the end of the stop will help preserve it and lessen the chance of planing into its surface.

Shooting flat miters. A double-ended bench hook lets you shave mitered work, such as this three-way miter joint, on the push or pull cut.

Shooting ends. This hooked shooting board lets you shave the ends of work straight and square. For end-grain cuts, a large plane set to take a light cut works best.

Clean cuts. A sharp iron takes full-length shavings and leaves a glassy, smooth surface on the work, even in end grain.

Shooting edge miters. Wide miters can be trimmed precisely using this angled jig clamped between dogs.

There are a couple varieties of shooting boards designed for tackling mitered work, which can be some of the most demanding joinery in the woodshop. We all know how frustrating it can be to accurately fit miters. Usually it's the last miter that needs some tweaking before the assembly comes together with all the joints nice and tight. For shooting the ends of miters, there are two jigs that cover the two common types. The **flat-miter shooting board** works in the bench-hook style, and lets you fine-tune miters on flat frames, such as picture-frame miters or even three-way miters, for a precise fit. (See top right photo, opposite page.) Because some mitered work has only one flat reference face (usually the back side), this jig is designed to shave miters from both directions. Size the board for the width of your workbench, and attach cleats or hooks at each end, then straddle the jig over the bench. This way, you can pull or push the plane depending on the orientation of the miter you need to trim.

For edge miters, where the miter runs across the face of the work, an **edge-miter shooting board**, also known as a **donkey's ear** for it's ridiculously floppy-looking shape, is an accurate trimming jig for tweaking long or short miters to precision. Typically this jig is clamped into an edge vise via a stout beam glued or screwed to the underside of the jig, or you can forgo the beam and grasp the jig between bench dogs. (See bottom right photo, opposite page.)

There are a few dedicated bench stops that you can build into practically any type of bench, and their greatest advantage is the fact that they're always there, ready to come to your aid at a moment's notice. The first is a pair of **slide-up stops** that pop out from the surface of your bench to register and stop your work, as shown in the photo below, left. Some woodworkers use a single stop, but I prefer pairs for their versatility. I use these stops for all kinds of work laid on the bench, but they're particularly useful for holding very thin stock, especially if you locate the stops on a solid, void-free area of your bench. Try holding thin work between bench dogs and you'll see the advantage of these stops: Dogging thin work will likely cause it to buckle and bow, and make it impossible to plane, since it has to span the gap between the tail vise and the bench itself.

Slide-up stops should be friction-fit into mortises cut square through the benchtop. You can rout the through-mortises, or chisel them out by hand, then thickness the stops for a snug, sliding fit. Make the stops themselves from a strong, dense wood—rosewood is an excellent choice. After much experimenting with their exact location, I've found it valuable to position the stops in line with each other as well as aligned with a bench dog, preferably at the far left end of the bench. This way, you can stop wide work against three points, preventing it from twisting and careening off the bench as you work its surface. (See photo below.)

Stopping thin stuff. You can adjust these slide-up stops above the bench surface so they register the edges of very thin stock.

Dog and two stops. Locating the slide-up stops in line with a bench dog lets you use all three stops to support wide work.

Edge support. To hold long boards on edge, this pull-out stop is housed in a grooved block screwed to the underside of the bench.

A **pull-out stop** on the underside of the benchtop is a great way to hold long boards on edge, and works to catch the end of the work when it's clamped in an edge or shoulder vise. (See photo, above.) You can install two or more of these stops along the edge of your bench to hold long or short boards. Make sure to use a dense, resilient wood such as hard maple or rosewood for the slide-out stick. Even though you'll only need a few inches of stick to support the work-piece, it's wise to make the stick about 8 to 10 inches long so you gain leverage as it contacts the underside of the bench for support.

Another type of built-in stop, a **flip-up stop**, is a handy device for small crosscutting and planing tasks, and works much like the cut-off bench hook on a slightly smaller scale. If you locate the stop at the end of your bench,

you can overhang work off your bench and use the stop to register the work. Like the slide-up stop, a single flip-up stop is handy, but two are handier, one for pulling and one for pushing cuts, as shown in the photo below. For strength, make the stops from a hard, dense wood such as maple or rosewood. And take your time laying out and positioning the parts so the stops rotate correctly into position. (See fig. 6.)

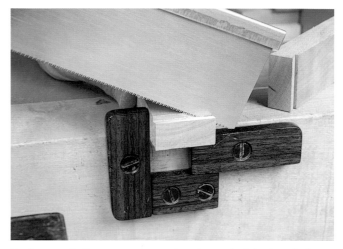

Push or pull. Two stops screwed to the end of the bench flip up for planing and sawing chores, depending on whether you're pushing or pulling in the cut.

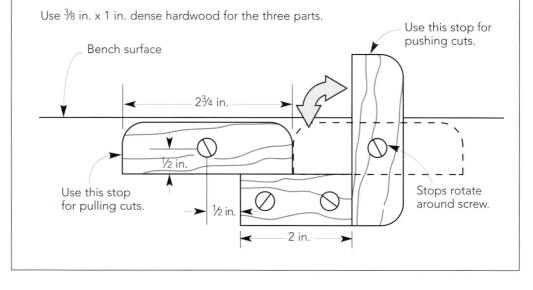

Fig. 6: Flip-Up Stops

Use ⅜ in. x 1 in. dense hardwood for the three parts.

Bench surface

2¾ in.

Use this stop for pushing cuts.

½ in.

Use this stop for pulling cuts.

½ in.

2 in.

Stops rotate around screw.

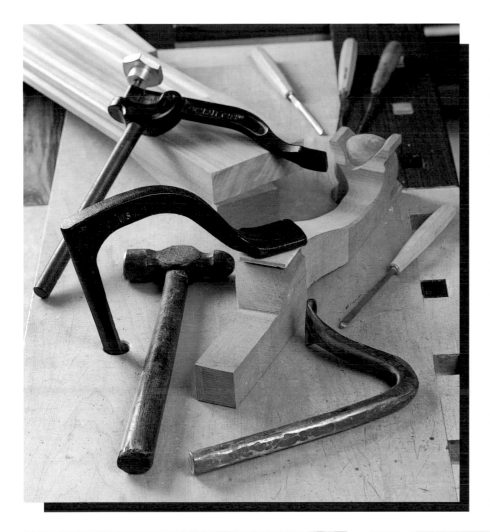

Holdfasts

Holdfasts can grip regular and odd-shaped work, such as carvings, anywhere on a benchtop and they do so quickly without a lot of fuss. A **traditional holdfast** is a length of malleable iron shaped to a hook at one end. You insert the holdfast through a hole in the benchtop and over the work, then hit it soundly to seat it. (See bottom photo, left.) To remove it, simply tap behind the crown and the holdfast will release. You can use the same type of holdfast for edge-clamping by incorporating holes on the side of a bench, either in the edge of the bench or through a leg, as shown in the photo, below.

It takes some deliberation (and guts!) to drill the necessary hole (or two) through your benchtop for the holdfast to engage. But

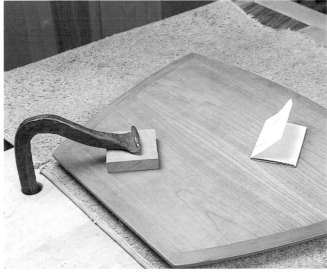

Quick hold. This hooked-shaped holdfast is made from malleable iron and works in conjunction with a hole drilled through the benchtop to grasp the top of a workpiece. It works great for odd-shaped pieces where standard clamps can't reach.

Edge holding. You can use a holdfast to support boards on edge when seated in a hole drilled through the leg of your bench.

I've found in practice that one or two holes won't compromise the surface of the bench. (See fig. 7.)

Similar to a standard holdfast, a fancier **screw-type holdfast** gives you the ability to regulate clamping pressure more sensitively via a large screw. You use it like a traditional holdfast, except you won't need to tap it down very hard. Once the holdfast is over the work, turning the clamping screw exerts an incredible amount of force onto the work. (See photo, below.)

Fig. 7: Traditional Holdfast

Made from malleable iron, a holdfast exerts tremendous holding power down onto the workpiece.

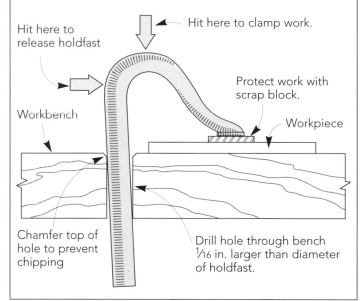

Hit here to release holdfast

Hit here to clamp work.

Protect work with scrap block.

Workbench

Workpiece

Chamfer top of hole to prevent chipping

Drill hole through bench $\frac{1}{16}$ in. larger than diameter of holdfast.

Screwed down. A large clamping knob on this hold-down allows you to fine-tune the clamping force over the workpiece.

Clamps

The old saw is true: You can never have enough clamps. After years of acquiring as many clamps as I can, I still run short on those occasions when I'm putting together really complex assemblies. Luckily, it seems that manufacturers are tuned-in to this predicament, judging by the hundreds of types of clamps on the market. Though it may take years to build up a decent clamp collection, you can get started with a much smaller stockpile. The most important advice is to know which ones are most vital to your woodworking, and where you can expect to use them.

Pipe clamps and bar clamps are by far the most reached-for type of clamp in the shop. Used to bring long or wide boards together, such as when clamping a tabletop, **pipe clamps** are an inexpensive investment. (See bottom photo, left.) You'll find two sizes of pipe clamps: ½ inch and ¾ inch, which refers to the size of the clamping heads and the corresponding pipe size you'll need.

The metal jaws made for pipe clamps slip over or thread onto metal pipe, which you can have cut to your desired length at a plumbing-supply store. Ask for "black pipe," which I find has less tendency for allowing the free clamping head to slip. Smaller ½-inch pipe (the measurement actually refers to the internal diameter) will bend if great force is used during clamping, effectively ruining the clamp. Larger-diameter ¾-inch pipe is much stiffer, although you'll be lugging heavier clamps around the shop. It pays to have both sizes on hand, one set for light duty clamping and one for serious pressure. Generally it's worth having sets of four to six clamps each in assorted lengths, from 2 feet up to 6 feet or more.

When you buy your pipe, be sure to have the store thread both ends of each pipe. One threaded end

accepts the fixed jaw. Then buy a few **pipe couplers**, so you can extend the effective length of your clamps by threading a coupler onto the end opposite the fixed jaw and attach another length of pipe. (See photo, right.)

Bar clamps are much stiffer than pipe clamps, and many woodworkers prefer them. Be warned: They're expensive! The traditional bar clamp has been around for a long time. Because the beam is rectangular in section, a bar clamp has much more beam strength, and is less likely to bow or bend under pressure. (See photo, below.)

Infinite length. To increase your pipe clamps' overall length, screw these threaded pipe couplers and extra pipe onto the ends.

Piping tight. These ¾-inch pipe clamps are inexpensive and stiff enough to withstand bowing even under heavy pressure.

Beam strength. The rectangular shape of a bar clamp makes it stronger, allowing you to apply more pressure without danger of bowing the beam.

A newer breed of bar clamp, **K-body clamps**, have jaws covered in glue-resistant plastic, and they have proven themselves to be very popular with cabinet-makers. (See photo, left) These relatively deep-jawed clamps can reach deeper, often allowing you to place one clamp over another while still gaining purchase on the work. One nice feature of these newer bar clamps is that their jaws remain square to the bar or beam, even under great pressure. This means you're less likely to twist or cock an assembly out-of-square, making this style of clamp especially useful when putting together cabinets.

For clamping smaller assemblies and locking down jigs and fixtures, **C-clamps** offer lots of clamping pressure in a relatively small package. Tried-and-true C-clamps are inexpensive, and come in a variety of sizes, based on their throat depth. Four-inch clamps prove the most useful, and it's worth investing in 10 or more of them. The most convenient style of C-clamp comes with a movable clamp handle that slides through its nut, letting you position the clamp close to the work without having the handle in the way. (See photo below, left.)

Similar to C-clamps, but faster to apply and release pressure, **quick clamps** have a sliding jaw that lets you position and tighten the clamp in a hurry. This feature is a real timesaver when a complicated assembly means

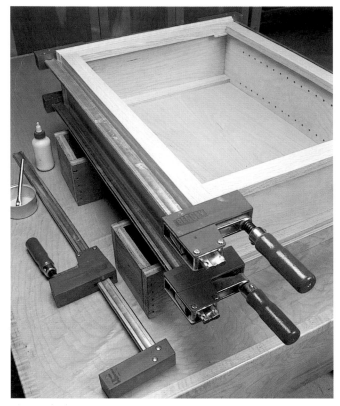

Strong and square. The deep jaws on K-body bar clamps let you reach farther over the work. They remain parallel as you apply pressure, preventing the work from racking out of square.

Old faithfuls. C-clamps are affordable and can be used all over the shop for a variety of clamping tasks. Sliding handles lets you use the clamps in tight spaces.

Quick to clamp. The sliding jaws of quick clamps make them well suited for complex assemblies, when you need to get lots of clamps on fast.

having to apply lots of clamps before the glue starts to set. (See bottom right photo, opposite page.) Look for quick clamps with stiff beams or bars, which can apply great pressure without bending. Heavy pressure can not only distort the clamp itself, but also mar the workpiece with small depressions in the surface. Clamps outfitted with protective plastic caps on their clamping jaws overcome this habit, and as a bonus they'll resist glue, too. (See photo, below.)

With jaws typically made from hard maple, **wooden handscrews** can grasp all sorts of items, including tapered work. Used with quick-clamps, holdfasts, or bench vises, a handscrew will readily grasp work and offer it up at a more convenient angle, as shown in the top photo, right. One of the great attributes of handscrews is their pivoting jaws, which allow you to grab angled or odd-shaped work. (See middle photo, right.) Look for handscrews in various-sized jaw lengths, from small 2-inch clamps up to 12 inches or more. The larger sizes act as deep-throat clamps, letting you apply pressure in the middle of wide work.

Spring clamps offer light-duty clamping action, and are great for temporarily holding jigs or parts together. Traditional spring clamps, with pressed-metal or plastic jaws and rubber grips, are affordable and quick to open and close. But larger spring clamps can be difficult to open, especially if you have small hands, as shown in the bottom photo, right. A newer breed of

Convenient clamping. By clamping a wooden handscrew in a bench vise, you can raise your work to a more suitable height.

Angled clamping. By pivoting the jaw, you can pull odd-shaped parts together.

Mar-free clamping. The plastic pads on these quick clamps resist glue and won't ding or scratch the work.

Big squeeze. Metal or plastic spring clamps are quick to hold, but large versions require a big reach and lots of muscle to overcome the spring tension.

STORING CLAMPS

Keeping clamps on hand can be a challenge. Where do you put 'em so you can get at 'em, then store 'em out of the way when not in use? A rolling clamp cart is a great solution, since it lets you bring the clamps exactly where you need them. (See fig. 8.)

If floor space is at a premium in your shop, hanging your clamps is another effective strategy. Wooden curtain rods or solid-metal

Clamps at a glance. Hanging clamps over a metal rod with a support stick below it gives you instant access, and lets you put camps safely away when you're done.

rods will support clamps and allow them to be draped quickly in place, ready for action, as shown in the photo, above. Don't overlook existing house fixtures as viable clamping spots. Basement stairs are likely candidates that offer various surfaces for creative storage. (See top photo, opposite page.)

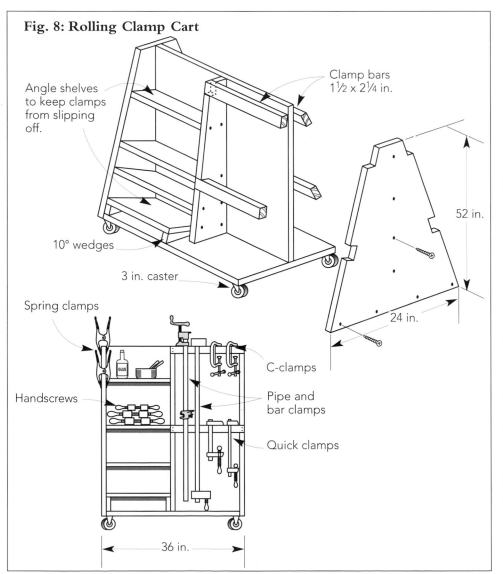

Fig. 8: Rolling Clamp Cart

Angle shelves to keep clamps from slipping off.

Clamp bars 1½ x 2¼ in.

10° wedges

3 in. caster

52 in.

24 in.

Spring clamps

Handscrews

C-clamps

Pipe and bar clamps

Quick clamps

GLUE

36 in.

Wall access. Plywood hangers make any large clamp collection easy to access.

Up and down. The stringers and the steps on these basement stairs offer lots of clamp storage space without intruding into the steps proper.

Another option is to hang your bar or pipe clamps on shopmade hangers, as shown in the bottom photo, opposite page. Make the hangers from plywood, and use heavy-duty screws or bolts to attach them securely to the studs in the wall. (See fig. 9.)

Fig. 9: Wall Clamp Hangers

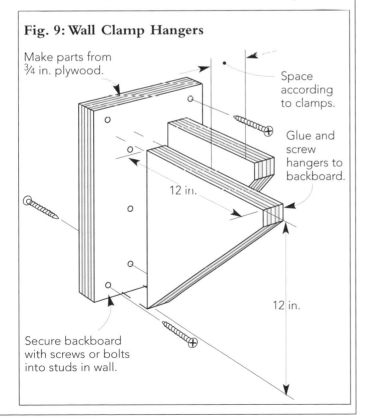

Make parts from ¾ in. plywood.

Space according to clamps.

Glue and screw hangers to backboard.

12 in.

12 in.

Secure backboard with screws or bolts into studs in wall.

plastic spring clamp offers ratcheting action to overcome the spring tension, letting you easily open and apply the clamp with one hand. (See photo, below.)

Band clamps or **web clamps** are designed to wrap around work and pull it together, and they're particularly useful when an ordinary clamp can't reach. (See bottom photo, below.) The ratcheting-style band clamp lets you apply more pressure than the less-expensive pull-style clamp.

Easy open. These small plastic spring clamps work via a ratcheting action, letting you easily open and close them with one hand.

Tight strapping. Band clamps can pull mitered joints together and wrap around hard-to-clamp items such as boxes, cylinders, or other irregular work.

Stretched together. When clamping curved laminated work, an inner tube—or any stretchy, rubber-like material—sliced into strips, pulls plies together while the glue sets.

For complex curved assemblies or laminations, stretchy rubber is just the ticket. You can buy **surgical tubing** from woodworking suppliers, or recycle old **bicycle inner tubes** or other **lengths of stretchable rubber** into strips to make very effective band-type clamps. Use a razor knife to slice an inner tube along its length to make two strips. You'll be surprised at how much clamping pressure you can achieve by pulling on the tube and wrapping it around the work. (See photo, above.) Start clamping by wrapping the tubing around the work and underneath itself, then continue wrapping around the work, stretching the band tightly with each wrap. For maximum pressure, double back on the work in a criss-cross fashion. Finish by tucking the last length of tube under itself, and pull tightly to secure it. One tip: If you're using a bicycle inner tube, position the powdered inside surface onto the work so excess glue doesn't stick to the band.

While you can use all sorts of small C-clamps, quick-clamps and spring clamps for holding little parts, nothing beats **toggle clamps** for speed and convenience when it comes to holding small-sized parts in jigs, or wherever you need great pressure and want your hands away from the cutting action. There's a bewildering assortment of sizes and styles available, but the most useful for jig-making and other fixtures are the hold-down varieties. (See photo below, left.) Unlike screw-action clamps, toggle clamps are quick to use. At the flick of your wrist, a toggle clamp will snap closed on a workpiece, cinching it tightly in place. Another flick of the wrist pops the clamp open, instantly freeing the part. (See photo, below.) You won't need many of these clamps, since you can mount and dismount them to any number of jigs with a few screws.

Not often thought of as a clamp, a collection of **heavy weights** can come to your rescue for those

Toggle selection. Hold-down toggle clamps are labor-saving devices when it comes to gripping parts in jigs and fixtures.

Lever action. A flick of the wrist is all it takes to instantly secure a part to a jig with a toggle clamp.

times when an ordinary clamp can't reach. (See photo, below.) I regularly use weights to clamp in the middle of wide work, position workpieces, or hold parts flat, as shown in the bottom photo, below. Chunks of iron and steel are best, and can be found at any number of places, some of them off the beaten path. Look for discarded window sash weights, or visit flea markets or tool auctions. My biggest score was attending a machinery auction at an old forge, where various metal cast-offs were laying a dark, dusty corner. Most of the weights you find can be free for the asking.

Roll it right. This hand roller lets you press narrow strips of laminate to an edge with great precision and control, and without the risk of breaking any overhang.

Weighty collection. Blocks of iron and steel can be used as weights to clamp or hold odd parts.

The last "clamp" in your tool repertoire is more of a pressing tool than an actual clamp. For adhering plastic laminate and edgebanding to substrates, it makes sense to have a **laminate roller**. I generally use a roller for plastic-laminate work, where I need to press pieces together using contact cement. But a roller is handy for various pressing jobs where you need pinpoint pressure to squeeze out glue or air bubbles. For moderate pressure, especially on edges, a small hand roller with a hard rubber roller affords more control, as shown in the photo, above. For broad surfaces, a J-type roller provides more pressure and covers larger surfaces with less effort. (See photo, below.)

Weight where you want. A series of weights placed on top of sticks helps distribute pressure for keeping parts stacked flat.

Big pressing. This J-roller lets you apply pressure on large plastic laminate surfaces for a consistent bond.

Layout Tools

The foundation for fine woodwork begins with careful layout, which divides itself into marking and measuring. You'll need accurate tools for dimensioning stock, laying out parts for joinery, and testing for true. There are many essential layout tools that accomplish these tasks, and they tend to run the gamut when it comes to quality and cost. You'll see lots of fancy rosewood handles, brushed brass, polished steel, and high prices when it comes to this category of tools. But some of the plainer, less expensive tools will do the job just fine, thank you.

The best advice is to look closely when you buy: While tropical woods and exotic metals may look nice, unless these materials affect a tool's use, you're often better off saving some money and buying a cheaper alternative. On the flip side, don't let the high cost of a tool prevent you from buying it when you can gain greater precision. Above all, a layout tool must be precise and smooth-working, since any errors at this stage of a project will only multiply and cause bigger headaches later on. Finally, it's OK to buy a tool for its beauty. I do all the time, because I love tools that look and feel good to my hand and to my eye. Just make sure you're not buying the bark without the bite: A snazzy-looking tool had better perform as well as its plain-Jane cousin.

Marking Tools

Marking your work requires many different approaches, from drawing straight and curved lines to locating hardware and laying out joints. And making these marks often demands varying degrees of accuracy. For example, marking a rough-sawn board to cut to rough length doesn't require the same degree of precision as when marking out a set of dovetails on dimensioned stock. Yet each operation requires a clear, legible mark using the appropriate tool. Read on to find out how to make the right mark on your work.

Marking Straight Lines and Points

Let's face it. The vast majority of woodworking is rectilinear, or involves straight lines. Even irregular-shaped work or round objects usually begin life in the shop in some rectangular form. Because of this fact, we need good tools that mark legible and accurate straight lines in our work. And some of these

tools are useful for marking dimples in work for drill bits and other tools to follow.

Pencils are a staple in any woodshop. Ordinary pencils carry the bulk of my marking work and, unlike a carpenter's pencil with its flat or rounded tip, a properly sharpened pencil marks a fine line. But for more consistent lines, I recommend using a **mechanical pencil**, which draws a thin line of consistent width. (See photo, below.) Available in fine (0.7 mm) or finer (0.5 mm) leads that fit into the shaft, a mechanical pencil provides a consistent line width as it wears. It never dulls, and it never needs sharpening. (How many tools can stake that claim?) It's best to use a mechanical

Fine marks. A mechanical pencil leaves a fine line of consistent width.

pencil with a light touch to avoid breaking the delicate leads. The trick is to extend the lead just a hair beyond its housing, and use light, even pressure as you draw.

When marking darker-hued woods like walnut or rosewood, an ordinary lead pencil can be frustratingly difficult to see even under good light. Here, it makes sense to use a finely sharpened **white pencil**, available at art supply stores. (See photo, below.)

Some woodworkers prefer to mark their work with an **awl**, scratching the pointed tip into the work. While this technique often yields better results than a pencil, I generally find it unacceptable for marking anything but the shortest lines, since the tip actually scratches a V-groove in the surface, leaving a somewhat ragged line. This is especially true when you draw an awl across the grain. But awls really shine with pinpoint accuracy when it comes to locating holes for hardware and such. By

pressing the tip of the tool into the work, such as when laying out for a hinge, you can leave a highly precise mark for a drill bit to follow. (See bottom photo, left.)

There are top-dollar awls available, with fancy rose-wood handles and brass ferrules, or you can pick up a simple plastic-handled awl at the hardware store. They all work the same, as long as their tips are sharp. One style of awl that works well for many operations is a small Japanese awl with a stout but stubby handle. The short handle brings your hand closer to the work for more fingertip control, as shown in the photo, right. If—or I should say *when*—the tip of your awl dulls, be sure to re-grind it on a bench grinder or with a file to keep it sharp.

Good grip. This stubby little Japanese awl fits into the palm of your hand and affords great fingertip control.

While an awl is a great aid for laying out hardware, if you've got *lots* of holes to mark, a **center punch** is less fatiguing, faster, and more accurate. Commonly used in the metalworking trade to punch a dimple in metal stock to keep drill bits from wandering, a center punch is just as useful to the woodworker. When you push the top of the tool, a spring-loaded tip drives itself into the work, leaving a very accurate mark, or dimple. The tip itself is chamfered, so it centers itself automatically if pushed through a narrow hole. (See photo, left.)

Visible lines. A white pencil leaves a fine but visible line on dark woods.

Prick and push. An awl can help locate the center of a screw hole for tasks such as laying out holes for a hinge.

Spring-action marking. The chamfered tips on these center punches align with the centers of small holes. Spring-loaded plungers drive the tips into the work when you push from above.

I often use center punches and awls in conjunction with jigs to help guide the tool's tip. One of the most useful jigs for the cabinetmaker is a shelf-hole jig, as shown in the photo, below and in figure 1. This homemade guide allows you to prick a series of shelf-pin holes with an awl or punch in a cabinet's side. After drilling on your marks with a drill bit, your shelf holes will line up precisely once the cabinet is assembled.

When it comes to rough layout lines on large workpieces, such as dividing lines for case parts on a sheet of plywood, you can use a **chalk line**, also known as a **snap line**. A traditional carpenter's chalk line is a plastic or metal container filled with colored chalk powder and a spool of string. As you pull the string from the spool it automatically coats itself with the chalk. A metal hook on the end of the string lets you position the string at one end of the work while you pull the string taut. To use the tool, you lift the string in the center and let it

"snap" down on the work, marking a dead-straight line made of chalk. (See bottom photo, left.)

Before marking a second line, make sure the entire line is well-covered in chalk by rewinding the string fully and shaking the container. A useful advantage of a chalk line is its reversibility. Should you need to erase your marks, simply swipe the line with a damp sponge or blow it with compressed air, and the mark disappears.

After laying out your parts and cutting pieces to rough size, eventually you'll need to produce a line with the highest degree of accuracy possible, such as when laying out dovetails or other fine joints. For the finest line of all, it's worth considering a knife. A fine knife line on your work is easy to see, yet much more distinct and accurate than a pencil. Plus, a knife edge severs wood fibers cleanly, unlike a fiber-tearing awl, and it leaves a small groove for registering a chisel or saw. The simplest and least-expensive type of knife to use is a **razor knife**, also called a **craft knife**. You can pick up these knives at craft stores or wherever art supplies are sold. With its thin and pointed blade, a craft knife will reach into tight spots and leave a very fine line. (See photo, below.)

Although practically any type of knife—assuming it's razor sharp— will mark a wonderful line, the finest line of all comes from a true **marking knife**, which is beveled on one side only, and is flat on the opposite side. With a marking knife, you can reference the flat side against a straightedge or other edges, and, even more important, you'll leave an accurate 90-degree wall, or shoulder, to cut to. This makes registering your

Pricking shelf holes. With a simple guide jig clamped to the work, you can use a center punch or awl to mark a series of precisely spaced holes for shelf pins. Blue tape defines the desired holes.

Pull up; let go. A chalk line lets you lay out long lines for rough work, such as dividing a sheet of plywood into parts prior to cutting.

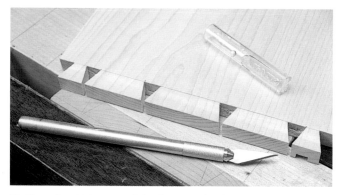

Knife point. Using a craft knife to mark a line is many times more accurate than using a pencil or other marking device.

One side flat. A true marking knife has a bevel on one side of the blade only, letting you register the flat side accurately against a straightedge to cut a precise 90° shoulder in the work.

Cut both ways. Double-bevel marking knives have a flat side for referencing against a fence, and two bevels so you can scribe from either side of the work.

tools—especially chisels—to the cut line more accurate than were you to use a blade with a two-sided bevel, which essentially cuts a less-accurate V-shaped groove. (See photo, above.)

Marking knives are most accurate when you pull them toward you, not the other way around. And they work best when guided by a fence or the edge of a thin, straight board. If you're cutting with the grain, make

several light passes instead of one deep cut to keep the knife from wandering with the grain. Light, cross-grain cuts are easy to see; cuts with the grain should be deeper to make the line more visible. Unlike a pencil, a knife mark has no width because you're cutting into the wood's surface. With such a fine mark, you can cut right on the line without having to favor one side or the other. These features make a marking knife a practical choice for demanding marking tasks, particularly when it comes to laying out joints.

While a good marking knife should have a bevel on one side only, for more versatility you can use a **double-bevel marking knife**, which has two bevels on the same face. The double bevel allows you to reference the knife on the left and right side of the work when you need to pull in the same direction. (See photo, above.)

Fig. 1: Shelf-Pin Hole Guide

Use this jig and an awl or center punch to accurately locate holes for shelf pins in the sides of cabinets.

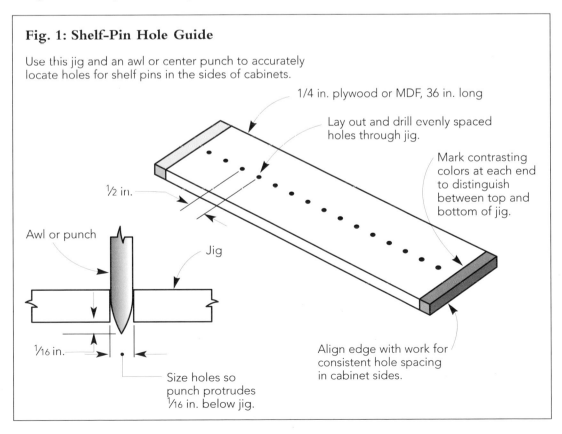

1/4 in. plywood or MDF, 36 in. long

Lay out and drill evenly spaced holes through jig.

Mark contrasting colors at each end to distinguish between top and bottom of jig.

1/2 in.

Awl or punch

Jig

1/16 in.

Size holes so punch protrudes 1/16 in. below jig.

Align edge with work for consistent hole spacing in cabinet sides.

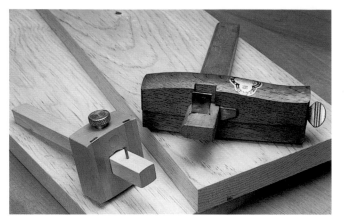

Two types of gauges. The marking gauge (left) sports a pin for scribing lines with the grain, while the cutting gauge (right) has a knife edge for clean cuts across the grain.

Employing the same degree of marking precision is the **gauge**. Essentially a fenced marking knife, the traditional gauge takes many forms, and is used for a variety of marking tasks where you need a straight line that's parallel to one edge of the workpiece, typically in laying out joints. Unlike a marking knife, once you set up a gauge it's quick to scribe a straight line because the fence registers and guides the tool against the edge of the workpiece. You move the gauge along the work, pushing or pulling it, depending on your preference. A pin or knife in the beam scores a straight line in your stock. You can adjust the distance of the cutter from the fence by loosening a thumbscrew and moving the beam in or out. While there are many styles of gauges for a

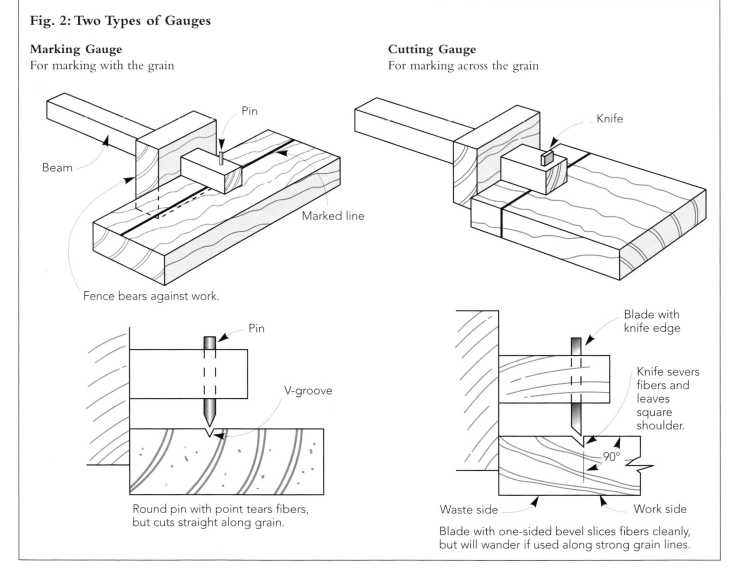

Fig. 2: Two Types of Gauges

Marking Gauge
For marking with the grain

Pin

Beam

Marked line

Fence bears against work.

Pin

V-groove

Round pin with point tears fibers, but cuts straight along grain.

Cutting Gauge
For marking across the grain

Knife

Blade with knife edge

Knife severs fibers and leaves square shoulder.

90°

Waste side

Work side

Blade with one-sided bevel slices fibers cleanly, but will wander if used along strong grain lines.

Marking with the grain. Start a marking gauge with the tool slightly cocked (above), and roll it into the work. Push or pull the gauge with the grain direction of the board to score a line parallel to the edge of the work (below).

variety of uses, there are two essential types, the marking gauge and the cutting gauge. (See photo, opposite page.) Each type of gauge has distinct cutting attributes that are important to note. (See fig. 2.)

The **marking gauge** has a hardened pin or spur that scores a small groove in the work. This gauge is designed to be used for marking stock across the grain, or on end grain, since the rounded tip cuts straight and true, and won't wander along deep or strong grain lines. I use a marking gauge any time I need to scribe the edges of boards for resawing, or wherever I need an accurate straight line close to the edge of the workpiece. (See photos, above.)

The **cutting gauge** differs from the marking gauge in that it holds a knife-type cutter instead of a pin. Like the marking gauge, the cutting gauge can be used to scribe lines in end grain, or for slitting thin materials, for example, slicing fine veneers into string inlay. But a cutting gauge's main purpose is to mark a straight line across the grain, such as when laying out the baseline for dovetails. (See top photos, right.) On a cutting gauge, the cutter is beveled on one side and flat on the other, with the bevel always facing the gauge's fence. The difference is significant. Should you try to cut along the grain in anything but fine-textured woods, the cutter will follow the grain lines and spoil the line. But used across the grain, the

bevel actually pulls the fence tight to the work, and the cutting edge severs the wood fibers cleanly, leaving a perfect 90-degree shoulder for your chisel or saw.

Similar to the marking gauge is the **mortise gauge**, which consists of a pair of pins that scribe parallel lines. This is the tool for laying out mortises and tenons in the edges or ends of stock. The pins are adjustable via a brass bar or a threaded rod. To use the gauge, adjust the pins equal to the width of your chisel and the mortise, or to the thickness of your tenon, and set the fence to reference against one side of the stock. Then pull or push the gauge to mark parallel lines. (See photo, below.)

Marking across the grain. The cutting gauge's knife-like blade cuts a clean line across stock (above), such as when marking out the baseline for dovetails. The broad fence makes it easy to scribe lines across narrow edges (below).

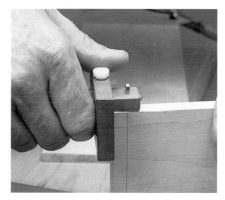

Marking mortises and tenons. The mortise gauge has a pair of adjustable pins that scribe parallel lines for marking out mortises or scribing the cheeks of a tenon.

Some mortise gauges come with an extra third pin on the opposite side of the beam, giving you essentially two gauges—marking and mortise—in one. While a dual-purpose gauge is useful and economical, you're better off buying a dedicated mortise gauge if you need to mark a lot of mortises or tenons, since the extra pin has an amazing knack for jumping up and pricking your finger when you wrap your hands over the tool.

One type of gauge that's used less these days in furnituremaking is called the **panel gauge**. Its geometry is identical to the marking gauge in that it sports a pin-style cutter, but both the beam and the fence are much longer, allowing you to mark the width of wide boards along the grain and parallel to one edge. (See photo, below.)

With any type of gauge, it's worth practicing for a few minutes to get a feel for the tool. You can push or pull a gauge, depending on your preference and the particular orientation of the workpiece. Don't try to make a deep line the first time. You can go back and forth as many times as you want to make a deeper line that's more visible. If you don't want the gauge lines to show in the finished work—which is purely a matter of personal taste—gauge a shallower line that you can erase later by planing or sanding.

SHARPENING A GAUGE

Like all cutting tools, you'll need to sharpen the cutters on your gauges regularly, or the lines they leave won't be sharp and crisp. For all gauges other than the mortise gauge, simply grasp the non-cutting end of the pin or knife with a pair of pliers and yank it out of the beam. Then hone the cutter on sharpening stones—the steel is too hard to attack with a file. The mortise gauge with its fixed pins is a bit trickier. Here, you'll need to work a small slip-stone around each pin until it's sharp. Be careful you don't leave one pin longer than the other, or the tool won't scribe accurately when you put it back to use.

Honing stick. A kerfed stick grasps the cutting gauge's diminutive cutting knife to aid in honing the bevel side. Hone and polish the back, too, by rubbing the blade flat on your stones.

Marking wide. Similar to the marking gauge but bigger, the panel gauge lets you cut accurate parallel lines on wide stock.

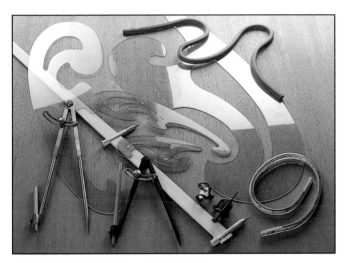

Marking Curves

There are several tools and methods for generating curves or other non-rectilinear marks and lines on your work. One of the simplest is to use your eye.

Often I'll sketch a curve freehand, refining it by eye until I'm satisfied that it's fair. The term is important to woodworkers: A fair curve means a line or edge that moves smoothly in one continuous motion, without bumps or dips. Using fair curves can raise the level of your work, whereas curves that aren't fair often look crude or ill-planned. While you can often use your eye to successfully produce a fair curve, there are times when using a tool is more appropriate or more accurate.

Big and little circles. Small compasses are great for drawing small arcs; a longer 12-inch compass holds a standard pencil and lets you draw arcs or circles up to 2 feet in diameter.

Remember your fifth-grade **pencil compass**, with its little yellow pencil? If you've still got it, it's time to move it into the woodshop for all sorts of jobs. Of course, compasses are great for drawing accurate circles or arcs of circles, and a small 6-inch compass is handy to have for just this purpose, and

affords good control when swinging through small arcs. A more versatile solution for grown-up woodworkers is a 12-inch compass, which lets you draws arcs as large as 24 inches, more suited to general furnituremaking. (See bottom photo, left.)

Another use for the compass is to generate an ellipse, which is essentially an accelerated curve with constantly changing radii. Ellipses are beautiful curves that can be used in all sorts of work, from inlay work and scrollwork to swooping table aprons and gently curving tabletops. While there are many ways to draw an ellipse on your work, one of the simplest involves using a compass along with a pencil and some string, as shown in figure 3.

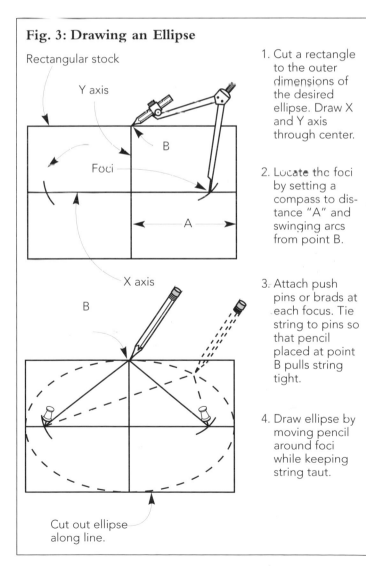

Fig. 3: Drawing an Ellipse

Rectangular stock
Y axis
B
Foci
A
X axis
B

Cut out ellipse along line.

1. Cut a rectangle to the outer dimensions of the desired ellipse. Draw X and Y axis through center.

2. Locate the foci by setting a compass to distance "A" and swinging arcs from point B.

3. Attach push pins or brads at each focus. Tie string to pins so that pencil placed at point B pulls string tight.

4. Draw ellipse by moving pencil around foci while keeping string taut.

Bigger circles. A beam compass fit with trammel heads can draw small arcs or really large circles of practically any size, depending on the length of your stick.

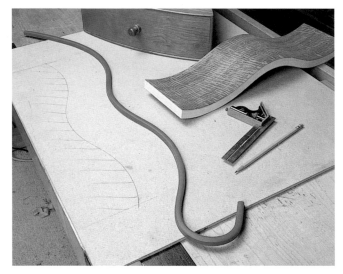

Molding a curve. Vinyl flexible curves come in different lengths, and can be flexed to match almost any curve, letting you draw curved lines or copy shapes.

Accelerated curve. You can bend a thin, 1/8-inch stick of wood to a desired ellipse and trace the shape onto your work. Clamps help hold the curve as you draw.

When I need to mark or scribe irregular parts so they fit together precisely, I use a compass as a very accurate scribing tool. The best example is when fitting cabinets to out-of-flat walls, or scribing complicated trim. (See Using a Compass for Scribing, opposite page.)

For really large circles or arcs of circles, a **beam compass** fitted with a pair of **trammel heads** is the answer. (See photo, left.) You can make the beam from scrap stock, and it can be as long as you like, giving you the ability to draw circles or arcs of an infinite number of sizes.

For circular and irregular layout, a **flexible curve** can be molded to radii as small as ½ inch without kinking, and lets you lay out irregular shapes as well. Look for them in woodworking catalogs, or at art-supply stores. These vinyl or rubber strips come in short or long versions and can be flexed into practically any position, making them handy for copying existing curves or drawing new ones. (See photo, left.)

Flowing curves. Plastic French curves let you adjust radii, draw transitional lines, or generate any number of curves in your work. Small French curves are good for small work; jumbo-sized curves let you work on a bigger scale, helping produce flowing curves and transitions over large areas.

If you want to draw parts of an ellipse, or accelerated curves (where the radius is not constant), you can make your own **flexible stick** from a thin stick of scrap wood. By bending the rule to the desired curvature and clamping it in position, it's a simple matter of tracing the curve onto your work, as shown in the bottom left photo, opposite page. It's important to select straight-grained stock, so your curves will be consistent, or fair. I generally mill the stick to around ⅛ inch thick, then test its flexibility. If I need more curvature, I simply thin the stick some more in a thickness planer or with a hand plane until it bends to the desired curve.

A **French curve** is another useful curve-generating tool, and acts as a tracing template to let you smooth a transition from a radius to a straight line, make small arcs, or generate practically any sort of curve. Commonly sold in art supply stores as a set of three, each with varying curves, these plastic templates can help you draw the tricky stuff without a lot of head-scratching. One of the drawbacks to the standard artist's French curve is its diminutive size. Recognizing this, you can now find **oversized French curves** made specifically for woodworkers. These clear plastic templates are great for bigger work, such as curved cabinetwork and tabletops, as shown in the bottom right photo, opposite page.

USING A COMPASS FOR SCRIBING

To fit irregular work, such as a piece of trim to an uneven wall, you can employ a compass as a scribing tool, letting you mark and trim your work so it fits exactly.

Fig. 4: Scribing with a Compass

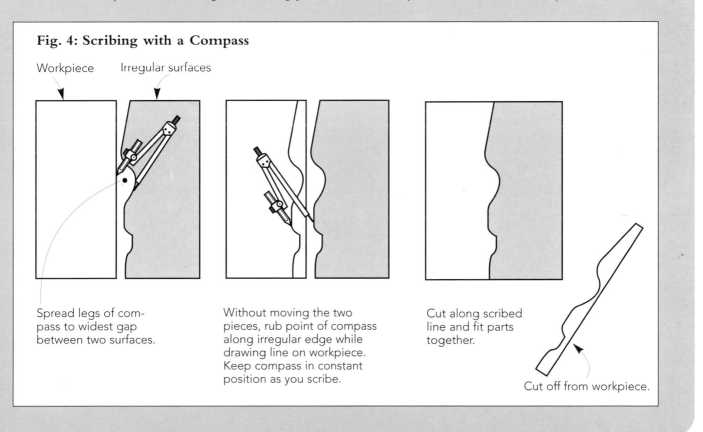

Workpiece   Irregular surfaces

Spread legs of compass to widest gap between two surfaces.

Without moving the two pieces, rub point of compass along irregular edge while drawing line on workpiece. Keep compass in constant position as you scribe.

Cut along scribed line and fit parts together.

Cut off from workpiece.

Measuring Tools

Accurate measurement is a cornerstone of woodworking, and sound measuring prevents mistakes while giving you greater control over your work. Taking the time to measure precisely results in better-fitting parts, and often alerts you to potential snags in the construction process. If you can measure accurately at the layout stage, chances are you'll reduce last-minute snafus later. There's nothing more frustrating than discovering a part that's too long or a wee bit short, especially at the glue-up stage when there's often no turning back. Good measuring tools used throughout the building stage prevent these hiccups and horrors, and help your woodworking go smoothly.

Determining the dimensional size of a workpiece, say, its width or length, is only one aspect of the measuring process. Some of the most-used measuring tools in the shop, such as straightedges and squares, let you read the quality of surfaces accurately for flat or square, an equally important aspect of woodworking. Other important tools help you find precise angles or contours for irregular or curved work, or let you know the precise moisture content in your stock. Let's start by looking at the tools used for dimensional measurements.

Dimensional Measuring Tools

Thickness, width, length, diameter—these are the dimensions we need to be concerned about when calculating our parts as we lay them out or cut them to size. And some very important tools will tell us the exact dimensions we need.

Rules are the most basic of measuring devices, and allow you to accurately gauge thickness, width, length, depth, height, or circumference. The **folding rule** is a traditional tool used by craftspeople in the building and furnituremaking trades alike. (See photo, below.) These classy sticks, usually made of boxwood, come in small and large lengths (up to 6 feet), and fold up in a

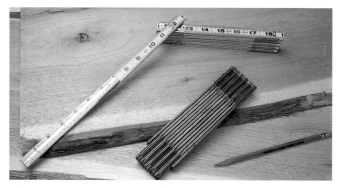

Wood rules. Wooden folding rules expand up to 6 feet for measuring long distances, and can be folded up to slip into a back pocket.

zig-zag fashion to fit in a back pocket. A brass depth gauge is a common feature on many of these rules, and lets you measure the depth of grooves, mortises and other holes. (See photo, below.) One of the advantages of the folding rule is its ability to span long distances with bending, letting you take long or tall measurements with ease.

The standard rule in most woodworkers' toolbox is a **tape measure**. Look for easy-to-read markings and divisions in $\frac{1}{8}$ and $\frac{1}{16}$ inch, with smaller marks down to $\frac{1}{32}$ inch along the first 12 inches or so of the rule. (See bottom photo, below.) More expensive tape measures are available with digital readouts, making it a cinch to see and read a measurement. However, these high-tech devices are heavy to lug around, and they tend to be better suited for taking long measurements.

Finding depth. A slide-out brass rule on this folding rule lets you easily determine accurate depths.

One of the benefits of using a tape measure is that you get a lot of measuring power in a small package. Tapes are available in lengths of 50 feet or more, letting you measure long distances such as room layouts or large outdoor projects. Keep in mind that bigger tapes are more suited to carpentry-type work, where measured spans are usually longer. And a bigger tape measure means a bulkier, heavier tool to carry around the shop, which can be a pain. For general woodworking, a 16-foot tape measure will cover most of your needs without becoming cumbersome. Smaller tapes—10 feet and under—are useful around the workbench for laying out and measuring parts.

An unusual yet practical type of tape measure that gets a lot of use in my shop is a **left- or right-reading tape**. This particular tape lets you measure with one hand while your writing hand does the marking, regardless of your hand preference, as shown in the photo below.

My pet rules are rigid **metal rules**, which are available in various lengths. Having a selection of these is useful for all sorts of measuring and layout tasks. Metal rules typically come with divisions as fine as $\frac{1}{128}$ inch for very accurate, detailed measurements. My favorite rule is a **6-inch steel rule** with etched markings. The markings are easy to see and won't wear away through use, and they're accurately placed right to the ends of the rule. Since the marks run full length, you can butt the end of the rule against work

Easy to read. The rule on this tape measure is clearly marked with divisions in feet and inches, down to $\frac{1}{32}$ inch for very precise readings.

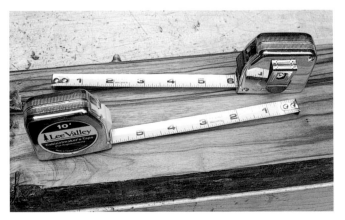

Southpaws, too. These left- and right-reading tape measures make it easier to measure and mark without needing a third hand.

Fine lines. The etched markings—as small as ¹⁄₆₄ inch—on this 6-inch rule are easy to see, and resist wear. Divisions are accurately marked to the very end of the rule, letting you make corner measurements with confidence.

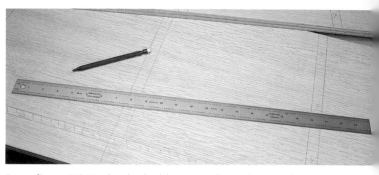

Long lines. A 24-inch rule doubles as a ruler and a straightedge, allowing you to lay out and mark long lines.

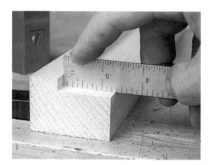

Find the height. End markings allow you to use the rule sideways to find the height of furniture parts as well as bits and cutters.

for precise corner or inside measurements, as shown in the photo, above. Another nice aspect of this small rule is its end markings, located on the short ends of the rule. End markings allow you to gauge heights accurately and easily on your work, and on your cutters and tools. (See photo, above.)

Longer rules, such as a **24-inch steel rule**, increase your measuring power, and can also be used as straightedges to measure flat surfaces, or as a ruler for laying out lines. (See top photo, right.)

An **architect's rule** is often used at the design stage, and is a highly accurate proportioning tool. If you've ever needed to produce a scale drawing, the architect's rule is the tool of choice. Most rules let you choose from six scales to suit your work so you can make an exact scale replica of the real thing in the most convenient size. (See middle photo, right.)

Commonly used in metalworking and fabricating shops for machine set-ups and other precision measurements, **dial calipers** are handy in the woodshop, too. Don't let a caliper's super-accurate dial (capable of measuring in thousandths of an inch) intimidate you.

While machinists need this high degree of accuracy in their work, woodworkers can take advantage of this precision tool without having to think in such microscopic terms. (See photo, below.)

With their outside-, inside-, and depth-reading capabilities, you can use dial calipers for laying out joints; gauging stock thickness, width, or diameter (such as measuring a round tenon or finding the exact shank size of a screw); as well as taking inside readings for

Scaled version. You can determine proportions or draw and make pieces to scale using an architect's rule.

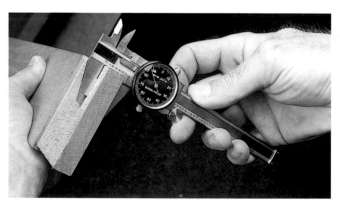

Direct reading. Close the jaws of a dial caliper over the work, then look at the dial face to find the exact measurement without guesswork.

round holes, mortises, rabbets, and dadoes. Not sure what size bit you have in your hand? Dial calipers will tell you in an instant, with an accuracy unmatched by any other measuring tool. (See photos, below.)

I don't think woodworkers need to decipher their work in terms of thousands of an inch, because wood is a moving, breathing material. More practical for the woodworker is to take comparative measurements to calculate the dimensions needed. For

Outside read. The inner faces of a caliper's jaws can read round work, such as the diameter of a drill bit, quickly and accurately.

Inside read. You can find inside diameters and widths with a dial caliper by using the inner legs.

Measuring depth. Extending the depth bar lets you quickly find the precise depth of mortises and inside areas.

example, one of the handiest ways to use a caliper is when comparing parts. You can check for minute variations in stock thickness among similar pieces, such as the rails and stiles for a door frame, by simply comparing the location of the needle on the face of the dial. When the needle reads the same for all the parts, you know your stock is dead-nuts on. This makes dial calipers a valuable tool for quick, precise feedback on all sorts of work.

Calipers come in a range of styles, and prices can top several hundreds of dollars for precision-milled, hardened stainless-steel varieties. But for shop use, woodworkers can spend much less and do fine with a fiberglass-reinforced plastic model, proving you don't need to spend a lot of money on an accurate dial caliper. (See photo, below.) For those of us with poor eyesight, and for the ultimate in convenience and readability, a more expensive electronic caliper with a digital readout is a good solution, as shown in the bottom photo, below.

Affordable and accurate. A plastic dial caliper is plenty accurate for a woodworker's needs, and costs peanuts compared to more expensive metal versions.

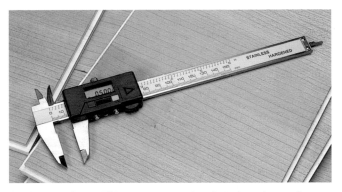
Seeing numbers. This more expensive digital readout caliper lets you choose between Imperial and metric numbers.

Simplified math. Calculate your work in feet, inches, or fractions with a dimensional calculator—a big improvement over standard calculators for the math-challenged woodworker.

When it comes to shop-math measurements, a **dimensional calculator** will let you add, subtract, multiply, or divide numbers—in feet, inches, and fractions. (See photo, left.) This type of calculator is expressly designed for woodworkers, so you won't have to go through the mental gyrations of translating decimal numbers into their more useful fractional counterparts. Who said math couldn't be fun?

Surface Measuring Tools

Measuring surfaces and areas requires specialized tools, and involves a host of essential shop chores from determining straight or square edges and flat surfaces or planes, to finding areas of a room or specific angles and contours. Luckily, long before you became a woodworker you acquired one of these tools—your eye. Master craftsmen place great importance on this natural tool. Through practice, the eye can read and measure surfaces with an amazing degree of accuracy. You can see this for yourself. Try sighting down the edge of a long, roughsawn board fresh from the mill. Immediately your eye will pick up any deviations from true, straight, or flat. This innate ability to read surfaces accurately with your eyes alone can be groomed through use, and eventually you'll come to rely on its accuracy as you would any other favorite shop tool.

In the following section you'll find all sorts of useful measuring tools that help you read the surface or area of your work. Some stand alone as useful aids for measuring in their own right; others rely on your eye to use accurately and efficiently.

Doubtless the most basic of all measuring devices, **straightedges** come in all sorts of shapes and sizes, but they all share one feature and one common goal: They're dead straight on at least one edge, and you use them to read whether a surface is truly straight or flat. (See photo, below.)

Reading whether a surface is flat with a straightedge is a crucial aspect of almost any woodworking endeavor. The reading technique is simple, and involves your eyes and the correct stance. Place the straightedge on the surface in question, and scooch down so your eyes can read the edge of the straightedge where it makes contact. Any light that appears between the work and the edge, or a dark gap (it depends on your

Straight sizes. The author's collection of straightedges includes tools with short and long edges, shop-made or commerical. They're used for gauging the surface or plane of your work.

lighting situation), tells you immediately that the work is out-of-flat. (See photo, below.)

I keep a large collection of straightedges for reading different surfaces. Small, 12-inch or shorter edges are useful for smaller work, where you are more interested in checking for cupping or out-of-flat areas across the face of a piece. Mid-size straightedges—2 to 4 feet long—handle the bulk of my measuring tasks, from reading boards for flat or straight to checking machine surfaces and fences, such as my jointer tables or the rip fence on my table saw. Long, 6- to 8-foot edges can check longer surfaces, and are also useful as very accurate rulers when you need to generate long lines in your work.

A good straightedge can be bought commercially or made in the shop. The best straightedges are precision-ground from steel, and offer more durability over softer metals or wood. If you make your own straight-

edge, select a stable hardwood with straight grain so the tool will remain straighter over time. Mahogany and hard maple are good choices. Periodically check your wooden edge against a reliable straightedge, and re-straighten it if necessary with a few prudent swipes from a hand plane.

One of the features to look for in a commercial straightedge or to incorporate in your homemade straightedge, particularly in mid-size and longer edges, is a taper or chamfer on the reading edge. By beveling the edge, you'll produce a thinner reading edge, which is more accurate since it's easier to see the contact point between the work and the edge itself. (See bottom photo, left.)

Essentially a pair of straightedges with parallel edges, **winding sticks** are shop-made sticks that let you check a board or other surface for *wind*, or twist, usually in roughsawn lumber. While your eye alone can detect twist in a board, winding sticks are far more accurate and let you determine when a board is perfectly flat. (See photo, below.) Winding sticks are also handy for checking other surfaces as well, such as your workbench or the tables of your jointer.

To use the sticks, place one at each end of the surface you want to read. Then hunker down until your eyes are level with the tops of the sticks. Sight over the near stick to the far stick, comparing their top edges for

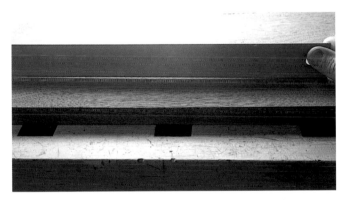

Looking for the light. A small sliver of light peeking between a straightedge and your work means something's not flat—and it ain't the straightedge, pal.

Narrow reading. This aluminum straightedge has a thinner edge on its reading side, making it easier to see the contact between the work and the tool.

Checking wind. Shop-made winding sticks let you check for twist, or wind, on boards. Place at stick at either end of the work and sight over the top of the sticks to read the surface.

Beveled contrast. Beveling the top edges of winding sticks makes reading them easier. Adding contrasting colors to the edges, such as black marker or white shoe polish, also helps in sighting them accurately.

parallel. If the two sticks are parallel to one another, the surface is flat. If one stick tilts in relation to the other, the surface is twisted. (See fig. 5.) After sighting with the sticks, correct any twist by working the high spots with a plane. Then keep checking with the sticks until the first stick is parallel with its neighbor.

Like a homemade straightedge, winding sticks should be fashioned from fairly thin, straight-grained wood. Although it's not necessary, cutting a bevel or chamfer

---

Fig. 5: Using Winding Stick to Determine Twist

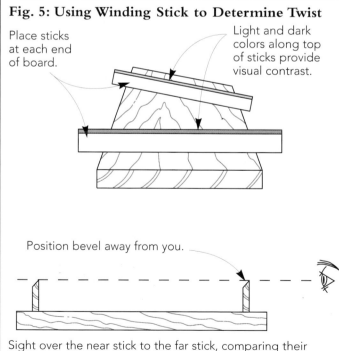

Place sticks at each end of board.

Light and dark colors along top of sticks provide visual contrast.

Position bevel away from you.

Sight over the near stick to the far stick, comparing their top edges. If the tops of the sticks are not parallel, the board is twisted, or exhibits wind.

---

along the top edges makes the sticks easier to read. What is mandatory is that each stick has two parallel edges, so take your time when making them to ensure these edges are accurate. The best method is to rip each stick a hair oversize on the table saw, joint the reading edge by hand with a plane, then rip the opposite edge parallel. Make sure the edges are straight, which you can do by holding two sticks edge-to-edge. You shouldn't see daylight between them.

Any thin hardwood stock will work fine for your sticks, although it's a good idea to make them thick enough to stand upright on their own; $5/16$ inch is about ideal. Sticks about 2 feet long will cover most of your needs, or you can make sets of sticks in varying lengths for different jobs. To make sighting easier, woodworkers traditionally make each stick from a contrasting wood, or inlay contrasting woods into their top edges. Species like jet-black ebony and bone-white holly are good candidates. A simpler, if less elegant, solution is to swipe the edge of one stick with a black marker, and color the opposite stick with white shoe polish, as shown in the top photo, left.

Another useful shopmade layout device is the **story stick**, sometimes called a **story pole**. (See photo, below.) This ancient tool, which dates back to the pyramid-building days of early Egypt, consists of a simple

Stick to your story. This simple stick of plywood can let you lay out and measure cabinet parts, or an entire kitchen or library. Here, the author transfers marks for cutting a door rail to length; the other side of the stick is marked with all the cabinet's vertical measurements.

length of wood with pencil marks scribbled on its surface. The information written on a single story stick can be used to lay out and construct a host of woodworking joints, a set of doors, or an entire kitchen. At the very least, using a story stick will prevent major measuring goofs in your work. After using one, you just might throw your tape measure in the trash.

A story stick relies on an empirical style of woodworking, a no-nonsense approach I try to adopt as much as possible in my work. Instead of depending on inch measurements and mistake-prone math, you use the stick by holding it up to the surface or object you need to measure, and you make a series of tick marks on the stick's face or edge that corresponds with key areas. By transferring these marks to the actual workpiece or to a cutting tool, you make a direct measurement without any chance for error. You can use story sticks for all sorts of measuring and layout tasks, from taking site measurements for installation work or deciphering the parts of a cabinet or chair, to laying out joints and hardware. (See fig. 6.)

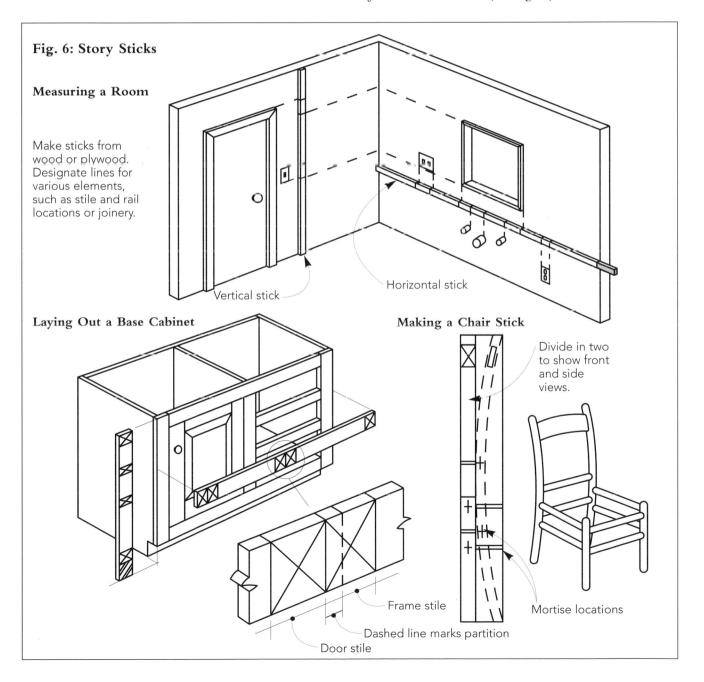

Fig. 6: Story Sticks

Measuring a Room

Make sticks from wood or plywood. Designate lines for various elements, such as stile and rail locations or joinery.

Vertical stick

Horizontal stick

Laying Out a Base Cabinet

Frame stile

Dashed line marks partition

Door stile

Making a Chair Stick

Divide in two to show front and side views.

Mortise locations

To keep a complex job from overloading a story stick with unintelligible marks, you can mark a stick with various colored pens to differentiate between parts or key dimensions. For example, when laying out a kitchen cabinet, I'll designate one color for all horizontal lines, such as rail lengths or drawer openings, and use another color for my vertical measurements, such as the stiles for a frame or a door, and so on. Another method is to use the front and back side of a stick for different measurements, or make up two or more sticks for a job, such as when laying out a big room or working on a large or complex assembly. One stick can contain all horizontal measurements; the other all vertical dimensions. To record a long measurement between two fixed areas, say the distance between two walls or the overall length of a long cabinet, use two sticks, each slightly longer than half the span. Measure the distance

Long recording. Measuring and recording great distances or complex assemblies sometimes warrants using two or more sticks. To span a long distance, slide two sticks past each other and record where they meet by striking a line on each stick.

Dovetail story. Using a story stick across the ends of a series of drawer sides lets you quickly lay out the tail spacing without having to reach for a tape measure.

by sliding the two sticks past each other, then mark across both of them to record them for later reference. (See middle left photo, below.)

For hand-tool enthusiasts, one of the best uses for a story stick is when laying out joints. For example, marking a series of dovetails on several drawers can be mind-numbing if you need to repeat the tail or pin spacing blank after blank. A story stick marked with the appropriate spacing will let you quickly tick off the correct sequence from piece to piece. (See bottom left photo, below.)

When it comes time to hang a cabinet or install your woodwork in a room or other setting, you'll need a **beam level** or **stick level** to get things straight. While levels make great straightedges, they're essential pieces of gear for reading surfaces for level or plumb. (See photo, below.) *Level* refers to any straight horizontal line, precisely parallel with the ground or floor; *plumb* means a vertical line that's in line with gravity, or square to a level line. These two measurements are vital for cabinetmakers or anyone involved in built-in work, which involves measuring existing room surfaces—walls, floors, and ceilings—for level. Beam levels have glass or plastic vials along their beams, and each vial is marked with two parallel lines and is filled with a liquid solution that contains an air bubble trapped inside it. You adjust the level up or down, or side to side, depending on whether you're reading for level or

Level lengths. Beam or stick levels are available in different lengths and materials, and let you measure surfaces for plumb (straight up and down) or level (parallel with the floor or ground line).

The bubble knows. When the bubble is centered over the hash marks on the vial, the level—and your work—is plumb or level.

Longer is better. To increase the effective length of a level, position it over a long straightedge placed on the work surface.

plumb. When the bubble is centered over hash marks on the vial, the surface you're reading is level or plumb, as shown in the photo, left.

Levels come in different lengths, from 1-inch line levels that hook onto a string (used mostly by masons and carpenters to gauge really long distances), and small 6-inch torpedo levels, to beam-type levels measuring 6 feet or more. The reason for such a proliferation of sizes is that you'll need a variety on hand for read various surfaces accurately. Ideally, a level should run the length of the surface you're measuring. For most work, a **4-foot level** is adequate. This is a good size for leveling most cabinets and reading the walls or floors they'll fit. For really tall or long cases, a longer **6-** or **8-foot level** is more accurate. However, if you have a shorter level and need to read a large surface, don't rush out and buy the biggest level you can find. You can increase a smaller level's capacity if you place it atop a long straightedge that has two parallel edges, then position this assembly on the work. (See photo, above.)

While a mid-size level is a good place to start, a **2-foot level** can come in handy in tighter quarters where a longer level won't fit. For really tight spaces, get a **torpedo level**, which comes in metal, wood, or plastic versions around 8 inches long. A torpedo level allows you to read for level in the smallest areas, and in a pinch you can use the straightedge trick I just mentioned to increase its effectiveness for bigger jobs. (See photo, below.)

There's quite a price range when it comes to buying beam levels. However, the old saying that you get what you pay for applies to this tool category. Less-expensive levels are made from aluminum or plastic (lightweight, but less sturdy) or heavier steel (built to last, but heavy in the hand). Pricier levels are made from lighter alloyed metals such as magnesium, and have the necessary stiffness and durability while remaining relatively lightweight in your hands. Remember, less weight is a good feature when you're measuring overhead or in difficult spots. Top-of-the line levels come with hardwood infill, typically mahogany, and are often edged and capped with brass wear plates and strips.

Make sure to maintain your level, or, like an out-of-square square, you won't be able to rely on its accuracy. Test the level by holding it up to a known level surface or against another level, and check that the bubbles read the same. Many bubble vials are adjustable by loosening a few screws. Fancier levels have a glazing compound to hold the vials in place (the same material used to hold the glass panes in windows), and you'll have to pry out the old glazing, fine-tune the vial, then re-seal the vial with fresh compound.

Small, but accessible. This torpedo level lets you read narrow confines where longer levels can't fit.

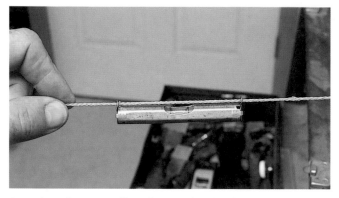

Long length in a small package. A line level slips over a length of string, and can read virtually any distance for level.

For measuring really long distances for level, such as an entire room or an entire span of kitchen cabinets, a **line level** is an inexpensive investment. You hook this device over a length of string, then pull the string taut between two points. Reading a line level is exactly like using a beam level: When the bubble is centered over the hash marks in the vial, your work is level. (See photo, above.)

The **plumb bob** has a long tradition in the construction and cabinetmaking trades. Many bobs combine practicality with great beauty, and are often highly ornamented. For this reason bobs are commonly sought after by woodworkers and tool collectors alike. Like a level, a plumb bob will find plumb, or vertical straight lines. But instead of relying on a straight and

Hanging straight. A plumb bob helps you find a plumb, or vertical line. When gravity brings the bob to rest, the points between the top of the string and the point of the bob are plumb with each other.

rigid beam, the plumb bob uses gravity and a simple piece of string. With its string tied or held above, the pointed end of a bob will eventually rest plumb if left to hang freely without obstruction. You gauge plumb by marking the two points, one where the line is fixed, and the other at the pointed tip of the bob. (See photo, left.)

A plumb bob is especially useful where a beam level might be awkward or difficult to employ, and works well for plumbing cabinetry or even setting up drilling operations for jigs or with the drill press. One of the challenges of

Flat bob. This particular model is designed to lay flat on the reading surface and has a slot for the tip of a pencil, allowing you to mark the work more precisely.

using a plumb bob is when reading the point of the bob itself. Because typical bobs are rounded, the point is often an inch or more away from the surface you're trying to read. For rough work, this is generally not a problem. But as woodworkers we generally need more precision in our work. One manufacturer has addressed this need by designing a bob with a flat face so it resides closer to the work. A vertical slot in the body of the bob lets you use a pencil for accurate marking, as shown in the photo, above.

While you're finding plumb and level, you'll probably want to locate studs and other hidden members in your walls and ceilings during the installation process. One technique involves tapping a small nail into the wall until it hits something solid beneath the sheathing. A neater method is to use an electronic **stud locator** or **stud sensor**, which works by monitoring different densities in the cavity of a wall. (See bottom left photo, opposite page.)

Stud locators are a snap to use by simply dragging them across the face of the wall. When the device passes over a material with a different density from the wall covering itself—a wood stud inside the wall, for example—a series of LEDs light up, telling you the exact location of that material. In fact, these sensors are so precise they'll locate each side of a stud, effectively telling you where the center of the material is. This makes is easy to screw or nail into the center of hidden metal or wood studs. Best of all, you won't be left with a series of nail holes strewn across the wall.

Another electronic device is a **moisture meter,** and it's an essential piece of gear if you do any work in solid wood. (See middle photo, below right.) Wood moves in response to changes in ambient moisture levels, swelling or shrinking in dimension. This movement is mainly isolated across the width of a board, and we need to design our furniture to allow for such movement. By monitoring your wood's moisture content with a meter, you can better plan for the eventual wood movement in your work. If you don't, joints are likely to crack or push apart.

There are many styles of moisture meters on the market, with hugely varying price tags, but they all fall into two basic types: pin and pinless. A pin-style meter has two or more metal pins that pierce the wood. Direct current travels through one pin into the wood and is picked up by another pin. The pinless variety lets you read the moisture content of a board without compromising its surface, and works by emitting electrical waves through a sensor that's pressed against the surface of the wood.

Luckily, you don't have to spend a fortune to get a meter accurate enough for home-shop use. Look for a meter that will take readings as low as a 7 percent or even 6 percent moisture content, and as high as 12 percent or more, since this is the moisture range that furniture makers need to be concerned about. While the pinless style of moisture meter is more convenient, it's most accurate when used on a smooth surface, making it awkward for reading

roughsawn lumber. I prefer the pin variety because I generally trust it to be more precise. To get an accurate reading using a pin-style meter, you'll need to read the center of your stock, preferably in from one end of the board. First crosscut 6 to 8 inches off the end of the board, then press the pins of the meter into the end grain to check its moisture content. (See bottom right photo.)

Once you begin the process of regularly monitoring your stock with a moisture meter, you'll be better equipped to understand the potential pitfalls involved in wood movement—and learn how to avoid them. To get the most out of your meter, it's worth reading up on the topic of wood movement. Fortunately, there's a lot of good information on the subject in books and magazines.

Reading wet and dry. The moisture meters on the left work via pins that penetrate the wood to read a board's moisture content. The pinless meter on the right can be used directly on the surface.

Finding studs. Passing an electronic stud locator over a wall tells you exactly where studs and other hidden framework lie beneath the sheathing. Lights appear when you've hit your mark.

In from the end. To use a pin-style meter, crosscut a chunk off the end of a board and read the board's end grain surface.

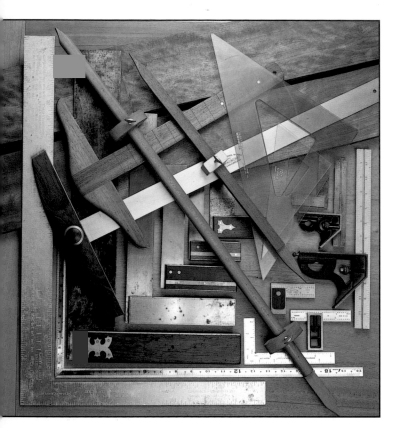

Squares

Determining square surfaces and right angles in your work is such an important aspect of the building process that it can sometimes affect the success or failure of an entire project. Joints need to be checked and cut for square, and the tools and machines that we use to make these joints, such as planes, jointer fences, or miter gauges, require checking for square, too. Even when your joints are cut properly, if you're not careful you can still introduce twist or racking in an assembly during glue-up. Checking for square at this stage shouldn't be overlooked. Learning to read for square takes many forms, and requires several different tools.

The essential tool for measuring square surfaces is the **square**, which consists of a blade and a handle, or fence, held at 90 degrees to the blade. By holding a square against two adjacent surfaces, you'll quickly know exactly where you stand by looking for daylight between the square and the work. (See right photo, above.) An accurate square is useful for all sorts of measuring, including reading when a board's edge is square to its

face, checking joints, setting tool fences, and the like. In addition, a square doubles as a great layout tool when you need to mark a square line, such as when laying out a joint. (See bottom photo, below.)

One thing to keep in mind with squares: They must be square to be reliable. Buying a new square is no guarantee you'll get an accurate square, and through use a square can become inaccurate. (Raise your hand if you've never accidentally dropped a square. No hands? I thought so.) To avoid trouble, it's best to regularly check your squares against a known square surface. The most practical approach is to use a reliable square, referencing the square in question against the known square. To do this, nest the two together and check both the inside and the outside edges, as shown in the middle left photo, opposite page.

Finding perpendicular. Determine square by positioning the fence of the square against one surface and sliding it until the blade makes contact with the adjacent surface. When both blade and fence make full contact, the work is square.

Marking joints. To mark a square line, place the offset fence against the edge of the work and follow the blade with your marking tool.

If you buy a square that isn't square, return it for a new one. And beware of squares that are square only on one side—usually the inside edge. While they can be useful for certain marking chores, squares with only one square edge can't be trusted to measure surfaces accurately.

Of course, to check a square with a square, you'll need to start with a reliable square, or a square that can reference all your other squares. Luckily, checking this square is simple. (See Finding a Reference Square, page 84.)

The traditional square in the woodshop is the **try square**. Try squares have a rather broad blade made of steel or brass that's riveted to a wood fence edged with brass wear strips. These squares are available in small and large sizes from 2 inches up to 12 inches or more.

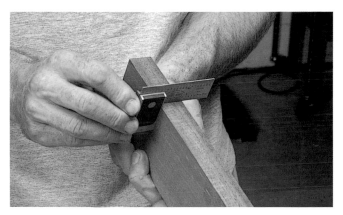

Hand Size. A smaller 3 inch square is easier to hold accurately across narrow work.

Checking a square. Use a reliable square to check a new or questionable square by nesting the two squares together, checking both inside and outside edges. Any light showing between the two blades indicates out-of-square.

The size refers to the length of the blade. The handiest size try square is a 6- or 8-inch model, which is useful for measuring and marking most joints. (See bottom photo, left.) When reading or marking a narrow edge, a small 2- or 3-inch try square is easier to handle, and therefore more accurate, as shown in the photo, above.

Similar in construction to the try square is a **machinist's square**, except that it's made from two pieces of steel soldered together instead of brass, wood, and rivets. (See photo, below.) Touted for their precision, these hefty squares are used by machinists and metalworkers where great accuracy is required. Both the inside and outside legs of these squares are machined perfectly square, and they usually come with a price tag that reflects this extra level of attention. Fortunately, these squares have become more available and more afford-able for wood-workers, and many woodworking cata-logs now sell them. I'm particularly fond of this type of square for all sorts of measuring jobs, and I keep a range of sizes from small 2-inch squares up to 12 inches for small and big measurements.

Wood, steel, and brass. Try squares have brass or steel blades riveted to wooden fences, and are available in various lengths, making them convenient for marking out and checking for square.

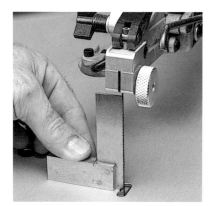

Precision metal. This small, all-metal machinist's square is good for checking joints and edges as well as machine set-ups, for example, when squaring a scrollsaw blade to a table.

One of the most versatile types of squares is a **combination square**, which has a blade that slides along the fence, or head, and removes entirely for ruler work. In addition to measuring right angles, the head has a 45-degree edge that lets you mark and measure very accurate miters. A small bubble vial in the head also lets you use it as a small level when you need to measure level or plumb in very tight spots. This degree of versatility lets you measure a wide range of work with just one square. (See top left photo, opposite page.)

A large 12-inch "combo" square is the most useful size for general marking and measuring, although smaller 6-inch and 3-inch combination squares have very practical uses. All combination squares have markings along their blades, letting you measure height and depth easily and accurately. A neat trick to learn with combination squares, especially with smaller squares, is to use them as edge guides for marking parallel lines at an exact width, as shown in the middle left photo, opposite page.

FINDING A REFERENCE SQUARE

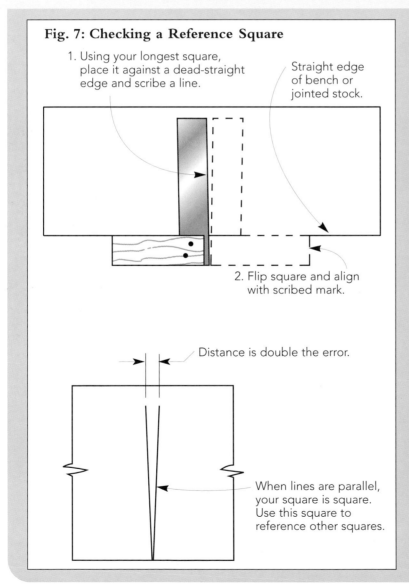

Fig. 7: Checking a Reference Square

1. Using your longest square, place it against a dead-straight edge and scribe a line.

Straight edge of bench or jointed stock.

2. Flip square and align with scribed mark.

Distance is double the error.

When lines are parallel, your square is square. Use this square to reference other squares.

New squares and—gasp!—squares that have been accidentally dropped or mistreated need to be checked for square. One way is to hold the square in question against a known square, or a reference square. But how do you find this original and accurate reference square? Figure 7 reveals a deceptively simple technique. Using your largest square, preferably one with a blade 12 inches or longer, place its fence against a straightedge that has a surface at least as wide as your blade is long. The straightedge can be the edge of your bench, a freshly jointed board, or a strip of plywood. The important thing is to have an edge that's dead-nuts straight.

Hold the square firmly against the straightedge, and scribe a line. Then flip the square over and align it with your mark, not quite touching it. If the lines match up, the square is okay. If not, the runout represents double the error. You might have to try this technique with several squares before you find one that's accurate. When you've found a reliable square, use this as your reference square for checking all future squares.

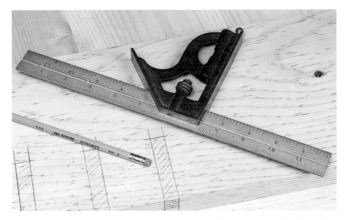

More than square. With its adjustable blade and 45/90 head, a combination square lets you mark and measure all sorts of work.

Either side will do. A small double square offers two 90-degree fences for layout work and checking worksurfaces.

Marking parallel. You can quickly gauge a parallel line of exact width by following a small combination square with a pencil.

Similar to a combination square is a **double square**. This type of square has two parallel fences—no miter edge—and it has a wonderful feel in your hand. I find it a useful as a try square for layout work as well as for checking surfaces with the accuracy of a precision square. The open fence is highly accurate while avoiding the heavy feel of a traditional machinist's square. (See top photo, right.)

Fenced squares are unquestionably the most useful types of squares in the shop, but sometimes the protruding or offset fence can get in the way of accurate measuring or marking. Here, a **small flat square** made from a single piece of stamped steel comes in handy, such as when marking a square line in the middle of a workpiece, as shown in the middle photo, right.

For larger measurements, a one-piece **framing square** is a tool that won't set you back big bucks like a large fenced square. Used primarily by carpenters and construction framers, this large square is very handy in the woodshop. (See photo, below.) With the longer of the two blades or legs at 24 inches, you can use this square to read large surfaces and mark

No-fence square. This small flat square lets you mark in the middle of the work by making full contact with the surface.

across wide panels and boards. This makes a framing square great for work such as laying out long dadoes or checking the end of a wide panel for square.

Big square. For large squaring work, a framing square is an economical choice. But be prepared to tune up this tool before relying on its accuracy.

Framing squares come in steel or aluminum, with the latter being lighter and easier to handle, although generally less sturdy and accurate. One word of advice: Framing squares in general are not known to be highly accurate in terms of squareness, so it pays to check one when you acquire it. While it may be fine for rough layout work, chances are it won't have the tolerances you need for your woodworking. Happily, you can adjust a one-piece square back to square with a few prudent taps from a hammer. (See Squaring a One-Piece Square, below.)

Another very useful type of one-piece square is a **Japanese carpenter's square**, which has longs legs like the framing square, but with a much narrower profile. (See photo, left.) This is a traditional tool used by Japanese carpenters and temple builders, and its light weight and slim profile makes it easy to carry to a jobsite. With its thin, flexible steel blades, this type of square is more suited to marking out rather than measuring. But the tool is such a delight to hold in the hand that I find myself reaching for this large square even when a smaller square might do.

Finding a large, affordable square for really big work can be frustrating. While framing squares are handy, their size is limited, and the lack of an offset fence can hamper some jobs. Laying out long dadoes or other 90-degree lines, for example, is best done with a longer fence that accurately registers against the edge of the workpiece.

Thin and flexible. A large Japanese carpenter's square is similar in size to a framing square. Its narrow flexible blades let you bend the square into position, making it particularly suited for marking chores.

SQUARING A ONE-PIECE SQUARE

Framing squares and other large, one-piece squares are not known to be particularly square when you buy them. And their longer blades or legs make them susceptible to accidental hits, which can move them out of square. A simple fix is to hammer the blade back to square, as shown in figure 9. Choose a round-faced hammer for the job, and use firm but light taps on the offending inside or outside corner. Placing the corner of the square on a hard surface, such the end grain on a block of hardwood, will provide a suitably resilient surface for hammering.

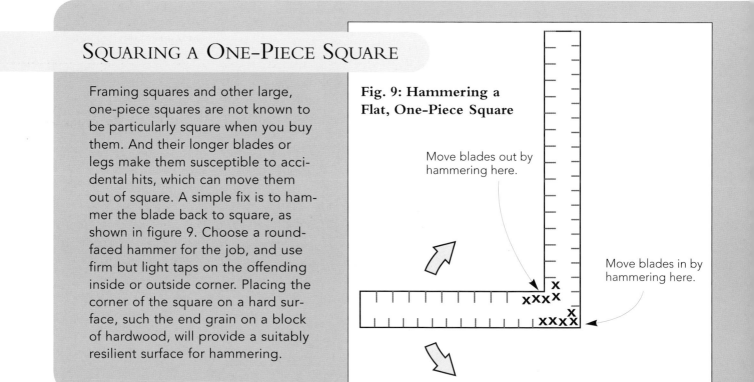

Fig. 9: Hammering a Flat, One-Piece Square

Move blades out by hammering here.

Move blades in by hammering here.

Squared to a T. A large shopmade T-square is simple to make, and lets you lay out accurate lines on wide or long work.

Divided and dotted. Divisions scribed every inch along the blade let you use a square for measuring and marking to length or width. Dots of mother-of-pearl inlay add a distinctive touch.

A **T-square** is the answer, but commercial versions are pricey. An economical solution is to make a solid wood T-square, with a long, offset fence and a blade length suited to your work. (See photo, above.)

You can make several sizes of T-squares, some with short blades a foot or so long, and others with blades up to 3 feet or more. (See Fig. 8.) Dense woods such as rosewood and hard maple are best, especially for the thinner blade piece. Use straight-grained wood for stability, and make sure to glue and clamp the fence dead-square to the blade when you assemble the parts.

Unlike a more rigid metal or metal-and-wood square, you'll need to treat this all-wood tool with special care so as not to throw it out of square. Plan on checking the square frequently with a reference square, as swings in ambient moisture levels can knock it out of whack. You can usually tune a wood square back to accuracy with a few judicious scrapes on the edge of the blade using a sharp chisel or scraper. If you want to get fancy, you can scribe divisions along the blade so the tool can be used for marking lengths as well as for square. (See top photo, right.)

When it comes to measuring an opening for square, you'll need something more accurate than a normal shop square, unless the opening is small, such as a small drawer box. The standard approach when squaring up large openings is to measure opposing diagonals by spanning the outside corners with a tape measure. When the two measurements are equal, the opening is square. But a tape measure is limited in two ways: Often the tape can't reach the outer corners due to clamps or other obstructions, and you can't effectively reach the back or the inside of the opening, where bowing from clamps can often twist an assembly, such as when gluing up a large cabinet. That's why most

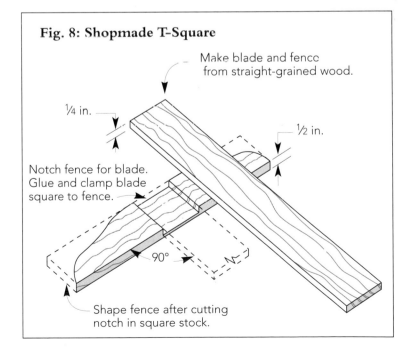

Fig. 8: Shopmade T-Square

Make blade and fence from straight-grained wood.

¼ in.

½ in.

Notch fence for blade. Glue and clamp blade square to fence.

90°

Shape fence after cutting notch in square stock.

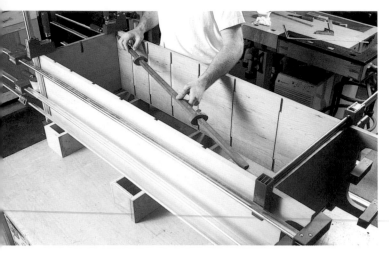

Pinch and compare. Pinch rods let you compare diagonal measurements deep inside a big case (above) or inside a small box, (below) checking for square as well as bow or twist. Wood blocks "pinch" the sticks via thumbscrews, locking the rods together so you can accurately measure diagonals.

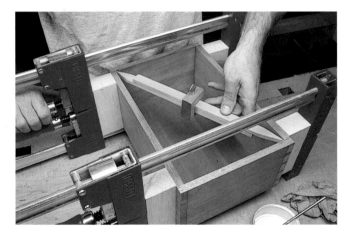

A rack of rods. An assortment of pinch rods in various lengths lets you measure small or large openings, from small boxes to large casework.

while you take a reading. You can buy commercial clamping heads, or make your own clamping pinch rod from two sticks and a block of wood. Larger sticks over 2 feet or so are best outfitted with a pair of heads to keep the rods parallel with each other. You can use practically any type of hardwood for the rods and the clamping heads. (See fig. 10.)

I keep an assortment of homemade pinch rods in different lengths. Short 12-inch-long sticks are good for reading drawers and small boxes, and rods 40 inches or longer, when fully extended, can measure a large cabinet opening that's 6 feet or more on the diagonal. (See photo, above.)

cabinetmakers and furniture makers keep a supply of **pinch rods** on hand. Instead of measuring outside the case or box, a pinch rod is designed to measure inside from corner to corner, and to any depth, as shown in the photos, above.

A traditional pinch rod is a simple affair consisting of two plain sticks, each pointed at one end. You slide the sticks past each other until each point contacts an inside corner, then you "pinch" or hold the sticks together to compare diagonals. However, I've discovered that a clamping arrangement that doesn't rely on hand strength and dexterity is superior, and makes reading for square much easier. The trick is to add a clamping head (or two on long rods) to hold the sticks in position

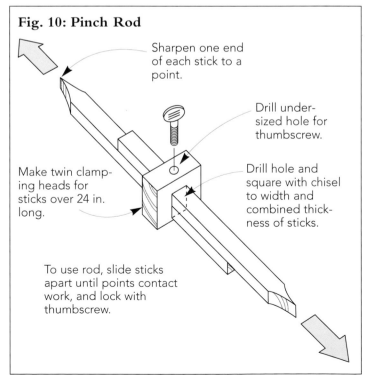

Fig. 10: Pinch Rod

Sharpen one end of each stick to a point.

Drill under-sized hole for thumbscrew.

Make twin clamping heads for sticks over 24 in. long.

Drill hole and square with chisel to width and combined thickness of sticks.

To use rod, slide sticks apart until points contact work, and lock with thumbscrew.

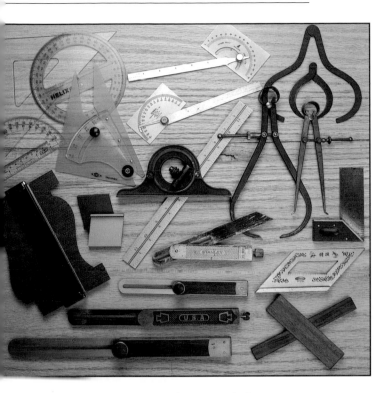

Measuring Angles and Contours

Although most woodworking starts out with stock that's straight, flat, and square, things can get more interesting as you introduce curves and angles in your work. For this kind of work, you'll need some specialty measuring tools that allow you to mark and cut these non-rectilinear surfaces and edges, from miters and other angles to round and contoured parts.

For accurate miter work, a **miter square** will pay big dividends. These tools let you measure and mark a true

45-degree angle, and come in two styles, as shown in the bottom photo, left.

Like a traditional try square, the offset fence on a miter square lets you reference the tool on the edge of the work for accurate marking and measuring. (See photo, below.) One benefit of the Japanese style of miter square is its ability to read accurate inside corners at 45 degrees. For example, I use the square to check the tilt of my table saw blade by nesting it between the blade's plate and the tabletop, as shown in the bottom photo, below.

Like the Japanese miter square, a **drafting triangle** can be used to mark miters or measure inside corners, making it handy for laying out work as well as for setting up angled cutters and other tools. Available from art and drafting-supply stores, these inexpensive plastic triangles come in large and small sizes, with your choice of three angles on each device, 45/90, 60/90, or 30/60. This gives

Up and over. The offset fence of a miter square lets you transfer edge marks to the face with great precision.

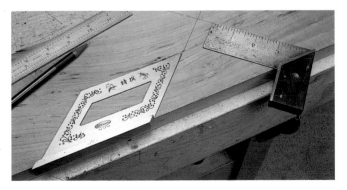

East and west miters. These two miter squares work in the same fashion for gauging accurate 45-degree angles. The all-metal square (left) is a Japanese version; a traditional English miter square (right) is a combination of wood and brass.

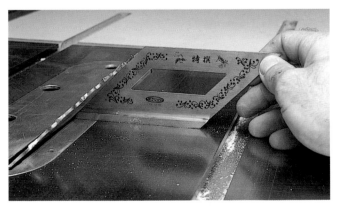

Inside miters. A Japanese miter square can gauge inside angles, handy for jobs such as measuring for true 45 degrees on a tilted saw blade.

you a square and angle-finding tool in one inexpensive package. (See photo, below.)

Since a drafting triangle has no fence or offset edge, it comes in handy for flat layout work where you need to measure or mark a line in the middle of the work. (See bottom photo, below.)

A commercial **dovetail gauge** has a fixed angle and lets you quickly lay out the correct slope for dovetail pins and tails prior to cutting dovetail joints. These types of gauges are available in traditional angle ratios of 1:6 or 1:8, about 9 degrees and 7 degrees respectively. A good dovetail gauge is designed to quickly

register on the edge of the workpiece, letting you strike an accurately angled line on its adjacent face. (See photo, below.)

I fashioned a rather versatile **adjustable dovetail gauge** in under an hour from scrap wood, and it's easy to make and a favorite to use. (See bottom photo.) This all-wood gauge has a blade that pivots between two fixed angles, allowing me to choose from a wider range of angles in a single tool. (See fig. 11.) Since the fence is offset on both sides of the blade, you can use the gauge as you would a normal dovetail gauge, marking opposing slopes by simply flipping the tool over.

Angled and square. Plastic drafting triangles come in a range of sizes and are available in three styles—45/90, 60/90, and 30/60—providing a square edge and a fixed angle in one tool.

Quick mark. Using a dovetail gauge speeds up the process of laying out pins or tails. You can mark both slopes of the dovetail by simply flipping over the gauge.

No-fence angle. Positioning a triangle on the face of the work lets you mark an accurate line where a fenced tool would get in the way.

Homemade angles. This easy-to-make, adjustable dovetail gauge has a blade that pivots inside the fence, allowing you to quickly pick a severe or shallow slope, or any angle in between.

Fig. 11: Shop-Made Dovetail Guage

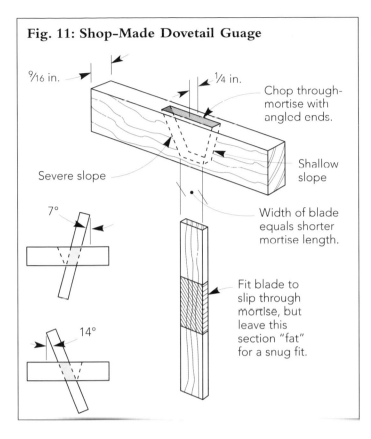

9/16 in.

1/4 in.

Chop through-mortise with angled ends.

Severe slope

Shallow slope

7°

14°

Width of blade equals shorter mortise length.

Fit blade to slip through mortise, but leave this section "fat" for a snug fit.

When you need to mark or measure beyond the standard fixed angle of a miter or the slope of a dovetail, there are a few tools to consider that provide more angle-making versatility. A **protractor** can handle angles from 0 degrees to 360 degrees. (See photo, below.) The plastic variety, available at office, drafting and art-supply stores, is useful for drawing or marking

Drawing angles. Circle and half-circle protractors let you draw angles from 0 degrees to 360 degrees on a flat surface. Place a ruler against the edge of a protractor when you need to lengthen the angle line.

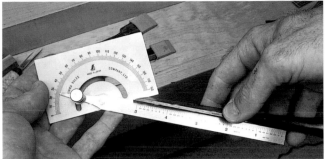

Measuring angles. While a fenced protractor can be used for marking angles, it's a wonderful tool for measuring them, too. Placing the tip of a chisel between the blade and the head gives you a direct reading on the tool's bevel angle.

angles, and works on any flat surface, such as a piece of paper or directly on the workpiece. The half-circle version provides angles from 0 degrees to 180 degrees; full-circle plastic protractors are capable of marking all angles from 0 degrees to 360 degrees.

For marking *and* measuring angles, an **adjustable protractor** is much handier. This type of protractor has a blade or arm that pivots to any angle from 0 degrees to 180 degrees, letting you wrap it around the actual workpiece to gauge its angle. (See photo, above.)

Although pricey, a **protractor head** fitted with a rule lets you find and mark virtually any angle. Fitted with a long rule, this device lets you mark really long angles. (See photo, right.) You can buy short or long rules made for combination squares (see page 84), and fit one to the head of this precision angle-finder. The head can be rotated from 0 degrees through 180 degrees.

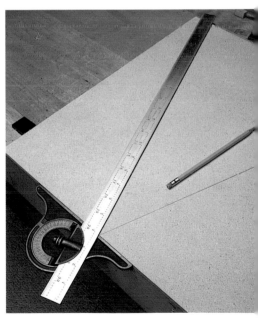

Long marks. A protractor head fitted with a 2-foot rule (borrowed from a combination square) lets you lay out long angles from 0 to 180 degrees.

By far the most effective angle-measuring tool in any shop is a **bevel gauge**. The tool consists of a fence and an adjustable blade that pivots in a complete arc around the fence from 0 degrees to 360 degrees. A knob or nut locks the blade at the desired angle. (See photo, below.) If you don't currently own one of these tools, run—don't walk—to get one. I can't stress enough the usefulness of this type of tool for measuring and marking practically any type of angle.

A bevel gauge's greatest asset lies in the fact that you use it as a reference tool for generating all the specific angles needed for a particular woodworking job. You set a gauge to a desired angle, then take it directly to the work to mark that angle. No measuring, no fuss, and no mistakes. For example, chairmakers will set a gauge to a known angle, say the necessary splay for the legs of a chair, and then use the fixed gauge for everything from setting up machine blades and cutters and laying out the joints, to transferring those angles to the workpiece or using the gauge as a visual drilling guide. (See bottom photo, left.) For this reason, it pays to own several gauges so you can lock them to all the angles needed for a job until you've completed the project.

Good from every angle. Bevel gauges can mark and measure any angle from 0 degrees to 360 degrees, including right angles. It's worth stocking up on more than one so you can set them for specific angles during the course of a project.

You can buy bevel gauges with various blade lengths and in various combinations of materials, such as brass and rosewood or aluminum and steel. But there are only two important features that can make or break a good bevel gauge: Look for a locking knob or nut that securely locks the blade, and make sure the knob itself won't interfere with the fence when it's positioned against a reference surface. (See photo, right.)

For measuring the area of circular work, such as turnings and other round items, **calipers** are indispensable. There are two styles of calipers you can use: outside calipers and inside calipers, as shown in the top photo, opposite page.

Good contact. The locking knob or nut on a good bevel gauge should be out of the way when the fence registers the work.

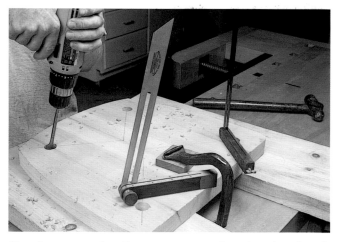

Gauging two angles. Two gauges set to the splayed angles of the legs act as visual guides when you're drilling compound-angled leg holes in a chair seat.

Outside calipers handle the bulk of my measuring needs when it comes to round stock, serving to gauge the exact diameter of a turning, or the thickness of a tenon or other joint. (See bottom left photo, opposite page.) By adjusting the two inward-curving legs of the caliper until they make contact with the workpiece, you can use outside calipers to transfer this measurement to a template, or take a direct reading from the legs to determine the diameter or thickness of the part.

Measuring in and out. Calipers are precision measuring tools for gauging the dimensions of round or circular work. They come in two styles: outside calipers (left) and inside calipers (right).

To find inside measurements, you spread the outward turned legs of an **inside caliper** in a similar fashion to gauge the exact inner dimensions of hollows or bowls in turned work, or to measure a mortise or other deep or angled hole where a ruler can't reach accurately. (See bottom photo, center.)

Calipers are made from steel, and as such will need occasional cleaning and oiling to keep their moving parts in good condition. If you use outside calipers on spinning work on the lathe, it's a good idea to gently round over the tips with some fine sandpaper to prevent any sharp edges from snagging the work.

Both outside and inside calipers are available with a spring and a threaded post, known as *spring-divided calipers*. These are the easiest and most accurate type of calipers to use. A nut on the post allows you to fine-tune the exact setting, and the spring keeps tension on the legs so you don't accidentally upset the setting.

Similar to calipers are **dividers**, which come in spring-divided versions. Instead of having curves, the legs on a pair of dividers are straight, and the tips are sharp and pointed. The sharp points let you scribe very accurate lines in the work. You use dividers whenever you need to accurately transfer dimensions, such as from a full-scale drawing to the workpiece, when marking dovetails, or when laying out equally spaced marks, say, for a series of holes. (See photo, right.)

Even divisions. Using a pair of dividers lets you transfer measurements or lay out equally spaced marks.

A **profile gauge** can tackle measuring complex patterns and shapes, and is made from plastic or steel with a series of wires or fingers that slide freely through a bar. When you press the tool against a surface, the fingers conform to the exact shape. This lets you measure or trace practically any curve for making patterns of complex shapes, such as turnings or moldings. (See photo, below.)

Gauging outside. An outside caliper reads thicknesses and diameters with a pair of legs that contact the work.

Inside reading. Inside calipers are handy if you do a lot of bowl work or other faceplate turning, and for gauging the inner dimensions of a mortise or hole.

Press and trace. This profile gauge is a nifty tool for measuring contours, and it lets you make templates and patterns for all sorts of complex shapes.

Striking Tools

Lumberjacks use axes, but that doesn't mean woodworkers have to fell trees to make good use of these potent striking tools. One of the most ancient of all hand tools, axes are swift and powerful. Yet in the hands of a skilled craftsman, an axe can sculpt, shape and otherwise transform a rough billet of wood into a recognizable furniture form, such as the leg or seat of a chair. A hammer is another invaluable striking tool. No shop should be without a good selection of these pounders for assembly work, driving nails, and general striking tasks. Smaller hitting tools such as nail sets and punches are handy for smaller jobs.

Axes and Other Cutting Tools

Several areas in furniture making require the keen edge of an axe for initial roughing work. A good example is in the "green" chairmaking trade, where the work starts out with green, or wet, wood, and needs shaping before the drying process can begin. Or perhaps you want to incorporate large sculptural elements into your work. There's no faster way to accomplish large-scale shaping of wood than with a good, dependable axe.

Axes and their smaller cousins, hatchets, are grouped into different categories depending on the job at hand. A basic **felling axe** is designed to sever wood fibers, and consequently has a thin but broad profile. The cutting edge must be very sharp to facilitate using the tool. Of course, if you need to chop wood limbs to length—or fell a tree—this axe can do the job wonderfully. But for furniture making, a felling axe is particularly useful for splitting large billets to rough size, such as splits for chair legs and other

spindles. Chairmakers use a felling axe to produce rived stock, in which the wood fibers are split with the grain. Instead of swinging the tool, you'll get more control if you use a large wood mallet or club to strike the head of the axe. (See photo, below.)

For finer shaping work, a carving axe has a thinner cross section. This type of axe is designed for finer cuts with the grain of the wood, in which you need more control, for example, general shaping work and detail cuts, hewing the outside of bowls, or architectural carvings. A small carving hatchet with a curved handle lets you produce a powerful stroke with a relatively short swing. (See top left photo, opposite page.)

For more splitting control, particularly when riving stock to produce straight-grained sections, a **froe** is used after the felling axe. The froe has a blunt cutting edge, and really doesn't cut

Rough split. While it excels at chopping trees or limbs, a felling axe also has the necessary mass for splitting billets to produce rived stock. Chairmaker Drew Langsner uses a large wooden club to start the split.

at all, but splits the work in a very controllable manner. The long blade is centered over the end of the

work, then given a sharp rap with a wooden mallet at the center of the blade. (See photo, right.)

Splitting finer. The long blade of a froe lets you create a very accurate split along the marked lines of a squared billet. Use a large mallet to strike the blade at its center.

Shaping and carving. The slim head and short, curved handle of a carving hatchet let you carve details and shape large chunks of wood in a hurry.

After initiating a split with a froe, you use the tool again to pull the split sections apart. Here, the wide blade comes into play as a

MAKING A CHOPPING BLOCK

From the mill. A leftover chunk of sawn and squared wood from the mill makes a great chopping block.

It's important when using an axe or other large chopping tool that you back up the work on a sturdy surface. While a solid benchtop can be utilized for this task, you risk destroying the bench in the process. A better solution is the hard end grain surface of a stump or log. Practically any log or large chunk of wood can be used for a chopping block, although softwood has a slightly more resilient feel and will cushion heavier blows. Be sure to check for bugs before bringing a stump indoors. Fresh-cut (green) logs are best; they'll split and crack, but that's OK.

If you're using a log, find the largest diameter you can. For general chopping work, a length of about 30 inches will make a block of suitable height when standing upright. Lower blocks are better for heavy chopping or splitting. Level the endgrain top of your log with a large plane, then stand it upright. Check that the stump sits solidly on the ground or floor. If it rocks, you can insert shims around the base, or install adjustable floor glides to level it, as shown in the photo, right.

Leveling logs. To keep a chopping stump level and free from rocking, install a few adjustable floor glides on the bottom surface.

lever, letting you control the split down the length of the work. (See photo, left.)

For sculpting hollows and other contours, especially on flat work, an **adze** can make short work of the job. With its upward-curving cutting edge, an adze will chop and sever fibers with or across the grain, leaving a faceted surface on the work. Traditionally used to hew and square up the sides of logs, this axe-like tool is a favorite among many chairmakers for its ability to quickly shape the flat surface of a chair seat into a curvaceous contour. (See photo, below.) There are short, one-handed adzes that can be used to chop work on the top of a bench, or you can use adzes with longer handles designed for ground-level work.

Lever apart. After starting a split, use a froe to lever or twist apart the sections along the grain.

Sculpting a seat. An adze makes quick work of shaping the hollows in a seat blank. Cuts are made by swinging the tool toward you in short, controlled arcs.

SHARPENING AN AXE

There's nothing complex about sharpening an axe, adze or other large striking tool, but it's important to keep these edges as sharp as possible to reduce the amount of work it takes to cut with them. Using a large (8 inches or longer) mill file, follow the tool's existing bevel angle and stroke the beveled faces toward the cutting edge. (See photo, above.) A gently rounded bevel makes a strong edge that resists dulling. If the tool is beveled on both sides, file both sides. You're done when the edge looks even and without any flat spots.

Filing sharp. A large mill file makes quick work of sharpening an axe. Use long strokes toward the cutting edge on each beveled side, rounding the bevel slightly over its face.

A filed edge will work fine for most chopping work, and is perfect for large axes that perform rough work. If you use the tool for more delicate paring and shaving tasks, you may want to further refine the edge. To do this, grab a fine slipstone and use the same procedure as you did with the file, running the stone over the bevel toward the cutting edge. (See photo, left.)

Honing sharper. For paring or shaving chores, use a slipstone on the filed edge to smooth and polish the surface.

Hammers and Other Pounders

Hammers are vital shop tools, and you'll need an assortment to tackle a variety of pounding and hammering tasks. The common claw hammer is a good tool to start with, but there are plenty of other useful hammer types that belong in the woodshop.

For woodworkers, an ordinary **claw hammer** is a necessity for all sorts of shop tasks. The claw at the end of the head is useful for pulling large headed nails, but I generally reserve this feature for my home carpentry jobs. (See Straight Claw Or Curved?, page 100.) Of more use to the woodworker is the business end of the tool, or striking face. You'll want to shop for a hammer by weight. I find that a somewhat light 16-oz. hammer is sufficiently heavy for most of the bigger pounding needed in furniture making, such as seating a tenon into its mortise, yet small enough for driving finishing nails and other lightweight tasks. (See bottom photo, left.)

Occasionally I'll tune up the striking faces of my hammers when they become gouged or chipped in use. You can file the surface with a large mill file, or take the tool to the grinding wheel and gently grind away any blemishes. Finish up by sanding the surface with some 120-grit paper wrapped around a felt block. Leaving a smooth, sanded surface will result in fewer blemishes when you strike your work. (See photo, below.)

Not too heavy. A 16-oz. claw hammer gets a lot of use in the shop, from tapping small nails and other hardware to assembling parts and driving joints home.

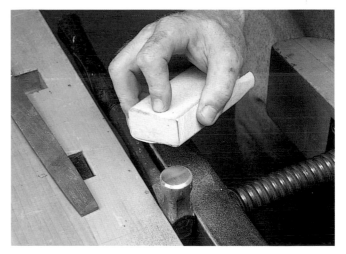

Smooth head. Filing and sanding the head of a hammer reduces the likelihood of dings and other blemishes in your work.

Used primarily by metalworkers for shaping sheet stock and other metalworking chores, a **ball-peen hammer** can be a very useful woodshop tool. (See photo, right.) Ball-peen hammers are available with small, 12-ounce heads, or you can use a sturdier 20-ounce or heavier hammer for really big jobs. With its rounded, or domed, face and heavy head, this type of hammer doesn't work well for driving nails, but it's ideal for pounding small or

Concentrated taps. The compact heads of ball-peen hammers are useful for tapping individual parts together, since the blow is focused over a relatively narrow area.

STRAIGHT CLAW OR CURVED?

While it's not an essential device for woodworking, the claw on the end of a common hammer comes in handy on occasion for pulling out stuff like nails and other obstinate hardware. Claws come in two styles: Straight and curved. I prefer the straight variety for most jobs since it affords more pulling power than the curved version, allowing you to remove stubborn nails more easily. Occasionally the curved claw comes in handy for removing less-stubborn nails, since you can rock the curved section on your work with less damage to the surface.

Straight gains leverage. The straight claw on the hammer at left offers more leverage for pulling stuff like nails and other stubborn hardware. The curved claw at right is better for removing smaller nails and is less likely to ding the work if you rock the head as you pull.

big parts together. I usually ignore the opposite ball-shaped end; its primary function is for peening or shaping the surface of sheet metal.

For setting small nails and brads, and for tapping small or delicate parts into position, a **brad hammer** affords great control without the risk of over-hitting. The flat face on one end of the head is used for general tapping and hitting, while the wedge-shaped end on the opposite side lets you start small nails. (See photo, right.)

Many chisels, such as plastic-handled chisels, Japanese chisels, or any wood-

Hitting nails, not fingers. The narrow wedge-shaped head on a brad hammer lets you start a small nail safely without risk to your fingers or the work.

handled chisel that has a metal hoop just below the striking surface, can be struck with a metal hammer (see Chiseling and Carving Tools, page 146). One of the best tools for this job is a **Japanese chisel hammer.** (See photo, right.) The dense hammer head packs a more powerful punch than a regular claw hammer, and the tool is balanced for more control. A slight crown on one face allows you to hit a chisel's handle with pinpoint accuracy. I find a 12- or 16-ounce hammer is good for lighter, more delicate cuts. Choose a heavier 20- or 26 ounce hammer for really big work or heavy cuts, such as deep mortising in hardwoods.

Hammering a chisel. A Japanese-style chisel hammer is a delight to hold and offers more control and more mass at the head than a conventional hammer—useful attributes when chopping with a chisel.

A good hard surface is a must in any shop as a back-up surface for pounding or shaping metal parts. Nothing beats the hardness and durability of metal, and an **anvil** nicely fits the bill. But you won't need a blacksmith's shop and a 100 lb. anvil; a small chunk of folded steel will do the job for most furniture making applications, such as straightening the leaves on a hinge or flattening the tip of a nail. (See photo, below.)

If you find you need a bigger surface for working large chunks of metal, it's worth looking into a small anvil. Anvils are sold by weight, and a 25- or 50-lb. anvil is big enough for most big wood-shop chores. If you find an old anvil in bad shape

BIG AND SMALL ANVILS

Bigger blows. A 50 lb. anvil clinched to a wood stump lets you play blacksmith when you need to flatten bits of metal, shape custom hardware, or perform other metal-working chores.

(many are mushroomed around the edges from repeated, heavy blows), use a mill file to level the top surface, then sand with fine-grit paper until the surface is smooth. To keep the hitting surface resilient, mount your anvil on a wood stump to absorb the blows. (See photo, above.)

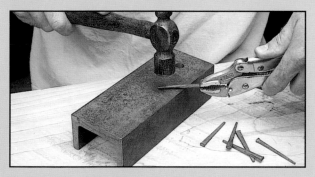

Small but hard. A short length of scrap channel iron makes a convenient anvil for tapping small metal gear such as hinges, pins, or nails.

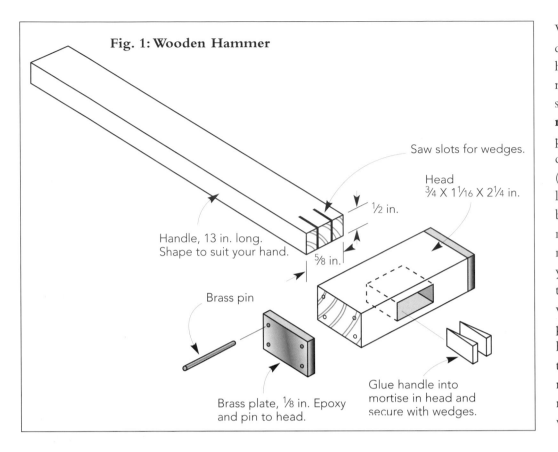

Fig. 1: Wooden Hammer

Handle, 13 in. long.
Shape to suit your hand.

Saw slots for wedges.

Head
¾ X 1¹⁄₁₆ X 2¼ in.

½ in.

⅝ in.

Brass pin

Brass plate, ⅛ in. Epoxy
and pin to head.

Glue handle into
mortise in head and
secure with wedges.

While some chisels can be struck with a hammer, many require the softer strike of a wooden **mallet**, which can pack quite a blow depending on its size. (See bottom photo, left.) Used extensively by carvers, a round mallet should be made from a dense yet resilient wood, typically lignum vitae. The round head promotes accurate hitting, since it's hard to miss a tool using a round face. Round mallets come in a variety of diameters,

Powerful but gentle. Round-head mallets made from a dense wood are best for striking solid-wood handles, providing a firm blow without crushing or deforming the tool upon striking.

Small taps. This homemade wooden hammer, made by wood-worker Yeung Chan, is faced with strips of brass and has the perfect heft for tapping delicate joints home or other small work, such as adjusting the cutting depth of a plane.

Consistent punch. The filled heads of deadblow hammers give them a big punch that transmits the force directly into the work, without bouncing back into your hand.

head on this style of hammer is filled with a loose, heavy material—typically lead shot. This unique head construction allows a deadblow to deliver great force without the ensuing vibration or bounce-back you experience from a metal hammer. (See photo, left.) The lack of vibration makes deadblows a good choice for case construction and other large panelwork, or wherever you need to hammer parts home in a controlled manner. But this style of hammer also excels at smaller work, too. Because it packs such a punch, I use a deadblow with light taps whenever I need to align or adjust small parts that resist the blows of a small hammer.

the larger 4-in. sizes being more useful for heavy chopping or carving chores, and the smaller sizes better suited to chisel work and other small-scale striking jobs. Don't try to fit furniture parts together with a mallet, because the round face will glance off any flat surface and offer little force to the blow.

A small **wooden hammer** is great for smaller jobs such as tapping a set of delicate dovetails home, or for adjusting wooden-style planes. This shop hammer, made by woodworker Yeung Chan, is lightweight and easy to maneuver. (See bottom right photo, opposite page.) The two hitting faces are lined with soft brass, giving the hammer the right heft without risk of damaging the work.

For a few hours work, you can have a homemade hammer that works and feels like no other. (See fig. 1.) You can use any hardwood for the hammer, although the best handle material is hickory. Denser is better for the head, so choose a hardwood such as one of the fruitwoods—apple or pear would be perfect.

When you need a serious pounder for large work, a **deadblow** is your best bet. There are many styles of deadblows, from all-plastic to wood-and-plastic versions, but they all share one common feature: The

Deadblows usually come with non-marring, plastic heads, allowing you to smack a surface soundly without denting the work. Some deadblows come with two different head caps on each end of the head, one end for heavy pounding and the other for lighter work. Another style of deadblow has interchangeable head caps made from soft, medium, or dense plastic. You can unscrew the caps from the main head and outfit the hammer with the right cap for the particular job at hand. (See photo, below.)

Head change. Interchangeable head caps, from hard to soft, let you fine-tune this deadblow for big or little jobs.

For really serious pounding, a **sledge** is the answer. Sledges come in short- or long-handled versions, and are generally rated by the weight (in pounds) of their heads. (See photo, below.) While my sledges certainly don't get daily use, having a really big persuader in the shop is handy insurance for all sorts of force-fit tasks and heavy pounding. Smaller, short-handled sledges are great for flattening or shaping metal parts on an anvil (see Big and Small Anvils, page 101); big, two-handed sledges can help move big beams into position, drive oversize joints home, or pound parts when all your other heavy-duty hammers fall short.

Carpenters use them, and so should you. **Nail sets** are lengths of hardened steel with narrow tips, and they're

Hide that head. A few taps with a nail set let you drive a nail below the surface of the work for a better grip. Size the set to suit the nail; the tip should be slightly smaller than the head of the nail.

just the ticket for setting the heads of nails below the surface of your work. (See photo, above.) Buy nail sets according to the size nails you use. Large penny nails and really big finish nails require a large-diameter tip; smaller finish nails and brads are better set with smaller

King-size hammers. Big and small sledges come in handy when no other pounder can do the job.

Punching set. Two varieties of metal punches, flat (left) and pointed (right), can perform a host of punching and pointing jobs.

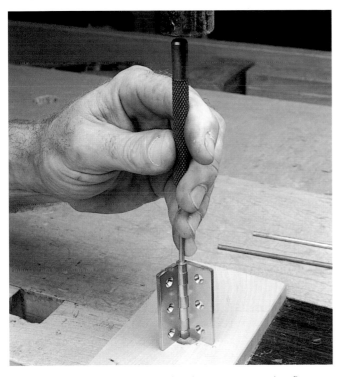

Punching a pin. Tapping metal hardware or pins with a flat-tipped metal punch affords great control and pinpoint precision without damaging the work. An end grain block of hardwood backs up your taps.

Punches come in various sizes, and differ by the diameter of their faces. It's worth investing in a few sizes so you can punch small items such as rods and small dowel pins, or larger objects like hinge leaves and bigger metal objects.

The hardened tip of a **pointed punch** lets you create small dimples in metal or wood, which is handy for starting holes when drilling metal to steer the drill bit and keep it from wandering. (See photo, below.)

Punching a point. A pointed metal punch lets you make dimples in metal or other hard surfaces for the initial steering of a drill bit.

tips. In a pinch, I've modified my bigger nail sets to suit smaller nails by grinding the tips to a point. On really small nails, this pointed tip creates a small dimple in the nail's head, and the nail set's tip is less likely to skitter off the nail (and into the work!) when struck with a hammer.

There are many times in woodworking when we need to flatten a small piece of metal, such as a slightly bent door hinge, or we need to drive a metal pin or similar hardware into or right through our work. Or, perhaps you want to dimple or punch a small divot in a hard wood or a piece of metal. While nail sets can be used in a pinch, a better alternative is to use **metal punches**, which like nail sets are designed for striking with a hammer. (See bottom right photo, opposite page.)

Unlike a nail set, a **flat punch** has a flat face, and is therefore better suited for tapping surfaces without dinging the surface, as shown in the photo above.

Pulling, Prying, and Twisting Tools

The gentle art of woodworking sometimes involves some astute ripping and tearing, or at least pulling a stray nail or two. And driving screws, or snugging up nuts on bolts, is part and parcel of the woodworking bag. Like any tool-using endeavor, it makes sense to use the right tool for the job, and this category of tools has plenty worth considering. Taking apart work or removing nails and other hardware can be handled by a variety of pulling devices, from small nail pullers to larger, more powerful pry bars. Turning screws and bolts requires a more dignified approach with screwdrivers and various wrenches, and also involves the right technique so you avoid damaging your work or the hardware you're installing.

way you came in, and pulling the nail is your one and only option. While a claw hammer does a fine job of pulling nails, the kinds of nails we run into in woodworking are generally unresponsive to a hammer. Either the nail is too thin (a wire brad, for example) and the head of the nail slips right through the hammer's claw, or the head doesn't protrude enough for the claws to get a decent bite.

When you're faced with removing a big nail or staple that's flush or even below the surface of the work, a **cat's paw** can save the day. These prying tools come in assorted sizes, and share one similar feature: At least one end of the tool is hooked, bearing a striking resemblance to the curled foot of a cat. With its rounded face, you can use the paw to gently pry out delicate brads and nails. Or, by hitting the crown of the paw with a hammer, you can set the paw into the work and under the head of a bigger nail, then use the bar's length as a lever to pull the nail up and out. (See photo, below.)

Pullers and Pryers

Pulling out hardware such as nails or wrenching apart an assembly because of a failed measurement is never any fun, but at least these tasks can be done with minimal stress and hassle if you select the right tool. If you're faced with pulling something apart, the first thing to do is stop and breath deeply. Above all, don't grab the nearest hammer and start swinging. Chances are you'll create more of a mess than you're already in. There are more prudent and efficient approaches, and they involve different pulling and prying tools to get the job done.

As much we hate to admit it, oftentimes we need to remove a misplaced nail or brad from a piece. The goal in this situation is get the nail out with as little damage to the surface of the work as possible. (Getting it out quickly is also a desire, before anyone notices your mistake.) One option is to punch the nail deeper into the surface, or even through its back, or non-show side. A metal punch (see page 105) and a good whack from a hammer make short work of this. But many times the only way out is the

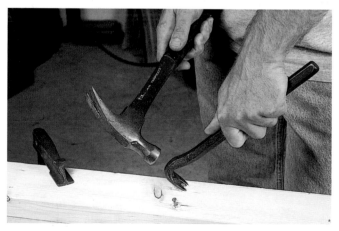

Digging deep. Cat's paws are available in large and small sizes. By tapping the hooked end under the head of a nail and pushing down on the opposite end, you can remove small or big nails with minimal damage to the surface.

Lever power. The bent end of a pry bar facilitates moving or repositioning heavy objects.

A **pry bar** is the answer for bigger pulling jobs or prying tasks, such as disassembling parts, lifting the corner of a heavy cabinet, or racking an assembly into square or level. While you can use this tool like a cat's paw for a limited amount of digging work, a pry bar's best feature is its ability to act as a fulcrum for levering heavy parts into position, such as when moving a heavy cabinet or piece of furniture. (See photo, above.) Notches at each end of the tool let you pull up nail heads that are close to the surface by tapping on the

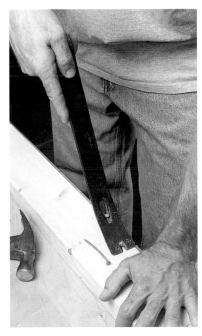

Big lift. A teardop-shaped hole in the bar's end lets you pull nails with more leverage than a conventional hammer.

hooked end with a hammer. Once you've pried the head upward, you can slip the head through a teardrop-shaped cutout in one end to lever the nail up and out. (See bottom left photo.)

For more delicate shop-pulling needs, your best bet is a pair of **nail pullers**. If the head of a nail is protruding from the surface of the work, relax. You're halfway there. The rounded head of a nail puller lets you grab the head while you pull it out with a rocking motion. By placing a thin piece of scrap under the head of the puller and levering the tool back and forth, you can ease the nail from the wood without marring the piece. (See photos, right.)

Nails set below the surface are trickier. For this job, a pair of **modified nail pullers** is far superior to the standard fare you'll get off the store shelf. I use my bench grinder to grind to a point one side of an ordinary pair of pullers.

Rock and pull. Get a nail out without a blemish by grabbing the head with a pair of nail pullers and gently levering the tool back on a piece of scrap (above). Keep re-gripping the nail at the surface to ease the nail out (below).

Fig.1: Modified Pullers

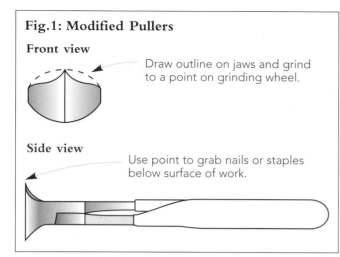

Front view

Draw outline on jaws and grind to a point on grinding wheel.

Side view

Use point to grab nails or staples below surface of work.

Different grips. Ordinary pliers (left) adjust to grasp small or big items; adjustable pliers (center) open wider and provide a better grip on bigger gear; and locking pliers (right) have square or pointed jaws and provide a more tenacious hold when you lock the jaws onto the work.

Get a grip. The modified tips of these shop-ground nail pullers let you grasp the head of a nail without having to dig into the surface of the work.

(See fig. 1.) By shaping the jaws to a point, you can effectively dig below the surface of the work to grab the head of the nail, then use the same rocking action to ease the nail out. (See photo, left.)

For grabbing, pulling, or twisting hardware, a pair of ordinary **pliers** is invaluable. The jaws on most pliers can be adjusted in two or more positions, allowing you to grab pins and other small items or bigger gear such as large dowels using the same pliers. (See top photo, right.) When you need to grip larger work, or want to grasp square or parallel-sided gear, look for a pair of **adjustable pliers**. These pliers have larger jaws that can be adjusted for bigger items, and the long handles provide more leverage for twisting or turning, giving you a good grip on tough nuts or other square stuff. **Locking pliers** are a must when all else fails and you need a grip that won't let

go. By adjusting the tension on a pair of locking pliers, you can grip an item without having to squeeze with brute force. Locking pliers are available in various sizes, with square or needle-nose jaws for big or small pulling jobs.

Really small pulling tasks require **tweezers**, the best example being pulling wood splinters out of your hand. Luckily, woodworking tool manufacturers have recognized that the old pharmacy-style tweezers just don't have the power for serious splinter pulling. They've designed well-made grabbers with precise mating jaws and pointed, sliver-finding tips. These are not the tweezers your mother used to remove those thorns after a rumble in the bramble bush. Indeed, these newer, more refined grippers can do double-duty as mini grabbers for delicate materials, such as when repositioning a sliver of wood or veneer for gluing. (See photo, below.)

Delicate grip. A pair of woodworking tweezers with precision-ground tips is great for pulling splinters from your hands, or for carefully positioning small work such as marquetry and other inlay.

Screwdrivers and Other Twisting Tools

Even with the advent of cordless drills and driver bits for power-driving screws (see Power Drive Your Screws, page 112), the homely screwdriver still has its place in the shop, especially when it comes to installing high-end hardware and delicate brass screws. And there are special screwdrivers available that can make your work much easier and prevent damage to the head of a screw. Other twisting tools such as wrenches also play a big part in the woodworking tool arsenal, and shouldn't be overlooked.

SEEING REALLY CLOSE-UP

We can all benefit from magnification in the woodshop—regardless of the quality of our eyesight. Seeing a truly sharp edge on a chisel or inspecting tiny teeth on a small saw are two examples; prying out a particularly reluctant splinter from a finger is another. Magnifiers are the answer. A **hand-held magnifier** is great for close inspection, such as reading the pores of wood, or when positioning inlay or other small work. (See photo, below left.)

When you need both hands on the work, such as when sharpening a hand saw, sawing marquetry, or performing any small-scale woodworking job, a pair of **binocular magnifiers** that fit on your head are just the ticket. (See photo, right.)

One-handed work. This 2½x hand-held magnifier lets you see up close when positioning small parts, such as the inlay shown here.

No-hands work. These 2x binocular magnifiers let you see the action while you use both hands. A small 2½x loupe on the side of the glasses pivots into view to increase magnification even further.

You might think that any old screwdriver will do when it comes to twisting screws into your work, but when you delve into the anatomy of screws you'll think again. It's vital to select the right size screwdriver for the size screw you're using, and it's equally important to choose the right type of driver for the style of screw. In addition, the standard hardware-store screwdriver is likely to have a palm-abrading handle that's too small in diameter for serious driving. For general-purpose screws in the shop, a set of **cabinetmaker's screwdrivers** fills the bill nicely. The long shanks on these drivers provide more torque and control, and the nicely shaped wood handles ensure a good grip and won't dig into your hands. (See top left photo, opposite page.) Cabinetmaker's screwdrivers have a couple more advantages over the ordinary fare. First, they're available in a wide range of sizes for small and large flat-head and Phillips-style screws. A good set should include flat-head and Phillips drivers, in sizes

POWER DRIVE YOUR SCREWS

When I need to snug up a delicate solid-brass screw, I reach for my trusty screwdriver to control the action and avoid snapping the soft metal of the screw. But for most of my screwdriving needs, an electric drill gets the job done in less time with less hassle. I prefer a **cordless drill** (see page 121), but any drill with a jawed chuck will work fine. The key to power-driving your screws successfully is to equip your drill with a couple of screwdriving accessories, and to employ a few simple driving techniques.

Chuck a magnetic **driver-bit holder** into the end of the drill, and insert a **driver bit** into the end of the holder. (See photo, below.) The magnetic holder magnetizes the driver tip, which keeps screws from falling off the tip—a handy feature when driving lots of screws.

In line, and lots of pressure. Prevent the driver bit from spinning by placing your weight over the bit, keeping the drill straight and aligned with the screw.

Be sure to pick the right driver bit for the screw you're using. A #2 bit in either flat-head or Phillips style is the most useful, and fits #6 and #8 screws.

Smaller #4 screws require a #1 bit. Above all, don't try to use a smaller bit to drive larger screws. Although it will certainly fit into the tip of the screw, the tolerances are sloppy and the bit will invariably slip during driving.

Bit and holder. For power-driving screws, it pays to equip your drill with a bit holder and the appropriate-size driver bit.

Once you've selected the right bit, good power-driving technique involves two essential approaches, both of which will help prevent *bit spinning*. That happens when the bit spins repeatedly in the screw's head and deforms the screw or the bit itself. The first key point is to align the driver and the drill with the shaft of the screw, keeping all the parts in a straight line. Second, place as much force as you can muster over the drill and onto the tip of the screw, even when backing out a screw. (See photo, above.) If you keep these two driving techniques in mind, your screws will go in cleanly and quickly, and your wrists won't suffer all the twisting and turning from those old-fashioned screwdrivers.

The king of drivers. A set of cabinetmaker's screwdrivers makes driving screws a breeze.

accommodating #4 up to #12 screws. Second, the steel shafts have wide flats on them just below the ferrule, allowing you gain more leverage by using them with a wrench to turn obstinate screws. (See photo, below.)

There are many times when a standard screwdriver is too long to access the head of screw, especially in restricted areas such as inside a drawer or cabinet. In these situations, you can turn to a **stubby screwdriver**, available in either flat-head or Phillips style. While you won't get the same amount of torque as you would from a long-handled screwdriver, these

Turning power. The flat area on a cabinetmaker's screwdriver accepts a wrench, allowing even more torque for difficult driving situations.

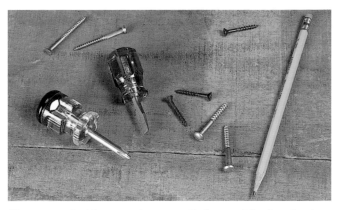

Short turn. Stubby screwdrivers, in Phillips and flat-head styles, let you get into tight spots where a longer driver can't reach.

short, palm-size drivers can get you out of a tight spot. (See photo, above.)

If you ever get into using European hardware, especially concealed cup hinges and commercial drawer slides, you'll notice right away that the Phillips screws used with this gear are shaped slightly different from ordinary screws. A standard Phillips driver can slip and damage the heads of these screws, so it pays to buy a **specialty screwdriver for Euro screws** to ensure a positive grip. The tip on this style of driver is specially shaped to fit Euro-style screws (one manufacturer calls it a "Posidrive"), and it's available to fit both #6 and #8 screws. (See photo, below.)

Small screws demand small screwdrivers, and even smaller screws, like those used for jewelry boxes or

Positive grip. This screwdriver has a special tip that fits European-style screws for a no-grip twist.

Tiny drivers. For really small screws, pick up a set of mini screwdrivers with flat-head and Phillips-style tips.

miniature hinges, require even smaller drivers. A set of **mini screwdrivers** will let you drive those tiny screws without damaging them. (See photo, above.)

When it comes to nuts and bolts, a set of **box wrenches** and **socket wrenches** will allow you to tighten or loosen six-sided nuts and bolt heads, which are the most common. Be sure to equip yourself with both Imperial (English) and metric wrenches, since these days many of our woodworking tools and machines come from all over the world and are assembled with both standards. A good starter kit would include wrenches from ¼ through ¾ inch and 6 through 19 mm. (See photo, below.)

When you get into a tight spot you can use a short, stubby screwdriver when a longer driver can't reach (see

previous page), but sometimes a short screwdriver can be downright impossible to turn with difficult screws. In cases like this, you can turn your socket wrench into a low-profile **socket screwdriver** that packs tremendous torque. The key is to equip the wrench with a ¼-inch socket, then slip a driver bit into the socket. (See Power Drive Your Screws, page 112.) Now you can access difficult-to-reach screws with maximum turning power. (See top left photo, opposite page.)

You're very likely to come across hex bolts in the shop, where the head of the bolt has a six-sided hole in its center. The tool that works to turn inside these hexagonal holes is a set of **hex wrenches** or **hex keys.** Hex keys come in a variety of styles, and are available in Imperial and metric sizes. One style folds into a compact set and contains essential wrenches into one convenient package. (See middle photo, opposite page.) Standard individual hex keys are available in T-handled versions that provide more torque, or short keys for hard-to-reach spots. (See bottom left photo, opposite page.)

Turning power. A set of box or open-end wrenches (left) and a set of socket wrenches (right) will let you tighten or loosen most nuts and bolts.

LUBING YOUR SCREWS

If you've ever driven a screw into hardwood by hand, you know the feeling of impending doom when the screw starts to get harder and harder to turn, and finally snaps off mid-turn. While nothing can replace a properly drilled pilot hole for your screws, a ball of **beeswax, candlewax,** or any relatively **hard wax** can help. By rubbing the threads into the wax prior to installation, you'll find that screws go in with ease and you're less likely to split the wood.

Waxing a screw. Lubricating your screws with beeswax will let you drive screws with less friction and can prevent the heads from snapping off.

Tough screw turner. By converting your socket wrench into a screwdriver with a ¼-inch socket and a driver bit, you can drive tough, hard-to-reach screws.

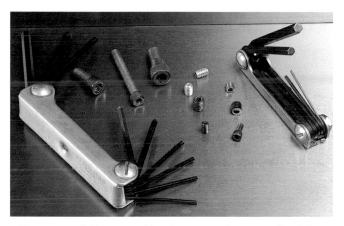

All in one. A folding set of hex keys provides you with a full range of wrench sizes in a single tool. Look for them in Imperial and metric sizes.

Individual wrenches. Long-handled hex keys (left) provide more turning power for difficult bolts; small L-shaped keys (right) let you access confined areas.

Nut power. A nut-driver bit chucked in a cordless drill makes a powerful and wrist-relieving way to install or remove bolts.

Nut drivers have saved me time and again from a sore arm by letting me spin tons of nuts with the power of a drill. These special drivers come with shanks that fit into a drill chuck, and the business end accepts the head of a nut. Buy them in common nut sizes, and you can use them in a power drill to turn those nuts in no time. (See photo, above.)

When your wrench doesn't quite fit that odd nut, look for adjustable wrenches to fill the gap. While a pair of pliers can work in a pinch, the movable jaw on a **crescent wrench** can be adjusted for a precise fit to the head of a nut. (See photo, below.) To prevent damaging the more delicate movable jaw, always orient the wrench so the stronger fixed jaw is behind and driving the nut.

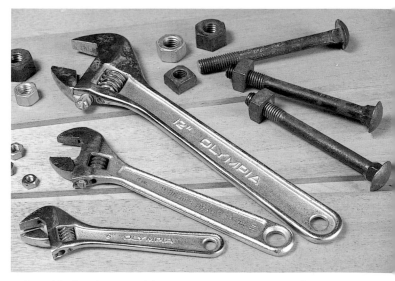

Adjustable fit. The moveable jaw on a crescent wrench allows you to grab odd-sized nuts with a precision fit.

20 Everyday Aids To Woodworking

Some of the most-used tools in my shop are from decidedly non-woodworking sources. In fact, there are all sorts of unusual but stone-simple items that make great tools or aids for woodworking. Chances are you won't find them in woodworking catalogs; they're more likely to be found in an ordinary supermarket, pharmacy, or even your local sporting-goods store. Here's a list of 20 of my favorites.

1 Toothpicks. Toothpicks are perfect for spot-gluing of parts; the round variety is great for filling oversized screw holes so your screws will fit correctly. Just tap in the pick with a dab of glue, snap the pick flush to the surface, then re-drill for the screw. Instant fix.

2 Golf tees. Pick up a pack of wood (not plastic) tees at a sporting-good store. To quickly fill a hole or other round blemish, dab a spot of glue on the tapered end of a tee and tap it home. When the glue has dried, saw or pare the excess flush.

3 Bamboo skewers. Buy a pack of ⅛-inch diameter skewers at the supermarket and use them for filling holes or pinning parts. These tiny dowels are incredibly strong, and flex without breaking.

4 School chalk. Make your mark stand out—especially on darker woods—and make it temporary by using blackboard chalk. It's great for making quick notes on your work, and removes easily with the swipe of a damp sponge.

5 Lipstick. This highly visible but easily removable stuff is just the ticket for locating hardware. Rub some on the tongue of a lock to mark where the strike plate will go, or use this glamorous stick to find obstructions when installing cabinets or paneling.

6 Sticky notes. Use these pre-glued slips of paper as temporary labels, such as for marking finished parts. Or keep 'em on hand for shim stock by inserting one or more pieces into the necessary spot. Notes peel off without a blemish.

7 Metal flashing. Flashing makes inexpensive and durable shim stock, and can be found at a hardware store or a builder's supply outlet. Cut this thin aluminum with tin snips or shears to the sizes you need.

8 Sand bags. For great clamps that conform where it counts, fill canvas bags with sand. These heavy yet supple bags mold to your work, making great clamps for curved work, wide panels, or other areas where standard clamps can't reach. Buy clean sand at a home center or building supply outlet, and get some bags at a home center or from a photographic or theatrical-supply house. Fill the bags with sand, them tie 'em shut with string.

9 Waxed paper. Prevent mistakes and messes by slipping a sheet of waxed paper between or under your work when gluing up. Available at the supermarket in a boxed roll, waxed paper repels glue, so you won't risk gluing the wrong parts.

10 Stretch wrap. Available in long or short rolls from home centers or shipping companies, this super-sticky wrap seals open jars or cans of finish and keeps wet brushes from drying out. Or use it like waxed paper to prevent gluing the wrong parts. Even better, wrap wood parts to temporarily seal them and prevent warp.

11 Cotton swabs. These soft cotton tips are great for spot-finishing, or for cleaning small parts and getting into nooks and crannies with solvent.

12 Cat food tins. Clean and recycle your old tins and use them for parceling out small amounts of finish or for holding glue. A low center of gravity means a parked glue brush won't tip over the tin, and it's easy to dip into one with a rag or wiping cloth.

13 Baby food jars. Great for storing small amounts of finish or for organizing small hardware, such as nuts and washers.

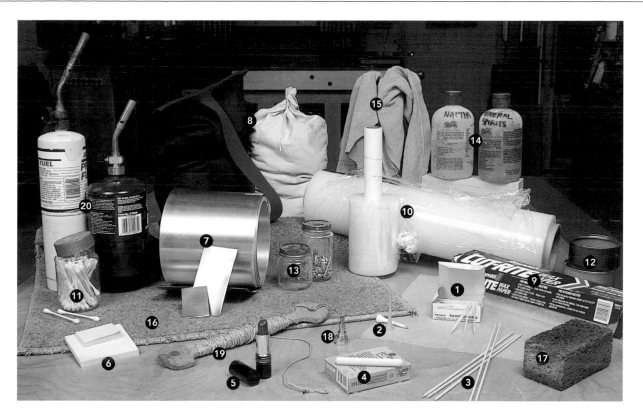

14 **Squeeze bottles.** Recycle your empty shampoo bottles for more control when measuring out liquids, such as shop solvents. Fill the bottles with fluids such as mineral spirits, denatured alcohol, lacquer thinner (test that it doesn't melt the plastic), and the like. Look for bottles with flip-up spouts, which are more convenient to use. For safety, be sure to label the contents clearly.

15 **Old cotton clothes.** Well-washed and scissored into strips or squares, soft cotton makes great rags for wiping finishes and for common clean-up chores.

16 **Carpet remnant.** Lay a scrap on the bench to protect finished work from dings and scratches, or to keep parts from sliding around, especially when sanding.

17 **A damp sponge.** Wipe off glue squeeze-out or clean up chalk marks with a moistened sponge. For the prefect wetness, fill a sponge with water, then squeeze away the excess until it's damp like the nose of a dog.

18 **Rare-earth magnets.** These powerful little magnets are available from woodworking catalogs, and can be used to make all sorts of clever contrivances for holding iron and steel parts in the right spot (such as a chuck key on a drill press). Or sink a couple of magnets into a door and case (make sure to reverse the polarities) and presto! Your door closes as if by magic.

19 **String.** Pull a length of string taut to check really long areas for flat, such as a conference table or a kitchen countertop. Or attach a line level to the string, and read long surfaces for level, such as a floor or a run of cabinets.

20 **Propane torch.** Pick up a bottle of propane and a torch tip at the hardware store or home center, and get ready to heat all sorts of stuff in the shop. Good uses include "aging" hardware such as steel hinges by heating them until they change to a darker color; annealing harder metals to soften them for bending or shaping; and "polishing" the sawn edges of plastics such as polycarbonate by passing a flame quickly over the surface.

Boring Tools

Drilling holes is a basic woodworking operation, whether we're boring pilot holes for screws, cutting tapered plugs or openings, drilling for bolts, fitting hardware, or any of the myriad boring jobs associated with woodworking projects. To drill a hole accurately, we need the right bits and the right tools to hold them. The drills that hold our bits come in a variety of shapes and sizes. While standard twist bits can cover most of our drilling needs, there are many specialty bits and jigs that can give us more precise holes in certain drilling situations.

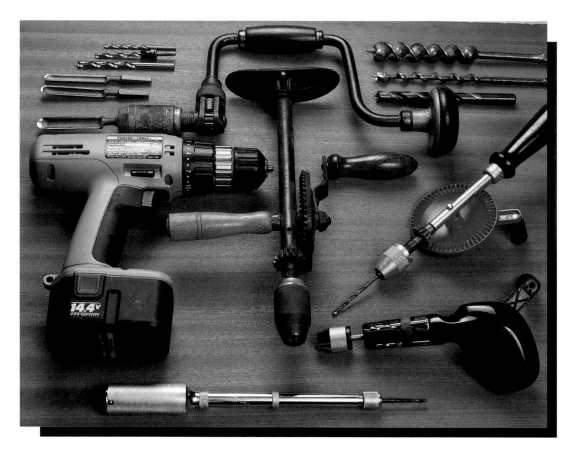

Drills

Holding a drill bit securely is the key to drilling accurate holes, and there are several bit-holding tools that you can choose from depending on the drilling job at hand. If you need a hole that's dead-square to the surface of the work, your best bet is to mount the bit in a drill press. But for many drilling operations, the freedom of a hand-held drill allows you to reach difficult spots or drill at odd angles.

For drilling small holes without a lot of fuss, you can use a **push drill**, often called a **Yankee screwdriver**. (See photo, right.) This particular type of drill is one of the first mechanical tools used by woodworkers, and instead of relying on electricity, it works with an up-and-down screwing action to spin a drill bit very effectively. Some Yankee drills have adjustable jaws that will fit standard round-shanked bits (up to about ¼ inch); other models accept special square-shanked bits.

Similar to a push-type drill, but able to hold larger bits and drill larger holes (typically up to ⅜ inch),

is a **geared hand drill**. This type of hand-powered drill has a jawed chuck that accepts regular bits. A geared handle lets you spin the bit while you grab the side or top of the drill and push into the work with your other hand. (See top photo, opposite page.)

For square- or tapered-shank bits, a **brace** is the tool of choice. (See bottom left photo, opposite page.) This ancient tool has been around a long time, and with good reason. Made of wood with metal facings or metal with wooden grips, this was the

Push and drill. For pilot holes and other small boring jobs, a push drill works quickly and quietly. To use the drill, push repeatedly on the top of the drill. An internal screw coupled with a spring inside the drill's housing rotates the bit back and forth.

Push, turn and drill. For light drilling of holes up to ⅜ inch, a geared hand drill is inexpensive and convenient to use. Simply crank the handle and push down as you drill.

Braced for action. A traditional brace holds square-shanked bits, particularly useful for chairmaking. Use pressure over the top of the tool and guide the bit by eye.

tool our forebears used for all of their drilling chores. Today, a brace is the only tool to effectively hold bits such as square-shanked augers, spoon bits, and other specialty bits. And with the right bit, you can bore holes 1 inch or larger.

By placing your weight over the brace's top, and rotating the C-shaped arm, you can drill all sorts of holes at practically any angle. Chairmakers favor this tool for drilling the compound-angled holes in seats or rungs typically found in chairs. I find the brace to be a handy tool whenever I need to drill large or angled holes, or other holes that involve complex joinery and specialty bits.

In stark contrast to the traditional brace, my hands-down favorite "hand tool" for hand drilling is a **cordless drill** equipped with a rechargeable battery. Without a cord, you have the freedom to take the drill anywhere you need to, and today's crop of battery-operated drills offer lots of power with long drill times before recharging. (See photo, below.) Make sure to buy an extra battery for convenience's sake; when one battery is depleted, you'll always have a fresh battery on hand without having to wait for recharging.

Battery power. A cordless drill is the author's favorite method for drilling holes by hand. Look for a comfortable grip, and keep a spare battery on hand for back-up power.

121

you're much better off using **brad-point bits**. Brad points are essentially twist bits with tiny cutting spurs on the business end of the bit. (See top right photo, opposite page.)

The spurs on a brad-point bit do an excellent job of scoring the perimeter of the hole before the bulk of the hole or waste is drilled, preventing tearout on both sides of the workpiece. The key to using a brad-point bit effectively is to begin your hole at a very slow feed rate. Once the spurs have scored the surface, you can plunge the bit faster. Then slow down

Bits

There are dozens of drill bits for us to choose from when it comes to the many drilling operations we encounter as woodworkers, and many of these are considered specialty bits for specific applications. But for general woodworking, you can get by with much less, and you won't sink a fortune in exotic bits that you'll use maybe once a year. One of the best ways of selecting a bit for the work you're doing is to examine the type of hole it leaves. (See fig. 1.)

Twist bits are the standard fare when it comes to drilling wood—and for drilling in metal. A full set of twist bits is a must, from $\frac{1}{64}$ inch up to $\frac{1}{2}$ inch. (See photo, right.) Typically, twist bits have shank sizes that correspond to the drill size, where the shank is the same diameter as the cutting tip. These bits work fine in a drill press or a drill with a $\frac{1}{2}$-inch chuck. But most hand drills have a $\frac{3}{8}$-inch chuck, and if you plan on doing most of your drilling by hand, you should look at a twist-bit set with shanks machined down to fit your drill's chuck capacity. (See top left photo, opposite page.)

Sometimes clean entry holes *and* exit holes are a must, for example, when drilling for a dowel joint where the dowel is exposed on both faces, or anywhere a through-hole is seen on both sides. In these cases,

Old standbys. A full set of twist bits, from $\frac{1}{64}$ inch up to $\frac{1}{2}$ inch, will cover most of your everyday drilling chores, including drilling holes in metal.

Turned down to fit. A machined shank smaller than the cutting portion of the bit lets you use a twist bit in drills with smaller chucks.

again as the bit emerges from the opposite side for a clean exit. In addition to cutting clean entry and exit holes, a brad-point bit will also leave a relatively flat-bottomed hole, which is handy for installing many types of hardware, such as countersinking pan-head screws.

Spur action. For a clean entrance and exit when drilling holes ½ inch wide or smaller, a brad-point bit is the answer. Tiny spurs on the rim of the bit score around the hole, severing the fibers for a cut free of tearout.

Fig. 1: Four Basic Bits

Twist	Brad Point	Spade	Forstner

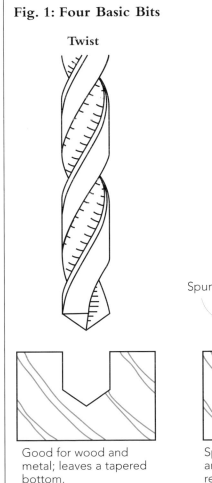

Spur

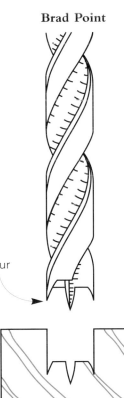

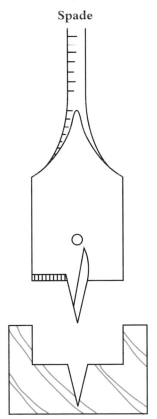

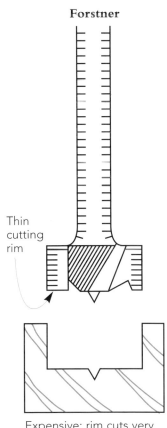

Thin cutting rim

Good for wood and metal; leaves a tapered bottom.

Spurs cut clean entry and exit holes; leaves relatively flat bottom.

Inexpensive; can drill deep holes, but long point leaves hole in work.

Expensive; rim cuts very cleanly and can make overlapping holes. Leaves flat bottom.

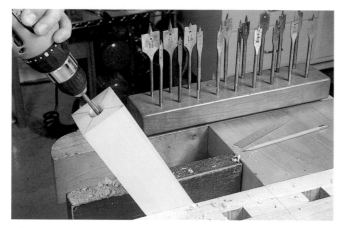

Cheap and effective. Spade bits make short work of drilling really deep holes, and are available in large diameters for drilling bigger holes.

For drilling deep or large-diameter holes, I keep a supply of **spade bits** on hand in sizes from $\frac{1}{8}$ inch up to 2 inches. Spade bits are affordable, and with their lead cutting point they can follow straight into a relatively deep hole without wandering. (See photo, above)

A big advantage with spade bits over other drill bits is the ability to shape the bit for a custom-size hole, as shown in figure 2. By modifying a spade bit to cut a slightly smaller hole, you can tailor the fit of custom hardware, pins, or undersized dowels.

One drawback with spade bits is that they don't produce particularly clean entrance or exit holes, since the geometry of the cutting edges produces more of a chiseling effect in the wood. To improve performance and get a cleaner cut, you can file small spurs at the outer cutting tips, as shown in fig. 2.

Like spade bits, **Forstner bits** can tackle large-diameter holes (or small ones, if needed). The geometry of a Forstner consists of a thin but razor-sharp rim with a brad-point center spur. Make no mistake: Forstner bits are expensive, especially in the larger sizes, which you'll find in diameters of $3\frac{1}{2}$ inches or more. There are two types of Forstners to consider: **continuous rim** or **sawtooth**, also called **multispur** bits.(See photo, below.) The continuous-rim style is best for bits under 1 inch; multispur bits have tiny saw teeth on the rim and cut very aggressively. Multispur bits are best used for large-diameter holes in which a continuous rim would heat up and dull the cutting edge. All large multispur Forstners should be used in a drill press only; smaller continuous-rim bits can be held in a hand drill, although accurate drilling using this method can be somewhat tricky and takes practice. The trick to getting either of these types of bits to drill clean holes is to combine a high feed rate with a

Fig. 2: Improving a Spade Bit

You can modify an ordinary spade bit for cleaner cuts, or for drilling undersized holes.

File notches in cutting edges.

Spurs sever wood fibers, leaving a hole with clean walls.

3/4

File sides to create custom, undersize bit.

Two styles of Forstner. Continuous-rim bits (left) cut exceptionally clean holes; multispur or sawtooth bits (right) can tackle larger holes without overheating.

low rotation speed—especially for large-diameter bits—to prevent the rims from overheating.

Forstners shine when it comes to cutting exceptionally clean entrance and exit holes, as well as producing smooth walls inside a hole. One of the best uses for a Forstner bit is when cutting overlapping holes, such as when drilling out a mortise, where edge-holding ability is key. The razor rim of Forstners allows the bit to hold without wandering, even if the center point is over a void, as shown in the photo, below.

Drilling side-by-side. Cutting overlapping holes without wandering, such as when drilling out for mortises, is no problem with a Forstner bit.

Another advantage to using Forstners is that you can drill a hole with a dead-flat bottom, something a twist bit or spade bit can't do. This feature makes these bits useful for creating flat pockets for custom fittings or hardware, such as when installing European cup hinges, for which you need a flat bottom for strength. (See top photo, right.)

Machinists often rely on **numbered bits** for the precision they need when drilling accurately sized holes. Instead of being grouped by size in fractions of an inch, these twist-style bits are graduated in numbered designations. With numbered bits, the higher numbers correspond to smaller-diameter bits. Differences between sizes can be measured in thousandths of an inch, a degree of accuracy needed for machine work such as when tapping holes for bolts, but not for general woodworking. However, as woodworkers we can take advantage of these numbered bits in their smaller sizes. A set of small numbered bits is a lifesaver in certain drilling situations. These tiny bits,

numbered from 61 to 80, are available in an index case of 20 and cost peanuts. They're great for drilling miniature holes when no other tool can do the job, from small decorative piercing cuts to drilling for tiny brads and other delicate hardware. (See photo, below.)

The bottom is nice, too. A Forstner bit will cut super-clean holes with smooth walls and no tearout on the face or back. And the bottom of the hole will be dead flat.

While it might be viewed more as a saw and not a drill bit, a **hole saw**, also known as a **sawtooth hole cutter**, has a series of saw teeth around its cutting edge, much like the teeth on a multispur Forstner bit. In fact, hole saws are a low-cost alternative to Forstners when it comes to drilling large holes, as long as you're not looking to make a stopped hole. And hole saws will drill most metals, including mild steel. You can't drill a stopped hole because hole saws are designed to drill *through* a workpiece, leaving the center as waste in the form of a

As small as it gets. A case of 20 numbered bits lets you drill tiny holes in your work for small hardware or for decorative effects.

Rim cutting. Used on the drill press, a hole saw will cut a large through-hole, leaving a wood plug as the waste. Slow rpm's are crucial for clean cuts and to avoid overheating the tool's cutting rim.

plug. A hole saw has a twist-style drill bit in its center, which centers the bit as the teeth on the rim do all the cutting. Like a Forstner, slow rpm's are key to clean cuts without burning. (See photo, left.)

One of the drawbacks to hole saws is a tendency for the wood plug to jam inside the bit once the bit is freed of the workpiece. Overheating a bit will almost guarantee this will happen. Luckily, the fix is painless. To remove a stuck plug, drive two screws into the plug until the tips of the screws push the block out of the bit, as shown in the top left photo, opposite page.

If you need to drill deep and accurately straight holes, an **auger bit** is a good solution. With its self-feeding screw on the tip, an auger bit is designed to be fed by

SHARPENING DRILL BITS

My general approach when it comes to keeping my drill bits sharp is to throw them away when they get dull, and replace them with new ones. While you can successfully sharpen most bits with a fine file or on a grinding wheel, the problem comes when you inadvertently offset the center of the bit during the sharpening process. If you don't maintain a bit's precise centricity, it will wander during cutting and drill a rough hole that's slightly oversize. Buying a new bit solves the problem.

Having said this, it's tough to toss expensive bits into the trash, so it's worth your while practicing on some spare bits to get a feel for the

sharpening technique. On most bits, you can use a fine file (see Rasps and Files, page 134) or the side and face of a grinding wheel. The general idea is to follow the existing bevel angles to remove any nicks and to re-establish a continuous cutting edge. Follow up your filing or grinding by honing the cutting edges with a fine slipstone.

By far the most challenging bits to sharpen are Forstner bits, and the price of these bits makes it worth your while to sharpen them. (See photos, below.) On a really dull bit, you'll have to hone both the inside of the throat as well as inside the rim. *Never* file or hone the outside of a drill bit, or you'll permanently alter its diameter. If you're left with a small burr on the outside of the bit from the sharpening sequence, rub the bit over a piece of hard leather such as a pants belt to remove it.

Inside the throat and rim. Use a fine slipstone to hone the face of the throat and sharpen the bevel above (left). Tackle the inner rim with a round stone, moving it around the rim in a continuous sweeping motion (right).

hand and will not work in an electric drill, hand-held or otherwise. Most augers come with square-sided shanks and are made for use in a brace. The self-feeding screw feature makes augers very easy to control, and their long length and overall stiff construction makes them well suited for drilling very deep holes. (See photo, below.)

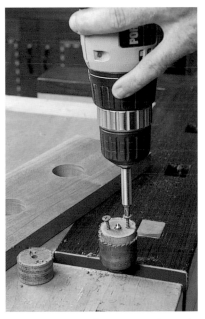

Unplugging the bit. Jammed wood plugs can be freed by driving two screws through the plug.

Long and deep. Held in a brace, an auger bit will drill deep holes with great precision.

Reamer selection. Old-fashioned reamers are hand-operated (left); modern reamers fit into a brace or an electric drill (right).

One specialty bit that cuts like no other is a **reamer**, and it's used to produce a tapered hole after drilling with a regular straight-sided bit. Chairmakers use them all the time to make and fit tapered, wedged tenons to join legs to seats and the like. You can find antique hand-operated reamers, or you can buy more expensive, modern reamers that fit into a drill or a brace. (See photo, above.) Reamers are available in a variety of different angles, but a total angle of about 10 degrees is the most common, and is the correct taper for a strong joint.

Drilling with a reamer is fast and fun. Chuck the bit in a drill or brace, and drill into your straight-sided hole until the tip of the reamer projects out the opposite face. Then check the fit to your tapered tenon. (See photo, right.)

Reaming a taper. To cut a tapered hole for a tapered tenon, first drill a straight-sided hole, then ream out the hole to the desired taper. Here, the reamer is chucked into a brace and held at an angle to create a tapered socket for a leg in the underside of a chair seat.

Spoon size. These round-ended spoon bits are available in a range of sizes for typical mortise work.

Often used by the same trade, a **spoon bit** is an another unusual drill bit that chairmakers often use to cut stopped mortises. Spoon bits are typically available in common mortise sizes from ⅜ inch up to ¾ inch. (See photo, above.)

With its spoon-shaped end and stubby profile, a spoon bit doesn't look like much, but in the hands of a skilled woodworker, these bits have amazing versatility. Designed for use in a brace or any hand-operated drill, you can start a spoon bit at practically any angle, then *change* angles or readjust the angle to suit once the full diameter of the bit is in the stock. Try that with another type of bit! This adjustability makes spoon bits well suited for drilling shallow mortises in legs, spindles, and other angled furniture parts. (See photo, below.)

Another useful feature of spoon bits is that they leave a round-bottom hole. This is handy when drilling narrow stock, such as when mortising a slender, round spindle. With a spoon bit, you can drill a relatively deep hole while leaving enough support material around the hole to avoid weakening the part you're drilling. (See fig. 3.)

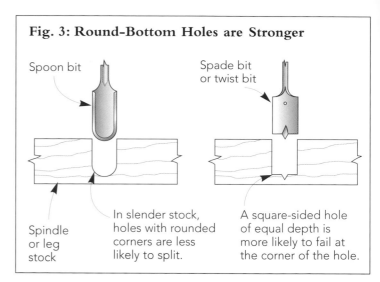

Fig. 3: Round-Bottom Holes are Stronger

Spoon bit

Spade bit or twist bit

Spindle or leg stock

In slender stock, holes with rounded corners are less likely to split.

A square-sided hole of equal depth is more likely to fail at the corner of the hole.

For dead-nuts accuracy, you can't beat a **self-centering bit**, which chucks into a hand drill and is designed to drill a pilot hole for screws through hardware. In one shot you can drill the hole and automatically center it over your hardware. Self-centering bits, sometimes called Vix bits, come in sizes to fit the particular screw you're using. A chamfered nosing at the end of the bit registers on the hardware, and then retracts when you push on the bit to expose a twist bit inside the housing. The best use for these types of bits is when installing hinges, especially for hinges where you have lots of holes to drill, such as a continuous, or piano, hinge. The drilling operation is fast and very accurate. Just position the hinge where you need it, place the tip of the bit into the hinge leaf, and drill. (See photo, right.)

Countersinking a hole is vital to many woodworking operations, and is often the best way to seat the head of a cone-shaped screw. Another common technique is to

Automatic pilot. Drilling precisely centered pilot holes in your work is easy using a self-centering drill bit. Just place the chamfered nose in the hole, push, and drill.

Angled holes. Chucked in a brace, a spoon bit allows you to drill angled holes by eye.

Sunken holes. A countersink bit chamfers the inside of a hole to accept a screw head. Various types include a multiple-flute countersink for drilling metal (left); single-edge wood-cutting bits in a small and large diameters for countersinking all your wood screws (middle); and a hand-held countersink for gently easing the sharp edges of holes or deburring holes drilled in metal (right).

lightly countersink around a shelf-pin hole or other visible hole to give a more refined look to your work. The right tool for these procedures is a **countersink bit**, which has a cone-shape cutter matched to the slope of the screw. Countersinks come a variety of sizes and angles, but for woodworking the best countersinks have an angle of about 82 degrees to match most screw heads. For drilling wood, look for a countersink with a single cutting flute to reduce chatter. (See photo, above.)

If you're driving a lot of screws, a faster method of countersinking is to drill the shank-clearance hole for the screw and countersink the same hole with a single bit. A **countersink/counterbore bit** will do just that, plus drill a counterbore if you need to recess the head of the screw for a design effect, or for fitting a wood plug. (See photo, below.) These drill bits come in a variety of countersink and drill-bit sizes. The most useful countersink/counterbore size is $\frac{3}{8}$ inch, which will accommodate screws up to #10, and accept a $\frac{3}{8}$ inch wood plug. Choose a

Bore and sink at once. A countersink/counterbore bit will drill a clearance hole for the shank of a screw, and countersink it, too. Drilling deeper will counterbore the hole with the same bit.

countersink/counterbore bit where the specific drill bit is sized to the screw you're using.

Wood plugs are a great way to conceal wood screws, and fit into a counterbored hole. The challenge is producing a tight-fitting plug that won't come loose or show gaps. The answer is to use a **tapered plug cutter** on the drill press. (See photo, below.) These cutters come in sizes from $\frac{1}{4}$ inch up to $\frac{1}{2}$ inch, and they produce a tapered plug that's guaranteed to fit tightly in a straight-sided hole when it's tapped home. (See fig. 4.) Like most hollow-style bits, plug cutters have a tendency to overheat and dull. A trick that can overcome this annoying trait is to drill your plugs so the

bit falls off the side of the work, which reduces friction. Using a fence on the drill press table helps align the workpiece. Be sure to glue your plugs into the counterbored holes, and tap them home soundly with a small hammer. Once the glue has dried, you can pare any protruding plugs flush to the surface with a sharp chisel.

Drilling plugs. A tapered plug cutter cuts a slightly tapered wood plug to fit snugly in a straight-sided hole. Reduce friction by aligning the work so a portion of the bit falls off the work.

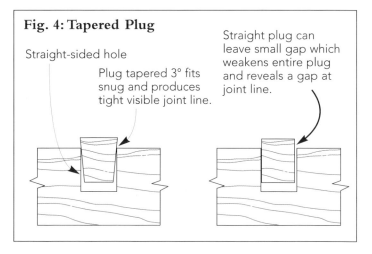

Fig. 4: Tapered Plug

Straight-sided hole

Plug tapered 3° fits snug and produces tight visible joint line.

Straight plug can leave small gap which weakens entire plug and reveals a gap at joint line.

Filling screw or nail holes with wooden plugs can

Tape 'em first. After drilling the plugs, keep them oriented properly by applying a strip of tape over their ends.

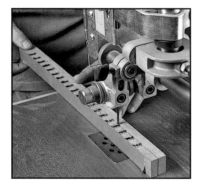

Freeing plugs. Free the plugs from the stock by eyeballing the cutline at the base of the plugs.

be an elegant solution—assuming the fitted plugs aren't glaringly obvious to the eye. To make them practically invisible, make them from similar stock as your work, and install them *with the grain*. Be sure to cut face-grain plugs for filling areas of face grain, and cut end-grain plugs for filling end-grain surfaces.

Once you've drilled the plugs in the stock, rub a strip of removable tape on the ends of the plugs, as shown in the top photo, left. After taping, free the

plugs from the stock by rotating the blank on its side and using a hand saw or the band saw. (See middle photo, left.)

Now for the really important part: Before pulling off individual plugs, be sure to mark them to indicate the correct grain direction. This is an important step because the saw marks run

Installing with the grain. Orient the marks of the plug with the grain of the work as you tap them home.

at 90 degrees to the grain and will often fool you into inserting the plug in the wrong direction. (See bottom photo, left.)

To install the plug, spread some glue around the plug and into the hole, then tap the plug home, making sure it's aligned with the grain of the work. (See photo, above.) Once the glue has dried, you can pare or sand the plug flush to the surface, where it virtually disappears! (See photo, below.)

Marking the orientation. To prevent mistakes later, use a dark marker to indicate the grain direction on the plugs.

Where did it go? Smoothed and sanded flush with the surface, the plug disappears.

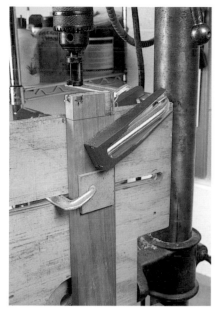

Quick tenon. Using a tenon cutter chucked into the drill press, you can shape round tenons quickly and accurately. Tenon length is usually limited to about 2 inches.

Cutting round tenons is easily accomplished on the lathe, but for those of us without access to a lathe, or for quick tenons without the set-up hassle, you can use a **tenon cutter** instead. (See photo, left.) Tenon cutters are available in diameters up to 3 inches for cutting 3-inch diameter tenons, and are designed for use in the drill press.

The main shortcomings to using these types of bits is that you usually can't cut a tenon longer than about 2 inches, and the bits are prone to burning, especially in hardwoods. To avoid scorching the bit and the tenon, keep the drill rpm's low, and make sure the cutting edges are sharp.

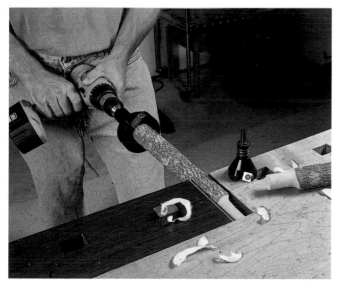

Rustic tenons. A power tenon cutter chucked in a hand drill lets you cut tenons on odd-shaped parts, good when forming limbs for rustic chairmaking.

For tenons on rustic work, such as when making chairs from round branches and limbs, a **power tenon cutter** offers more control over a standard tenon cutter. These bits are hefty pieces of gear designed to work in a hand-held electric drill or a brace—the choice of power is up to you, although the bigger bits are easier to control with a hand-operated brace. A large opening at the front of the bit helps align the cutter to the stock. To keep your tenons straight, align the bit and drill with the centerline of your work. (See bottom photo, left.) Power tenon cutters will cut tenons up to $4\frac{1}{4}$ inches long, and are sized in typical tenon diameters from $\frac{5}{8}$ inch to 2 inches.

Dowel joinery can be a quick, effective method for the small shop when building all sorts of frame-type work, such as doors or face frames. And dowels can help align edges or other workpieces for critical glue-ups. Accuracy when drilling the holes for the dowels is vital for a successful dowel joint, and a **doweling jig** can take the hassle out of the job. Hardened steel bushings in different diameters guide a drill bit. By clamping the jig to the work, you can drill a series of dowel holes in both

Accurate dowels. A doweling jig clamped to the work lets you drill precisely perpendicular dowel holes spaced evenly between mating pieces. Assorted sizes of hard-steel bushings allow you to drill different sized holes for thick or thin work.

mating pieces precisely perpendicular to their surfaces and equally spaced. (See photo, above.)

Scraping Tools

Working wood often calls for scraping rather than slicing cuts, especially when the potential for tearout is high. The action of scraping offers more control over the worksurface, since the fibers don't lift and tear as they can when you slice through the wood. A good example of scraping is cleaning away a bead of partially dried glue. If you try to slice off the glue with a chisel, the slicing action can lift the wood fibers along with the glue, leaving a torn surface— and a mess of your carefully prepared work.

Scraping comes in many forms, and there are specific tools for specific types of scraping cuts. Rough scraping, when you need to shape or remove large amounts of material (like the glue example) is best tackled with a rougher scraping tool that has a more aggressive cutting edge. Rasps and files fall into this category, as does a glue scraper. Fine scraping, when you want to smooth and polish the surface of the wood, requires a more refined tool with a finer cutting edge. For this type of work we'll look at hand scrapers, scraper planes, and other specialty scraping tools.

Rasps and Files

You probably won't find rasps and files in most wood-workers' toolkits, but you should. While files are most often associated with working metal, we can take advantage of some of their unique attributes for woodworking. Files and rasps (the latter can't be used on metal) excel for shaping and smoothing tasks since they cut in a controllable, scraping manner and won't risk tearing out wood fibers, unlike a chisel or a plane. And their broad surfaces register on the surface of the work, giving tactile feedback. These characteristics make files and rasps perfect for shaping and fitting parts, or wherever great precision is needed.

For general shaping and fast removal of stock, **rasps** are precise and powerful hand tools. (See photo, right.) Tiny teeth cut into the surface of rasps scrape wood fibers in a controlled manner, letting you shape con-toured surfaces or fine-tune and fit profiled or flat parts. Rasps are available in coarse or fine-cutting styles, in all sorts of shapes from rectangular to round. Because a rasp cuts to a controllable depth without

tearing wood fibers below the cutline, I use one all the time for precision fitting of parts, such as refining a tenon, as well as for general shaping work.

While any type of rasp will remove wood in a hurry, a **patternmaker's rasp** has a distinct advantage. Because the teeth of a patternmaker's rasp are hand-cut and thus arranged in a random pat-tern, the result is a much smoother surface with fewer groove marks—and that means less time cleaning up the rasped surface. My favorite styles of pattern-maker's rasp are two rasps made by Nicholson, the Nicholson #49 and #50. Both these rasps are flat on one side for smoothing flat or convex surfaces, with half-round backs for tackling shallow concavities. (See top left photo, opposite page.)

A Nicholson #49 will cut quickly, and is great for general shaping work. The Nicholson #50 follows

Sculpting with precision. Rasps will shape contoured or flat work quickly, yet cut in a controllable manner with great precision.

Shape and smooth. Two pattern-maker's rasps, the Nicholson #49 (right) and the #50 (left) make swift shaping cuts with their flat and half-round faces.

where the #49 leaves off, cutting less aggressively but leaving a smoother surface. If I were just starting out, I would pick the #50. With this one rasp you can shape curved surfaces in no time, yet leave a surface that needs very little in the way of cleanup.

One drawback to using rasps is their tendency to quickly clog with wood dust and shavings. If you get into heavy shaping work, you'll need to keep a **file card** nearby to clean the teeth frequently. (See Cleaning and Storing Files and Rasps, page 138.) And while the smooth-cutting capacity of patternmaker's rasps will reduce your time spent sanding and refining the surface, keep in mind that this virtue doesn't come cheaply: This particular style of rasp is expensive.

Swift cuts with a light touch. Punched-metal rasps are inexpensive, yet cut very aggressively, especially in softwoods. Use very light pressure to avoid bending the flexible blades.

Two-handed control. Using a rasp requires light pressure and short, forward strokes. Lift the rasp on the return stroke to prevent dulling the teeth.

A less costly alternative to patternmakers' rasps are **punched-metal rasps**, which have small razor-sharp teeth. One well-known brand is Sur-Form; other manufacturers make similar styles but with rust-resistant stainless-steel blades. Like traditional rasps, punched-metal rasps are available in various shapes, from round and half-round to flat, square, or V-shaped, and they cut very aggressively. However, you'll need a lighter touch to avoid bending the thin, flexible blade, making this style of rasp more suitable for working softer woods. (See photo, left.) An advantage with punched-metal rasps is that they won't clog with shavings as a solid rasps do. Plus, the stainless-steel variety won't rust, which quickly dulls cutting edges.

Using a rasp effectively takes practice. Grasp the handle with one hand and place your thumb and forefinger of your other hand on the tip. Cuts are made on the push stroke, with light pressure. Lift the rasp on the return stroke. For more aggressive stock removal, increase pressure or switch to a coarser-cutting rasp. (See photo, above.)

While a rasp will cut quickly, it still leaves a relatively rough surface. The next step is smoothing the surface with a **file**, which dramatically reduces the amount of sanding you'll have to do. Plus, you'll want to keep files on hand for working metal, for example, leveling dents and dings; smoothing drill bits; and sharpening

All shapes and sizes. Files are a boon to woodworkers for their ability to cut and smooth surfaces with great precision. They come in a variety of shapes, sizes, and teeth patterns.

saws, scrapers, and axes. There are many of types of files available today, and while most are used in the metalworking trades, numerous files are handy in the woodshop. (See photo, above.)

Whether you're working wood or metal, a file is a high precision tool for truing up a surface. Files are similar to rasps in that they contain rows of teeth, but instead of individual cutting edges, the teeth extend across the entire face of the tool. This make files less aggressive, but much more smooth cutting. Typically I'll start sanding a filed surface with 180-grit paper or finer, which saves time. (See photo, left.)

Precision filing. Files, like this single-cut mill file, are great for truing and fitting parts, and for general shaping work. While not as aggressive as rasps, they leave a much smoother surface that needs little sanding.

There are two primary teeth patterns on files we need to know about: *single-cut* and *double-cut*. (See fig. 1.) Single-cut files have a single

set of parallel teeth running diagonally across the face, require light pressure to cut, and leave a fine surface. Double-cut files, with diagonal rows of teeth running across the width of the file in opposite directions, cut faster but leave a rougher surface. You can also determine the coarseness of the cut by choosing between *bastard cut*, the coarsest cut; *second cut*, which removes material less aggressively but leaves a smoother finish; and *smooth cut*, which is even finer. The length of a file makes a difference in the smoothness of the cut, too. Since tooth spacing is proportional to file length, the longer the file, the coarser and faster cutting it will be. Conversely, the shorter the file, the finer the surface it will leave.

You'll need to pick the shape of the file that suits your work. Like rasps, files are available in many shapes, including flat, square, triangular, round, half-round, and knife-shaped. Plus, you can get safe-edge files in all sizes and shapes, which have at least one edge without teeth, so you can file up to adjacent surfaces without scratching the surface.

Of note for the woodworker is the **mill file**, which is a single-cut file with a rectangular profile. If I had to own just one file, this is the one I would choose. I find it's the most useful type to have in the shop for refining and truing surfaces, cutting edges, working metal and plastics, and for general sharpening. A double-cut

---

Fig. 1: File Teeth Patterns

Double-Cut

Fast cut; leaves rough surface

Single-Cut

Slower cutting with more control; leaves finer surface

Teeth

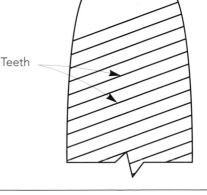
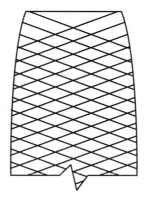

file that has the same profile as a mill file will cut more aggressively and is called a **flat file**, and it's also very hand to have around. But before you go out and spend a small fortune buying every file you can find (there are literally hundreds of types available), check out my list of 10 basic files, below.

Rifflers are available as both rasps and files, often with one end coarse and the other fine on the same file. These S-shaped tools, with rectangular, round, triangular, or pointed ends, are great for very small detail work, such as refining carvings. (See photo, right.)

Refining with rifflers. These curved and pointed files are perfect for smoothing carvings or other detail work.

The following files and rasps are the ones I use most in my shop. With this selection, you can tackle most of your shaping and fitting chores.

❶ **10-inch smooth-cut mill file.** My most-used file, it quickly trues up surfaces and tools, leaves a smooth surface on wood, cuts overhangs on plastic laminate, and is good for leveling scraper edges prior to sharpening.

❷ **6-inch second-cut tapered flat file.** Probably my second-favorite file, it's great for quick stock removal yet leaves a fine surface. The narrow point gets into nooks and crannies where larger files can't reach.

❸ **#50 Nicholson patternmaker's rasp.** For heavy cutting and shaping of sculptural furniture parts, such as curved legs or bowed edges, and for fairing curves.

❹ **6-inch double-cut, smooth-cut flat file.** For extra-fine cuts on metal, this file leaves a surface finish that needs little or no sanding.

❺ **10-inch double-cut, second-cut half-round file.** For aggressive cutting on flat and broad, curved surfaces.

❻ **8-inch single-cut, bastard-cut round file.** For shaping small or large holes and tight inside curves.

❼ **Set of rifflers.** For refining small sculptural detail, such as smoothing carved moldings and finishing ball-and-claw feet.

TOP-10 FILES

❽ **7-inch auger file with safe edges.** For sharpening all sorts of bits, such as augers, Fortsners, and brad points, and for working up to adjacent surfaces without damaging them.

❾ **Single-cut saw file.** When filing the teeth of hand saws, buy these triangular files according to the number of teeth per inch of the saw you need to sharpen.

❿ **Feather-edge file.** In small or large sizes for sharpening the deep gullets and teeth on Japanese-style saws, and for refining notches and other details in really close quarters.

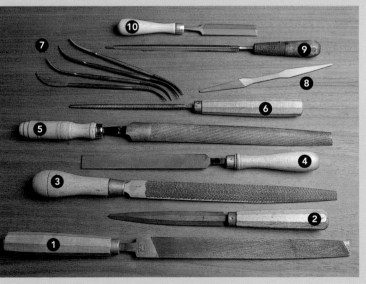

Scrapers

Most of us are familiar with glue scrapers, tools with hooked blades that are great for removing dried glue or glue squeeze-out between joints. But in the vast world of scraping, the lowly glue scraper is considered the bottom of the barrel in terms of precision and finesse. The fact is, some of the finest wood surfaces possible can be produced by correctly sharpening and using a unique tool called a hand scraper. This simple yet very effective tool is part of a family of scraping tools that are well-worth learning how to use because of the speed and efficiency with

CLEANING AND STORING FILES AND RASPS

A clean file or rasp will cut quickly. Clogged files impacted with dust, chips, or metal filings will skip over the surface and can leave marks in your work. Regularly cleaning your files and rasps with a **file card** will keep them cutting efficiently and aggressively. (See photo, below.)

The hard but brittle cutting edges of files will dull quickly if they come into contact with a metal surface—especially another file. And rust will quickly dull and ruin a file's sharp teeth.

Always store your files and rasps apart to prevent them from rubbing or banging together. You can hang files on wall-mounted racks, build dedicated slots in drawers for them or simply separate them in a drawer lined with cloth. A few packets of **desiccant** such as silica thrown in the drawer or storage area will prevent rust. (See photo, below.)

Safe storage. Keep files separated to keep them sharp, and place packets of desiccant nearby to dissuade rust. A layer of felt in a drawer will protect files and keep them from jangling together.

A file card removes clogs. For general cleaning, use the brush side of the card by rubbing in the direction of the teeth, or on the diagonal. Use the wire side for more stubborn debris.

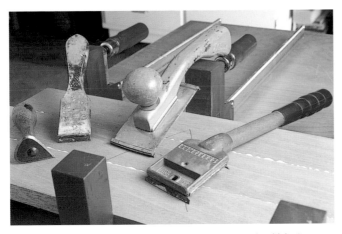

Removing excess glue. Glue scrapers have hooked blades, and are designed to remove beads of hardened or semi-hardened glue from the surface of the work

which they can smooth and level the surfaces of your work. Some scrapers can even shape moldings, and all depend on hand-power alone to work. The key to this unique style of tool is in the scraping action itself, which by its geometry cuts and refines wood surfaces with virtually no tearout—a trick no other cutting tool can claim. Read on to find out about some of the most efficient wood-cutting tools of our craft.

The most basic of scraping tools is the **glue scraper**, and I'd be lost without one in the shop. When it

comes to removing dried or semi-dried glue, this is the tool to reach for. With its hooked cutting edge, a scraper can remove glue from the surface of your work without removing wood fibers in the process. (See photo, above.)

Leverage and pressure. A good glue scraper, with a long handle for more control, lets you place pressure over the cutting edge.

Typically, I wait for the glue to form a rubbery film, which usually takes about 30 minutes, then I use a glue scraper to scrape away the glue before refining the surface any further. While a glue scraper can remove fully dried glue, the dried glue is harder on the cutting edge of the tool, and there's always a risk of pulling out small wood fibers along with the glue.

There are numerous styles of glue scrapers on the market. My favorite scraper is one with a relatively long handle, and a point of purchase over the cutting edge of the blade on which I can bear down with a hand to place pressure where it's needed. (See bottom photo, left.)

Roughly sharp. The cutting edge of a glue scraper works best if you file the bevel, then leave it alone. Filing produces a small burr on the back of the blade for an aggressive cut.

It's important that you keep your glue scraper clean and sharp. Wipe away any fresh glue from the cutting edge, and pop off dried glue with an old chisel or the tip of an awl. Sharpening is easy: You can run a fine mill file over the beveled cutting edge, following its angle, or grind the bevel on a bench grinder. That's it. The filing or grinding action produces a small burr, or hook, on the back of the blade, which makes for a very aggressive cut. (See photo, above.)

Leaps and bounds above a glue scraper is a **hand scraper**, which can be used to scrape dried glue very effectively…but I cringe at the very thought of using a carefully sharpened hand scraper for such rough work. Properly tuned, a hand scraper will leave a smooth, glassy surface on hardwoods, free from the tearout that a hand plane might produce. And the resulting surface is so smooth that only minimal sanding is necessary in preparation for finishing. A typical hand scraper is a simple piece of flat, rectangular steel

Simple, but effective. Hand scrapers let you tackle difficult woods without tearout, and are available in all sorts of shapes and sizes.

that's sharpened on all four edges to produce a small hook, or burr. Hand scrapers vary in thickness, hardness, length, and width, and you can buy contoured or curved scrapers as well. (See photo, left.) Or make your own scrapers from any type of hard steel, such as an old hand saw, band saw, or hacksaw blade. (You'll want to use the harder portion near the cutting teeth.)

The more common rectangular-shaped scraper, often referred to as a **card scraper**, is my favorite and most-used scraper when all my other cutting tools, such as chisels or planes, fail to produce a smooth surface. I use a thicker card scraper for wider surfaces, and a thinner, more flexible scraper for reaching tight spots or for scraping in smaller areas. You push or pull a scraper, depending on your preference, while tilting the tool slightly forward over the surface of the work. Bending or bowing the scraper slightly with your thumbs often helps to take a deeper cut. The telltale mark of a good scraper is that it actually cuts the surface, making very fine shavings, instead of abrading the wood and leaving a pile of dust. (See photo, left.)

Hand scrapers are also excellent leveling tools for tasks such as smoothing bumpy

Shavings, not dust. A hand scraper won't tear fibers, and shaves the surface of the wood. Properly sharpened, a scraper leaves very fine shavings.

Edge leveling. You can quickly make joints flush and smooth without the risk of tearout, using gentle strokes in either direction.

finishes, bringing edgebanding flush to delicate veneered surfaces, or flushing up joints such as where a rail meets a stile in a frame or where a set of dovetails protrude. (See photo, above.)

The key to using scrapers is to get a feel for the way you hold them, and to learn how to sharpen them correctly. (See Sharpening a Hand Scraper, opposite page.) You can pull or push a scraper using the same technique: Hold the scraper on the surface at a slight forward angle, and move it in a steady, sweeping motion. This sweeping movement is important, because hand scrapers have a tendency to dig into the surface and create small hollows if you work only one small area at a time.

If at first the scraper doesn't cut, increase the forward angle until you get a shaving. Also try slightly flexing or bending the scraper for a more aggressive cut. Generally, it's best to follow the grain for the smoothest cut. But scrapers are masters of difficult grain, and working against the grain is sometimes your only choice. (See photo, below.)

Against the grain. The crotch area of this walnut board, with grain going everywhere, would be difficult to plane. Working a scraper in all directions over the crotch leaves a smooth surface free from tearout.

Fig. 2: Hooking a Scraper Blade

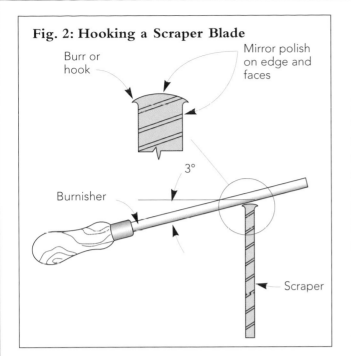

Burr or hook

Mirror polish on edge and faces

Burnisher

3°

Scraper

SHARPENING A HAND SCRAPER

For a scraper to cut well, it requires a small hook or burr on each of its four cutting edges. You use a burnisher, which is a tool with a polished rod or shaft made from hard steel, to form the hook. (See fig. 2.) In order for a scraper to leave a smooth surface, the cutting edge needs to be highly polished before you create the burr. The higher the polish, the finer the surface your scraper will leave, and the longer its edge will last. Sharpening a new scraper is a six-step process that takes about 10 minutes. (See photos, below.) When a scraper is dull (it will make dust, not shavings), it's time to re-sharpen. With a dull scraper, simply repeat steps 5 and 6.

1. Flatten the sides. Using a medium waterstone or soft Arkansas oilstone, apply pressure to the outer edge of the sides to remove any scratches or defects.

2. File the edges straight and square. Take full-length strokes over the edge with a smooth-cut mill file, concentrating on keeping the file square to the sides.

3. Hone the edges. If holding the scraper freehand intimidates you, use a thick block to help keep the edge perpendicular to the stone. Hone up to 6,000 grit on waterstones; for oilstones, finish the edge with a hard Arkansas. For the finest cut, hone the edge until it's mirror-bright.

4. Hone the faces. This removes the burr left from edge-honing and filing. Be sure to work up to your finish stone and spread pressure evenly over the scraper.

5. Burnish the faces. With the scraper laying on a hard surface, hold the burnisher flat and draw it toward you to consolidate the material at the edge.

6. Burnish the edges. Make a few passes perpendicular to the edge, then slowly increase the angle to about 3°, until you feel a small hook with your fingers.

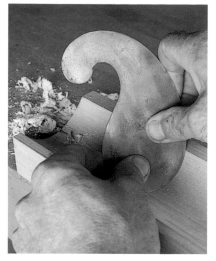

Smoothing inside profiles. A goose-neck scraper makes quick work of removing saw and millmarks from moldings and other concave surfaces.

Other useful hand scrapers include a **gooseneck scraper**, which has contoured edges that let you smooth concave curves or profiled stock. (See photo, left.) For tight convex curves, a **curved-end scraper** will help smooth blemishes and fair out shapes.

(See middle photo, left.) Sharpening contoured scrapers is similar to sharpening a card scraper, but takes more patience and time. To hone and polish the curved edges, you can use a slipstone instead of a benchstone. Then burnish as you would a regular scraper with a burnisher.

For really broad surfaces, such as the top of a desk, I switch to a **cabinet scraper**, often called a "gull's wing" scraper for its outstretched handles. With its handles and sole, a cabinet scraper is less tiring to use than a hand scraper, and the blade won't burn your thumbs the way a hand scraper does when it heats up from friction. (See bottom photo, left.) If you're faced with a large surface to scrape, reach for one of these workhorses. Since the cutter is limited by the scraper's sole, you're less likely to dig into the surface and create dips or a washboard effect.

A bigger cousin to the cabinet scraper is the **scraper plane**. These are pricey tools, available new or old. Be prepared to shell out some serious dough. But this type of bodied scraper is more comfortable to handle for extended periods of scraping, and its extra mass helps in pushing the tool over large surfaces. (See top left photo, opposite page.)

Working outside profiles. A curved-end scraper will reach convex areas, such as bullnosings and other rounded shapes.

Gull's-wing scraper. This cabinet scraper can be pushed or pulled, and offers good control over large flat areas.

WAXING A SCRAPER

When using a scraper, swipe the edge occasionally along a stick of paraffin or other hard wax. The wax lubricates the cutting edge, reducing chatter and keeping the edge sharp.

Wax swipe. Help maintain a scraper's sharpness by rubbing the cutting edge over a block of hard wax.

Plane scrape. This large scraper plane takes the sweat out of scraping large surfaces. Adjusting the knob behind the blade allows you to fine-tune the cutting angle for light or aggressive cuts.

Smaller scraping. Smaller scraper planes are more maneuverable than their bigger cousins. A commerical metal version (top) has a surprising amount of heft for its size; a homemade wooden-bodied scraper has a lighter feel (bottom).

Smaller metal- and even wood-bodied scraper planes are available, and they can fill the gap between a bigger bodied scraper and a hand scraper. Like its larger cousin, a **small scraper plane** affords more control over the work to prevent dips and hollows, yet is light and maneuverable like a hand scraper. (See photo, above.)

If you need to take very fine cuts, both the cabinet scraper and the scraper plane can be sharpened exactly like the hand scraper. (See Sharpening a Hand Scraper, page 141.) But for aggressive cuts, which are useful on large surfaces, you'll need to approach the sharpening job somewhat differently. (See fig. 3.) If the blade doesn't already have one, you'll need to grind or file a 45-degree bevel on the cutting edge. Then hone and polish the bevel and the back of the blade, using the same technique you would for a hand scraper. Finish by forming the burr of the back of the blade by burnishing at a more aggressive angle of about 15 degrees.

A variation on the standard scraper is a **scratch stock**, sometimes called a **scratch router** or **scratch plane**, which can be bought new or made in the shop from scrap material. Used primarily as a shaping tool to cut moldings and profiles such as grooves, beads, reeds, and flutes, a scratch stock works with the same scraping action as any scraper, yet is guided by a fence to control the cut. While a router or a shaper and the appropriate cutter can make short work of cutting moldings, a scratch stock offers the advantage of more control, such as when making stopped cuts, and the ability to make custom profiles by grinding your own blades. In addition, some curved cuts, such as the curving bead in an arched rail, are impossible to make with a rotating cutter

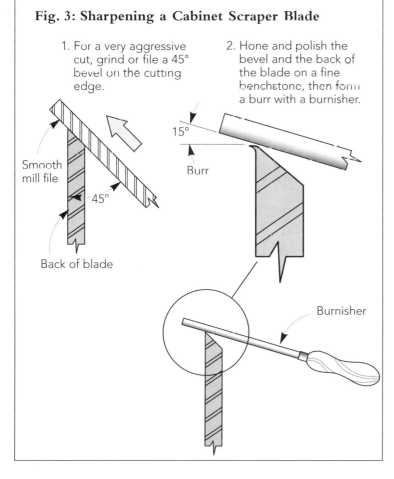

Fig. 3: Sharpening a Cabinet Scraper Blade

1. For a very aggressive cut, grind or file a 45° bevel on the cutting edge.

2. Hone and polish the bevel and the back of the blade on a fine benchstone, then form a burr with a burnisher.

Smooth mill file

45°

Back of blade

15°

Burr

Burnisher

A SHOPMADE SCRATCH STOCK

Wood and steel. This homemade scratch stock is easy to make from leftover scrap wood. The cutter, ground to the desired profile, is made from an old scraper blade.

A traditional tool used by cabinetmakers to create moldings and other architectural details, a scratch stock is easy to make from leftover hardwood in the shop. (See photo, above.) Any mild-grained, dense wood such as maple or cherry will suffice for the body. The overall size will depend on the type of profile you're cutting. Figure 4 shows a general-purpose size that will work for most profiles. You can make palm-sized stocks for cutting tiny beads, or beefier blocks with large blades for cutting wide or really deep profiles.

Blades can be made in virtually any profile. Any piece of steel that's soft enough to file, yet hard enough to keep an edge, will work. Good candidates are old scraper blades, hand saw blades, hacksaw blades, and band saw blades.

Grinding close. Follow your marked line on a grinding wheel to create the rough profile.

After finding a suitable piece of steel, trace the profile on the metal by drawing it with an indelible marker or by scratching into the blade with an awl. Then grind the rough shape on a wheel, being careful not to overheat the metal and ruin its temper. (See photo, above.)

Finish the profile by filing to the precise layout using an assortment of files, depending on the shape of the cutter. I use round and half-round mill bastard files and triangular saw files to refine the edge, then finish up with smooth mill files. Be sure to file straight across the edge, or drawfile, to get the smoothest possible edge. (See photo, below.) After filing, hone both flat faces of the blade on medium- and fine-grit benchstones to remove any burrs and smooth the surfaces. When the cutting edge dulls, simply re-file again, taking pains not to alter the original shape.

Fig. 4: Making a Scratch Stock

Use a dense wood such as maple or cherry for the body.

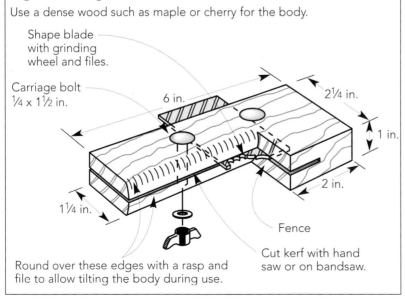

Shape blade with grinding wheel and files.

Carriage bolt ¼ x 1½ in.

6 in.

2¼ in.

1 in.

2 in.

1¼ in.

Fence

Cut kerf with hand saw or on bandsaw.

Round over these edges with a rasp and file to allow tilting the body during use.

File to the line. An assortment of round and flat files lets you shape the exact profile to your layout line. File straight across for the best possible cutting edge.

Scraping a bead. A scratch stock, such as this commercial version with an adjustable fence, can scrape a curved bead where a router bit can't reach.

such as a router bit. (See photo, left.) And because the stock cuts in a scraping action, you won't risk tearing figured wood the way a router or shaper can.

Many woodworkers make their own scratch stocks, then file and grind blades with a variety of profiles for different cuts. (See A Shopmade Scratch Stock, opposite page.) Commercial versions—past and present—are available with an assortment of blades in various profiles, including blade blanks that allow you to make custom shapes. (See photo, below.)

Using a scratch stock is simple: You tilt the tool slightly just as you would a hand scraper, then scrape back and forth in long strokes, keeping the fence in contact and the body square to the work. Start with overlong stock, since you'll probably waste a few inches at both ends due to the challenge of starting and finishing the cut. On the final pass, hold the tool perpendicular to the surface for a finishing cut. (See top photo, right.)

The fine edge of a **single-edge razor blade** is wonderful for leveling small finish blemishes and other minute inconsistencies in a wood surface. To keep

fingers safe, use a razor blade held in a plastic holder, available from paint and automotive-supply stores. Pull or push the blade across the surface using a scraping motion, taking very light cuts until you've leveled the surface. (See middle photo, right.)

You might be surprised to learn that your teeth aren't the only candidates for dental tools. **Dental picks, chisels,** and **scrapers** make superb mini-scrapers for detail work. The hardened stainless-steel tips on these tools are incredibly wear-resistant, very sharp, and are great for getting into small crannies and crevices. (See photo, below.) You can buy dental scrapers from woodworking catalogs, or ask your dentist. These surgical-steel tools are usually thrown away, so here's your chance to recycle them for a marvelously less painful cause.

Clean moldings. Like any scraper, a scratch stock can tackle difficult woods and makes shavings, not dust.

Finish scraping. To level drips in a dried finish, hold a plastic holder fitted with a razor blade perpendicular to the surface and pull or push the blade gently across the work.

Groove, bead, reed, and flute. Commercial scratch-stock blades are available in a number of profiles, including square blades you can grind to suit yourself.

Dental scrape. Recycled dental tools make great scrapers and picks for small detail work. They're often free for the asking.

Chiseling and Carving Tools

A good set of chisels will make a big difference in the quality of your work. And using the right type of chisel for the job at hand gives you more control over your cuts. Bench chisels, which include standard bevel-edge chisels, paring chisels, and mortise chisels, will cover all of your straight cuts, from paring delicate shoulders and grooves to chopping mortises and excavating other deep holes. Other specialty chisels let you make specialized cuts, such as dovetail chisels for paring and chopping dovetails, and corner chisels for cutting precise 90-degree shoulders or corners. For curved or profiled cuts you'll need a set of carving chisels.

It's important that you make an investment in quality chisels. A good chisel will hold a keen edge and feel comfortable in your hand. Generally, the higher the price, the better the steel. Probably the most important buying advice is to hold a chisel and get a feel for its balance and heft. More than any other hand tool, a chisel needs to fit your hand like a glove and become an extension of your body.

Bench Chisels

Bench chisels are staples for everyday use. They include a variety of styles, from bevel-edge and paring chisels, to firmer and mortise chisels, to more specialty chisels such as dovetail chisels and corner chisels. A set of chisels in a range of sizes is important, so you can tailor the width of the chisel to the work you're doing. For most woodwork, you'll do fine with a range from ¼ inch up to 1 inch wide. Occasionally you'll need a narrow chisel when working tight quarters, but these smaller chisels can be hard to find. If you can't find a slim chisel in the style you need, you can make your own. (See Thin Chisels, opposite page.)

The workhorses of the shop, **bevel-edge chisels**—so-named because of the wide or narrow bevels alongside the top of the blade—are the go-to tools for the majority of chisel work. With a properly sharpened bevel-edge chisel, you can make delicate paring cuts, clean up corners, and chisel joints. The bevel edges of these tools let you reach into the sloping sides of dovetails. And the sturdy handles and blades can withstand hits from a mallet for many chopping tasks, like cutting a hinge mortise. This versatility makes bevel edge chisels a must for any shop. (See photo, right.)

A bevel angle of about 25 degrees is ideal for most of the work you'll do with bevel-edge chisels, although a lower angle would be more appropriate if you're working with softwoods. Handle material differs from brand to brand (wood or plastic), and overall chisel length can affect performance. Older chisel blades were usually joined to the handle via a tapered socket that the handle slipped into; newer versions have tangs that fit into the end of the handle, and usually come

Utility chisels. General-purpose bevel-edged chisels are the workhorses of the shop, capable of making fine paring cuts or tackling aggressive mortise work. My old socket-style Stanley No. 750 still gets daily use (left); the steel in these Scandinavian chisels keep a keen edge and the handles are comfortable to grasp (middle); and newer plastic-handled versions are inexpensive, but have good heft and feel (right).

with a ferrule around the joint to strengthen the connection and prevent splitting. (See fig. 1.)

Beware of bevel-edge chisels—or any type of striking chisels—that have rounded ends on their handles, a feature found on many plastic-handled chisels. When you strike the rounded area, the mallet or hammer is likely to skitter off its surface, ruining the effectiveness of the blow. The fix is to flatten a sharply curved end to a gentle hump or a small flat spot. You can carve wood handles, or sand the plastic versions by hand or on a disc sander, and gain more control over your heavier chisel work. (See photo, right.)

Paring chisels, also called **patternmakers' chisels**, are the same basic design as bevel-edge chisels, except the blades are thinner and much longer, and they come with a low bevel angle. The long blade of a paring chisel makes it particularly useful as a reference

Safer pounding. On a chisel with a rounded end (left) you can improve the sweet spot for hitting by shaping the end to flat or a slight curve (right).

tool when making long, flat cuts. Bevel angles of 20 degrees are typical, although it's not uncommon to find lower angles of 15 degrees for more control when making delicate slicing cuts or cutting end grain. Because of this extra-low angle, paring chisels are designed for use with hand pressure alone for the

Fig. 1: Chisel-Handle Connections

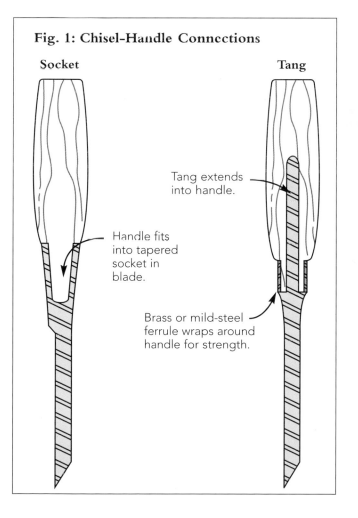

Socket

Tang

Tang extends into handle.

Handle fits into tapered socket in blade.

Brass or mild-steel ferrule wraps around handle for strength.

THIN CHISELS

Narrow ⅛-inch or even ¹⁄₁₆-inch chisels are very handy to have on hand, such as when paring the narrow space between twin mortises or cleaning up a set of dovetails, or anywhere a wider chisel won't fit. The problem is that many chisel makers don't manufacture chisels this thin.

If you can't find a narrow chisel width, don't despair: You can make your own. Simply grind the edges of a spare chisel, then sharpen it as you would your bigger chisels.

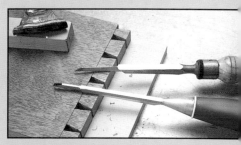

Skinny chisels. A narrow chisel is handy for working tight spots. Old chisels, such as the ones shown here, can be re-ground to a narrow profile on the side of a grinding wheel.

USING A CHISEL

Bevel up. Use the back of the chisel as a reference surface to maintain a flat face on your work.

Bevel down. Prying cuts in tight spaces require that you work with the bevel facing down, such as when you remove the waste from a set of dovetails.

Using a chisel effectively requires the correct grip and the proper orientation of the chisel to the work.

It's usually best to place the bevel up, using the flat back as a reference surface, as shown in the photo, far left. The exception is when making digging cuts or working in tight quarters. Here, you work with the bevel facing down. (See photo, near left.)

When chopping with a chisel, eyeball the flat back of the chisel to align the cut with your work, especially with 90-degree cuts. You'd be amazed at how accurate your eye is in this situation if you trust it. (See middle photo, far left.) For paring cuts, work across the grain. Paring with the grain involves fighting interlocked wood fibers and risks tearout. For the smoothest cuts and the most precision, take multiple light cuts. (See middle photo, near left.)

Use your eye. Align the straight back of the chisel square to the work when making square chopping cuts.

Pare from the side. Whenever possible, pare with light cuts across the grain for the best control and smoothest finish. Use your forefinger as a stop to regulate the cut.

Always clamp the work and use both hands on the chisel. Two hands give you much more control over the cut. Your rear hand powers the chisel while your front hand is as close as possible to guide the cutting edge. (See bottom photo, far left.)

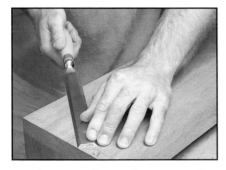

Two hands are better than one. With the work securely clamped, use one hand on the handle to power the cut while the forward hand steadies the blade and controls the cutting action.

Lean into it. With your elbows locked, use your upper body to power the cut by swinging your shoulder. This position generates great control and a more sensitive feel.

Body English is everything when using a chisel, particularly when paring. The idea is to push with your upper body, not your arms. Lock your elbows, and use your upper torso to transmit power. In this position you can lean into the cut, swinging your shoulder to power the cut through your forearm. (See bottom photo, near left.)

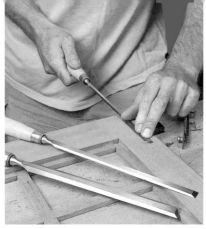

lightest of cuts. (See photo, left.) Never strike a paring chisel with a mallet, or you'll crumble its cutting edge and risk snapping the delicate blade.

Hand pressure only. The long blade of a paring chisel references the work when making long, flat cuts. Never strike a paring chisel with a mallet or you'll crumble the fragile edge.

You won't need many, but a couple **skew chisels** are indispensable for light paring cuts where you need lots of control, or to get into a corner of the work. You can buy a left and right skew chisel, or make your own from spare chisels you might have lying around. (See bottom photo, right.) The pointed cutting edge of a skew chisel doesn't have the tendency to dig into the

CHISEL MITER JIG

This is a helpful jig to keep around for fitting and shaving miters, and it takes only a few minutes to make. I'll typically use the device after rough-cutting a miter with a power tool by clamping or holding the jig up to the sawn

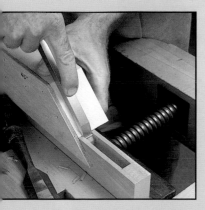

miter and paring with a chisel. Use a hardwood such as maple for the jig, and cut a miter on one end. Then nail a plywood fence to one side. You can make several of these jigs with different miter angles for specific jobs, but I find that a 45-degree slope covers the majority of my hand-fitting needs.

Shaving guide. A miter jig lets you shave accurate miters or angled mortises. Use the jig with a long chisel, taking light paring cuts.

SAND YOUR CHISEL BLADES?

That's right, but only near the handle. The idea is to ease over the super-sharp edges on the back of the chisel, *only* at the rear. This makes your chisels much more comfortable to hold, and prevents the sharp corners from slicing into your fingers. Never sand the forward part of the blade. Sanding this area would round over the sharp corners of the cutting edge itself, which are vital for good chisel work. Don't worry about ruining the back of your good chisel. As the blade gets shorter from repeated sharpenings, you'll eventually re-flatten those sanded areas to create sharp cutting corners once again.

Ease over. To make a chisel more comfortable to hold, use some 220-grit sandpaper to cut the sharp edges on the back. Only sand about 2 inches toward the handle, never near the cutting edge.

surface like a regular square-edge chisel, and the leading point makes them well-suited for shaving end grain. As with any paring chisel, never strike these tools; always push them by hand.

Corner cuts. Left and right skew chisels (the ones shown were ground from standard bevel-edge chisels) are particularly adept at shaving end grain, and allow you to pare deep into corners or up to left or right-handed junctions, such as rabbets.

JAPANESE CHISELS

Japanese chisels are a breed apart from Western-style chisels, and many woodworkers, myself included, have fallen in love with their wonderful feel, heft, and somewhat eclectic metallurgy. The shorter blades make them very maneuverable, and the super-hard laminated steel can be honed to an extremely fine edge. Traditional Japanese chisels are available in the same configurations as Western chisels, from the bevel-edge and paring chisels to heavier firmer and mortise chisels. (See photo, below.) One caveat: Quality Japanese chisels are very expensive, and it can take several years to build up a decent collection.

Made in Japan. Expensive—and worth it—these laminated-blade Japanese chisels are a joy to hold and take a keen edge.

Japanese chisels are much shorter in overall length and are designed for striking with a metal hammer (except for paring chisels). Their wooden handles are hooped with a thick ring of metal to prevent splitting, and the blades are tanged *and* socketed to the handle, giving these chisels a decided robustness. (See fig. 2.) The shorter length of a Japanese chisel gives it a great heft

Chisel types. Japanese chisels come in all the major styles; left to right: bevel-edge, paring, firmer, and mortise chisels.

Bright and brighter. The unique two-piece laminated blade of a Japanese chisel can be seen on its beveled side, where the harder cutting layer shows up as brighter line right at the cutting edge.

Hollowed backs. The backs of Japanese chisels have single or multiple hollows to facilitate sharpening and make it easier to maintain flatness.

Fig. 2: Socket-and-Tang Connection

Japanese chisels combine both socket and tang-style construction for maximum strength to the handle.

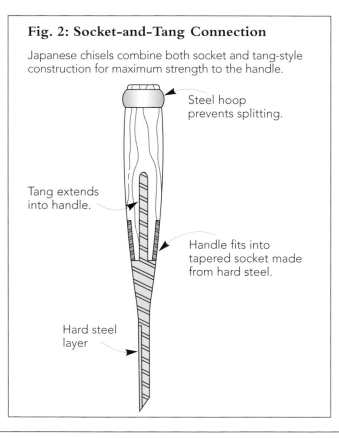

Steel hoop prevents splitting.

Tang extends into handle.

Handle fits into tapered socket made from hard steel.

Hard steel layer

and feel, making it well-suited to handwork. The drawback is a shorter blade that won't provide as much reference surface on the back when you're paring or mortising.

What really sets Japanese chisels apart is their unique blade construction. Each blade is made from two pieces of laminated steel, a very hard back (which in effect is the cutting edge) forged to a soft-steel or wrought-iron face. The harder back layer, or cutting edge, shows up as a brighter gleam under good light, as shown in the bottom left photo, opposite page. The softer steel provides damping qualities and a toughness that protects the hard but brittle cutting edge. To protect the delicate cutting edge even more, bevel angles are more obtuse than Western-style chisels, typically around 30 degrees. The result is a chisel with a very hard, keen edge.

Another unique feature of Japanese chisels is their hollow-ground backs. (See bottom right photo, opposite page.) The hollows help in easing the sharpening process, but there's a flip side to the equation: Sharpening a Japanese chisel takes more work because the steel is so hard.

One of my favorite styles, which is unique to Japanese chisels, is the **dovetail chisel**. This paring chisel has a steep triangular cross-section that's more effective than typical bevel-edge chisels for chopping or shaving dovetails and other inside areas without risk to adjacent surfaces. (See photo, right.) Generally, it's best to have a selection in smaller widths so they'll fit into the smaller openings typical of dovetail work. A set from ¼ to ½ inch should cover your dovetailing needs.

Clean tails. The steeply beveled edges of Japanese dovetail chisels let you successfully chop the baseline of dovetails and other inside cuts without damage to adjacent surfaces.

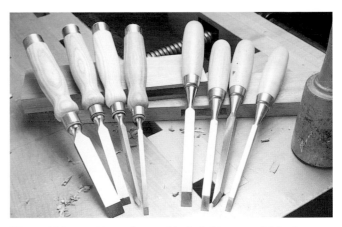

Big and bigger. Heavy firmer chisels (left) are useful for heavy chopping work, even in end grain; beefier mortise chisels (right) can withstand the heaviest cuts, such as deep mortises in the hardest of woods.

Mortise chisels and **firmer chisels** have tough, stout blades and more obtuse bevel angles (typically 30 to 35 degrees) to withstand the hard pounding required for end-grain cuts such as chopping deep mortises. A set of one or the other is a good idea for heavy work. (See photo, above.) If you plan on doing a lot of mortising by hand, a set of mortise chisels is probably a better choice. That's because the heavier and wider cross-section of a mortise chisel has a secondary function, which is to help align the blade accurately in the mortise as the cut progresses, as shown in the photo, right.

When mortising with a chisel, the width of the blade should correspond to the width of the mortise. Since we rarely cut mortises wider than ½ inch, I recommend starting with just a few chisels. A selection including ¼ inch, ⅜ inch, and ½ inch will cover the majority of your mortising needs.

Mortise work. For accuracy, use the width of the blade itself to reference the chisel parallel to the mortise as you cut.

Corner work. Large and small corner chisels are a bear to sharpen, but they leave clean, square corners with a few taps from a mallet.

Two specialty chisels are worth mentioning. The first is a **corner chisel**, which is used to clean up and square the corners of mortises or stopped rabbets. (See photo, above.) A somewhat abrupt bevel angle of around 30 to 35 degrees is best for this type of chisel to maximize its edge retention. Steeper angles are likely to blunt quickly during end grain cuts. And pray your edge lasts; sharpening a corner chisel is tedious and often disappointing. You'll need to use a diamond file or slipstones to hone the inner two faces, while attempting to keep adjacent cutting edges straight and square to each other and at 90 degrees to the spine, or back corner, of the blade. Good luck! But for those times when you want to quickly square a corner, a sharp corner chisel can't be beat.

Another useful specialty chisel is a **cranked-neck chisel**, which has a 90-degree bend in the blade, or a **swan-neck chisel**, which has a gentle S-curve. Made in Western or Japanese styles, a cranked-neck chisel is used as a paring chisel for light cuts on flat stock. The bent blade lets you get in tough spots where the handle would normally get in the way. (See photo, left.)

In by a crook. When a regular flat chisel can't reach and the handle gets in the way, turn to a cranked-neck chisel to pare hard-to-reach spots.

Carving Tools

You don't have to be a full-time carver to appreciate the usefulness of carving tools. Cabinetmakers and furnituremakers regularly use **carving gouges** for detailing molding and trim, cleaning up cuts left by router bits and other power tools, and anywhere they need to introduce a curve or accent in their work. This type of detail carving can often turn an ordinary piece into something extraordinary.

There are hundreds of different carving gouges available, and like clamps, you can never have enough of them. But for general woodworking, a basic carving set of about 10 chisels is all you need to get started. If you get into serious carving work, you can supplement this initial set with more specialized chisels as your work gets more elaborate.

A decent starter set of carving gouges includes a variety of chisels with curved cutting edges. Gouges are numbered according to their degree of curvature, or sweep: the higher the number, the greater the curvature. You'll want a few shallow curves for shallow cuts, such as small moldings and detail cuts, and

Carving basics. A good starter set of carving chisels includes gouges in a variety of widths and sweeps (or curves), from shallow to deeply curved (left to right); as well as large and small V-groove chisels (far right) for cutting grooves and lines into your work.

more deeply curved gouges for deeper, more complex carving, such as deep crown and cornice work. In addition to a variety of sweeps, look for gouges in a range of widths, from ⅛ inch wide up to 1 inch or more. Having a selection of curves in different widths lets you tackle a variety of carving details. Then add a couple of V-groove chisels in large and small sizes for incising small grooves, and you're set. (See photo, above.)

One interesting style of carving chisel is a set of **flexible carving chisels**, as shown in the photo, below. This style of chisel has a blade made from a springy steel that flexes as you place pressure in the cut. By flexing the blade, you can effectively change the sweep, or curvature, of the cutting edge. These paring chisels are designed to be pushed by hand, never struck with a mallet. But the springy steel and comfortable handles afford lots of control when carving details.

In addition to my basic carving set, I keep a few **palm chisels** in the shop for working really small details. These short-handled chisels fit into the palm of your hand, offering more control for close-up work. (See photo, right.)

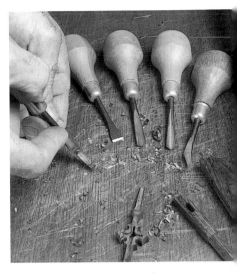

Palm-size push. A set of palm chisels lets you bring your hands close to the work for detail carving and other small cuts.

Flexible carving. This set of carving chisels has thin, spring-steel blades that flex as you press them into the work. Flexing the blade gives you the freedom to alter the curve as you cut.

PROTECT YOUR EDGES

Storing your chisels safely is important to maintain their razor-sharp edges. While a drawer or tray can make a safe resting spot, many times we keep our chisels lying on the bench during the workday. To protect them from accidental bumps or nicks, keep a supply of **chisel guards** on hand and slip them over any unused chisel. It's an inexpensive investment that will keep you from making unnecessary trips to the sharpening station to redo a damaged edge.

Guarding edges. Chisel guards protect delicate cutting edges and are available in widths to match your chisels.

SHARPENING A BENCH CHISEL

There are three ways to sharpen a chisel: hone the entire bevel; hone the back and front, or leading edge, of the bevel; or hone just the front of the bevel. (See photo, below.) Your chosen methodology depends on several things, including the tools you use to sharpen, the type of work the chisel will be doing, and your degree of proficiency. The good news is that it doesn't matter which method you choose: All three work well to give you the truly sharp edge you need.

Three types of sharpening. Bright reflections tell the story. The chisel on the left has been honed across its entire bevel; the center chisel is honed at the back and the front; and the chisel on the right has a microbevel, having been honed only at its cutting tip.

The process of sharpening a new chisel involves flattening the back on a medium-grit stone, then honing both the back and the bevel to a mirror polish on a fine stone. The procedure is the same for old or dull chisels that need re-sharpening, except that you won't need to initially flatten the back.

Assuming the bevel has been ground to your satisfaction and there are no major nicks in the cutting edge, you can begin on a medium-grit stone by lapping the back of the chisel. The idea is to produce an even sheen on the majority of the back, especially near the tip. This uniformity tells you all the deep scratches are gone and the back is now dead flat. (See top photo, right.)

Now flip the chisel over and rub the bevel on the same stone. You have three options here: You can hone a microbevel; you can hone the front and back edge; or you can hone the entire face of the

bevel. Honing a microbevel is faster, but the choice is up to you since the techniques won't make a bit of difference in the chisel's cutting performance. Occasionally I hone the entire face of the bevel, especially for my most demanding chisels like the bigger mortise ones, which are struck

Flat back. An even, dull sheen on the back of the chisel after lapping on a medium-grit stone means you're ready to move on to the bevel.

hard into the wood. Honing a full bevel takes more time and skill, but if done correctly provides the longest-lasting and most durable edge. What follows is the technique for honing the front and back edge of the bevel. The technique is the same for honing the entire face, except that you'll spend more time at it. For more on honing a microbevel, see Sharpening a Plane Iron, page 178.

Begin by rocking the face of the bevel on the stone until you feel that it makes even contact, then hold it steady in that position. (See photo, below.) Your goal is to keep the bevel flat on the stone as you move the chisel. Flatness counts as much on this face as it does on the back, because two dead-flat surfaces that meet produce a sharp edge with the best edge-retention possible. Any curvature will result in a blade that dulls quickly, so be sure to keep a steady hand. You can use a circular, figure eight motion as you rub the bevel, or move the tool from front to back or side to side. There's no "right" way. I recommend you choose the movement that feels the most comfortable and natural for you, and try that. Practice *will* make it perfect.

Flat bevel. Hold the bevel to the stone and keep a steady hand as you rub it back and forth to hone the front and back. Use the entire stone to avoid creating a hollow in its surface.

If you're nervous about hand-holding the bevel, try a honing guide, which holds the chisel at the correct angle. (See page 29.) Luckily, you don't need to hone the entire bevel; if the bevel was ground on a wheel, the resulting hollow means you're only going to flatten the leading and top edge, or front and back of the bevel. Check your progress often, and stop when about 1/8 inch of the leading edge is flat. At this point, feel the back of the cutting edge with your fingers. You should notice a slight "wire edge" or burr, on the back.

Back polish. After honing the bevel on a medium stone, switch to a fine stone and rub the back of the chisel until the wire edge is gone and the tip is polished.

Once you feel the wire edge, move to your fine stone and repeat the lapping procedure to produce a mirror polish on both the back and the bevel. Start with the back, but this time you only need to concentrate on the area right at the cutting tip, not the entire back. (See photo, left.) Stop when the tip is highly polished.

Once you've polished on the back, switch to the bevel and hone as you did on the medium stone, again feeling for the wire edge. It should be much finer than before. If all goes well, you should see two glaringly bright polished lines—one at the tip, the other at the back of the bevel—that are uniform and of even sheen. (See photo, right.) The last step is to alternate between honing the bevel and the back with very light pressure, finishing up with a few strokes on the back.

Bright and even. Final honing on the bevel should produce a pair of bright, uniform bands when held up to a light.

SHARPENING A CARVING GOUGE

Unlike regular bench chisels, carving chisels and gouges require a different approach when it comes to sharpening their curved edges. You use slipstones to hone the cutting edge, and instead of bringing the tool to the stone, you move the stone over the tool. Honing in this manner takes more time, but you can speed up the process if you start with a medium-grit stone to remove nicks or work a particularly blunt edge, then finish up with a fine stone to polish the surface. (See photo, right.)

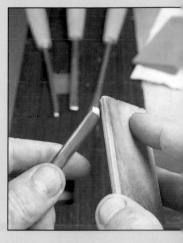

Honing a curve. Gouges should be sharpened on the outside of the bevel only. Use a medium-grit slipstone to remove nicks, then finish with a fine stone to polish the cutting edge.

The main consideration when sharpening gouges is to never hone the inside curves, or you'll blunt the cutting edge. After you've honed the outside bevel, use a fine slipstone to remove any burr or hook on the inside of the tool. Use very light strokes, and be extra careful to keep the stone flat on the surface to avoid rounding the cutting edge. A few swipes is all it takes. (See photo, right.)

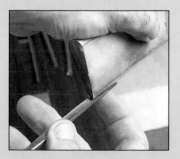

Cut the burr. After honing the outside, rub a slipstone very lightly along the inside curve to remove any burr. Hold the stone flat to avoid rounding over the cutting edge.

Edge Tools

My favorite hand tools are what I call edge tools: drawknives, spokeshaves, hand planes, and other tools with a knife-like cutting edge. The fine cutting edges on these types of tools give them the ability to shape, fit, and smooth wood in a very precise manner, giving you more control and pleasure in your work.

Drawknives and Spokeshaves

For quick stock removal, drawknives and spokeshaves are indispensable hand tools. What sets these tools apart is their ability to tackle curved work, including convex or concave surfaces. For this reason, chairmakers use them for the bulk of their seat-shaping work, as well as for rounding spindles and the like.

If you want to remove a lot of wood in a hurry, pick up a **drawknife**. (See photo, below.) This heavy-bladed tool has a single bevel along its cutting edge, and can quickly

shave curved and square stock. A drawknife can tackle both convex and concave surfaces, although deep hollowing is best done on narrow edges. Grasp the handles at either end of the blade and pull the knife toward you to make the cut. (See photo, below.) By changing the angle of the blade relative to the work, you can increase or decrease the depth of cut, taking large splits or making fine shaving cuts. Keep the bevel up for most work; deep concave cuts are best worked with the bevel-side down. Handling a drawknife takes practice, but once you get a feel for the tool you can sculpt undulating curves in just about any wood.

To scoop out a chair seat or any curving form, you can chop away with an adze (see page 98), or go directly to the wood with a specialty tool called a **scorp**. In essence a curve-bladed drawknife, the scorp lets you quickly dish out chair seats and other blanks for a sculptured effect. (See top left photo, opposite page.)

Both the scorp and drawknife are sharpened in similar fashion as you would a gouge by bringing the sharpening stone to the tool, instead of the other way around. Use a fine file to work a really rough edge. Once you've removed nicks, rub a medium-grit slipstone or even a benchstone on the bevel. (See middle left photo, opposite page.) After smoothing the bevel with the medium stone, use a fine stone to polish it, then finish by lapping the back lightly with the fine stone to remove any burr.

Big knife. The broad edge of a drawknife has a single bevel on its top edge, and can tackle straight or curved cuts.

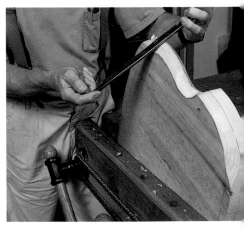

Big slice. You can make large, swift cuts with a drawknife by pulling the tool toward you. Keeping the blade at a low angle lets you maintain great control.

Rough hollowing. A scorp is a workhorse for hollowing seats, quickly dishing out the profile, but leaving a rough surface.

Flats *and* curves. A versatile performer, a flat-bottom shave is great for flat work or gentle curves (above). Adjusting the depth of cut lets you quickly rough out round stock (below) or make fine cuts to round over workpieces.

Hone the bevel. Curved bladed knives require honing on the bevel only. Start with a medium stone, then polish with a fine stone. Remove any burr on the back by lapping with a fine stone, being careful to keep the surface flat.

Spokeshaves come in many styles and configurations, including metal or wooden-bodied versions. (See photo, below.) The sole on a spokeshave works like a miniature hand plane, letting you make very precise cuts with great energy and speed. The blade is positioned with the bevel side down. These features make a shave less aggressive than a drawknife, but much more controllable.

A **flat-bottomed shave** is a good general-purpose shave, useful for chamfer work or anywhere you want to smooth or round a surface. If you're just starting out, this is the shave to get. While a flat-bottomed shave excels at smoothing flat surfaces, it's the tool of choice for shaping shallow curves as well. (See photos, above.)

For deep concave cuts, try a **curved-bottomed shave**. This type of shave takes more practice to master than a flat shave, but once you get the hang of it you can smooth deep curves or carve out hollows. If round convex curves are part of your work, a shave worth acquiring is a **concave shave**. This specialty shave makes quick work of shaping and smoothing round stock, such as spindles, while affording lots of control in the cut. (See photo, right.)

Shaving styles. Wooden-bodied shaves (left) have a wonderful "feel" to them; metal-bodied versions (right) are more rugged and are easier to adjust.

Smooth rounder. A concave shave will smooth legs and other round parts, and leave a tactile surface with subtle yet pleasing toolmarks.

Another specialty curved shave, the **travisher**, is typically used by chairmakers after initial shaping of seats and the like with rougher tools. The blade on a travisher is deeply curved along its length, allowing you to work deeper curves than other spokeshaves. Like most shaves, a travisher is designed to take light shavings, so it's a good choice for refining previously shaped surfaces, such as the dips and toolmarks left by an adze or a scorp. (See photos, below.)

Deeper curves. The broad, curved blade of a travisher can reach into hollows where a shallower spokeshave can't (above). This is a traditional tool used by chairmakers to refine and shape the curves in chair seats (below).

Hand Planes

Of all my tools, hand planes are my hands-down favorites. While it's satisfying to know that our woodworking ancestors used these hand planes extensively, far more pragmatic is the fact that planes continue to work just as well today in modern shops across the globe.

Before the advent of power tools, hand planes were used to prepare rough stock, making it flat, square, and of even thickness. Today, we can power up a jointer and a thickness planer to achieve the same results in a fraction of the time. But for certain situations, hand planes remain versatile tools for rough work in a contemporary shop. More often, however, I reach for my planes for very fine work. For example, planes really shine when it comes to surface preparation, or smoothing and refining a board's finished surface. In addition, a properly tuned plane is a reliable fitting tool, since it can remove whisper-thin shavings, letting you accurately size stock or refine joints for a perfect fit. And some specialty planes let you shape all sorts or work, from making moldings and trim to cutting chamfers, deep hollows, or smoothing circles.

Bench Planes

My favorite planes are my bench planes, and they get the most use in my shop. Essential bench planes consist of several smooth planes in long and short versions (both wood and metal) for truing and smoothing surfaces; and a block plane, which is small enough to fit in one hand and nimble enough for quick cuts. If you don't have a machine jointer, consider a scrub plane for removing lots of wood fast. With this assortment of planes, you can tackle all sorts of planing tasks from flattening and smoothing to decorating and refining surfaces.

Another advantage with hand planes is that once you've learned the art of planing, you'll be kissing your rougher-grit sandpaper goodbye. Instead of tedious sanding you can smooth wood in half the time with a sharp plane without clouds of dust swirling around your head. All you'll have to contend with is a pile of beautiful shavings at your feet.

Once an indispensable tool, the **scrub plane** has for the most part been supplanted by the power jointer and planer. But for small-scale roughing work, a scrub plane is a lifesaver. With its curved-edged cutting iron, a scrub plane can remove more wood in less time than any other type of plane. This makes the scrub plane a good choice for surfacing wide boards by removing any cup or twist. The flattening technique involves setting the blade for a deep cut, then planing diagonally to quickly dress a surface roughly flat. (See photo, right.) After straightening with a scrub plane, you move on to smooth planes to refine the surface.

I keep several racks of planes, but **smooth planes** form the core of my bench-plane stockpile. (See photo, below.)

Dressing quickly. The curved cutting edge of the scrub plane removes a lot of wood and leaves a scalloped surface in its wake, allowing you to quickly dress a warped surface to flat.

There are old and new metal-bodied versions available. Wood-and-metal *transitional planes* are another choice, but you'll have to hunt tool dealers or flea markets since they're not made anymore. Or you can choose smooth planes with all-wood bodies. (See Wood Planes, page 166.) For the beginner, my advice is to start with the metal-bodied variety, which is easier for the novice to master.

Smoother medley. Smooth planes are available in a variety of materials, and are generally 5 to 10 inches long. From left to right: An old Stanley No. 3, with cast-iron body and rosewood handles; a modern Lie-Nielsen cast-iron and brass No. 4; antique wood-and-metal transitional plane; a German-made Primus wood-bodied plane; two "coffin" planes, one modern and one antique; and a Japanese wood-bodied smoother.

As their name suggests, smooth planes excel at smoothing surfaces. These planes are sized by the length of their soles, which are anywhere from 5 to 10 inches long. Their relatively short soles can be worked in tight spots and will follow slightly out-of-flat surfaces, allowing you to smooth surfaces more easily than a longer plane.

Old and brand-new metal-bodied planes are commonly cast or stamped with numbers on their bodies, from No. 1 to No. 8, that correspond to the length of the plane, a practice that has been well-established by the Bailey-pattern, or Stanley brand, of planes, as well as by other makers. In general, the higher the number, the longer the plane, as shown in the chart, right.

While a short plane might suggest certain advantages, such as nimbleness or swiftness, it's important to realize that other critical dimensions change as the plane's length changes. As the numbers get smaller, so does the width of the blade, the body, and, more importantly, the handle size. For practical purposes, you should consider a No. 3 or No. 4 smooth plane. The tiny No. 1 plane is more of a curiosity than a real working plane (although it's revered by antique tool collectors), and the small No. 2 is great for children but will cramp an adult's hands. My favorite size—and I have small hands—is a No. 4. It has a $2\frac{1}{2}$-inch-wide body and is fitted with an 2-inch-wide iron. With this size plane, I can work all day without tiring my hands. (See photo, below.)

STANLEY BENCH PLANES

Size	Type	Iron Width (in.)	Length (in.)
No. 1	Smooth	$1\frac{1}{4}$	$5\frac{1}{2}$
No. 2	Smooth	$1\frac{5}{8}$	7
No. 3	Smooth	$1\frac{3}{4}$	8
No. 4	Smooth	2	9
No. 5	Jack	2	14
No. 6	Fore	$2\frac{3}{8}$	18
No. 7	Jointer	$2\frac{3}{8}$	22
No. 8	Jointer	$2\frac{5}{8}$	24

One interesting size of smooth plane is the No. $4\frac{1}{2}$, which is about the same length as a standard No. 4, but has a $2\frac{7}{8}$-inch-wide body with a $2\frac{3}{8}$-inch-wide iron. (See photo, below.) With its wider body and bigger iron, a $4\frac{1}{2}$ is a good choice for working long surfaces or whenever you have a lot of planing to do, as you can take wider shavings. And the additional heft (which is about another pound) helps to power the plane through the stroke.

Like any hand tool, a plane takes skill to master. But the biggest hurdle to overcome is ensuring that your plane is properly sharpened and tuned, often referred to as *fettling*. Don't expect to take a new plane out of the box and use it right away; and it's wise to

Smooth size. A No. 4 smoothing plane fits small and large hands, and has the right mass and heft for making precision cuts and planing all day long.

Wider smoother. The No. $4\frac{1}{2}$ smooth plane (left) is $\frac{3}{8}$ inch wider than a standard No. 4 (right). This extra width provides more mass to power the cut and lets you take a wider shaving.

Power down. Start with the blade off the work and push down on the front of the sole to keep the plane level. Then push forward in one swift movement.

expect old planes to need the same degree of attention. (See Making a Bench Plane Perform, page 172.)

Once you've tuned up your plane, set it for a fine cut and try your hand at face planing. As your skills progress, you can tackle more demanding tasks such as shaving end grain, truing an edge, or tackling figured or gnarly woods. Start out with an easy wood, such as clear pine, to get a feel for the action. Before you begin to plane, make sure the board is held securely to your benchtop. (See Holding Your Work, page 30.)

Hand planing is a dance, but only above the waist. Plant your feet in a comfortable stance, then pivot your upper body as you push the plane. The idea is to plane in one fell swoop, without start or stop marks. Start at the near end of the board with the front of the sole down on the work, and apply lots of pressure onto the front of the plane. Now push the plane in one decisive movement, maintaining downward pressure as you go. (See top photo, left.)

Follow through. Extend your arms and allow your upper body to power the stroke.

Clean getaway. As you reach the end, place more pressure at the back of the plane to avoid stop marks or chatter.

On long boards, extend your forearms as you push to make the stroke as long as possible, and reach with your upper body. All the while, keep even pressure down on the work. (See top photo, right.) As you near the end of the board, exert heavier pressure on the back of the plane to keep it from tipping down as it exits the surface. (See photo, above.)

When smooth-planing, it's vital to cut with the grain for the smoothest possible surface. (See fig. 1.) Watch the surface of your work as you plane. If you start to get tearout, try reversing the planing direction, or back off the iron to take a lighter shaving. Even in really difficult woods, such as curly maple, you can plane successfully by setting the blade for a super-

---

Fig. 1: Cutting with the Grain

Against the Grain

Moving the tool in this direction lifts and tears fibers, leaving a rough surface.

Chisel, plane iron, or other cutting tool

With the Grain

Like stroking the fur on a cat's back, cutting with the grain leaves a smooth, unruffled surface without tearout.

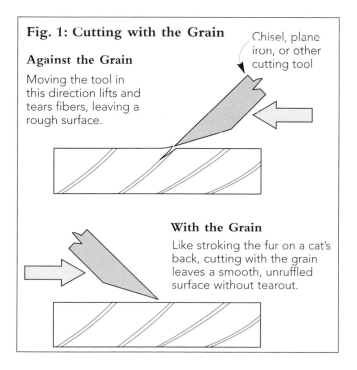

There are many types of all-wood planes in short and long versions, including shop-made planes. They all work great for all sorts of planing jobs.

But the big debate among woodworkers is whether to choose a metal-bodied plane or an all-wood plane. Is one style superior to the other?

Wooden choice. All-wood planes come in many styles, but are they superior to metal planes? From left to right: two Japanese pull-style planes; block plane; Primus smooth plane; modern coffin smoother; old jointer plane; two homemade planes.

The advantage of using wooden planes is their undeniable sensitivity. Wooden planes have a wonderful feel to them, since you get more tactile feedback from the wooden sole as it rubs wood-on-wood over the surface of your work. (See photo, below) One style of wood plane, the Japanese plane, incorporates another feature besides a wooden sole: you pull the plane instead of pushing it to make the cut. (See center photo, below.) The irons on Japanese planes have the same wonderful keen-edged steel found in their chisels (see Japanese Chisels, page 152). But adjusting the iron is a trial-and-error affair, requiring that you tap the plane block with a hammer and make test cuts before planing.

While I enjoy the feel of using wooden planes, they do have two distinct drawbacks: They lack the mass of metal planes, requiring more force to push and making them less practical for taking heavier shavings. And every time the humidity changes, so can the shape of the plane block and the sole. The fix for an out-of-flat sole isn't difficult, but it does require some skill. You can re-flatten the sole by scraping it with a scraper, or you can sand the sole. To sand a wood plane, back off the iron and rub the plane evenly over some 180-grit sandpaper adhered to a flat surface, such as a table saw or a jointer table. (See photo, right.)

Wood on wood. This wooden Primus smooth plane takes wonderful shavings, has internal metal parts for lateral adjustment and depth-of-cut, and provides tactile feedback. But occasional tuning is required to keep the sole flat, and you'll have to push hard to take thicker shavings.

Pulling shavings. A wooden Japanese plane cuts on the pull stroke, requiring a different grip and a distinctive arm orientation.

Sole fix. Re-flatten a warped wooden sole by rubbing it back and forth over a strip of 180-grit sandpaper glued to a flat surface. Maintain even pressure over the entire length of the plane as you rub.

Super thin. Backing off the iron for a super-light cut reduces tearout, and results in the finest finish on wood. Look for shavings that seem to float on the benchtop like puffy clouds.

thin shaving. The telltale sign of a plane set for a really light cut is when your shavings are gossamer-thin and look like puffs of clouds. (See photo, above.)

One variety of bench plane, the Stanley Bedrock series, is no longer made but worth seeking out at flea markets and old tool dealers. Distinguished by the flats that run along the top edges of the sides, a Bedrock has the distinct advantage of letting you adjust the frog to open or close the mouth without having to remove the cap lever or iron. Expect to pay a premium for this style of plane. (See photo, below.)

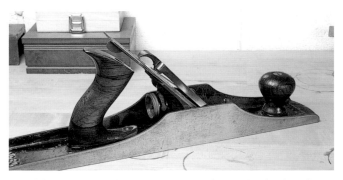

An oldie but a goodie. This No. 6 Stanley Bedrock, identifiable by the flats that run along the top sides of the body, has a single screw that lets you adjust the frog, closing or opening the mouth without having to remove the cutter.

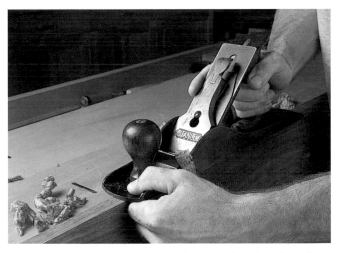

Shooting on a tightrope. A jack plane's midsize length and weight gives it the versatility for making heavy cuts in big work or precise planing, such as shooting a narrow edge on narrow stock. Keep the sole square to the face by letting your fingers rub the work as you plane.

Longer and heavier than smooth planes are **jack planes, fore planes,** and **jointer planes.** These bigger planes aren't generally used for smoothing surfaces (although there are many instances in which they excel at this task) but primarily for truing faces and edges, or making wood flat, straight, and square. The reason these longer planes work so well for truing and leveling is because their longer soles initially take off only the high spots on a board, skipping the "valleys." As planing progresses, you eventually take a full length shaving, which indicates that the entire surface is flat. This type of surfacing work would take much longer, require more effort, and be less accurate if attempted with a smaller smooth plane.

At 14 inches long, or roughly the length from your shoulder to your elbow, the smaller **jack plane,** or No. 5, has many great features. If I had to choose only one plane, a jack plane would quickly find its way into my hands. The great thing about a jack plane is that it's long enough for truing surfaces and has enough heft for big cuts, yet it's nimble enough for small cuts and precise edge work, such as shooting a board straight while perched on its precarious thin edge. (See photo, above.)

Longer **fore** (No. 6) and **jointer planes,** (No. 7 and No. 8), which are 18, 22, and 24 inches long, respectively, are king when it comes to truing broad surfaces. (See top left photo, opposite page.) While you can collect all three sizes, I find it myself reaching for a No. 7 when I need to make big truing cuts. If you had to own just one big plane, this middle-size jointer plane is probably the most useful of the bunch.

The truing and flattening technique using a fore or jointer plane involves initially bringing the surface to flat, but with a slightly rough texture, by moving the plane at about 45 degrees to the grain. Since you're shearing the fibers at an angle, you can set the iron for a fairly heavy cut. (See middle left photo, opposite page.) Once the surface is flat overall (check it with winding sticks and a straightedge), readjust the iron for a light cut and plane with the grain to finish the surface. (See bottom left photo, opposite page.)

BENCH PLANE MECHANICS

It's important to understand the workings of a metal-bodied bench plane in order to know how to tune one and use it. The blade assembly consists of the plane iron fitted to the *chip breaker*, which helps dampen vibrations at the cutting edge and prevent tearout. (See fig. 2.)

All metal-bodied smooth planes have a *frog* upon which the blade assembly sits. By adjusting the frog forward or aft of the mouth (the opening in the sole), you can close or open up the mouth for fine or thick shavings, depending on the type of planing you're doing. The advantage of closing the mouth becomes apparent when you're planing highly figured or difficult woods, since a tight mouth helps reduce tearout.

A *lateral adjustment lever* moves the plane iron sideways so you can adjust the blade square to the sole, allowing you to take shavings of even thickness. By rotating the *depth adjustment knob*, you can fine-tune the depth of cut for aggressive or fine planing.

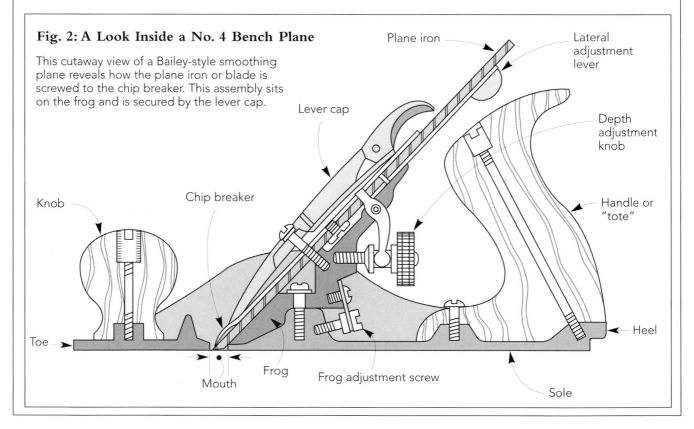

Fig. 2: A Look Inside a No. 4 Bench Plane

This cutaway view of a Bailey-style smoothing plane reveals how the plane iron or blade is screwed to the chip breaker. This assembly sits on the frog and is secured by the lever cap.

Plane iron

Lateral adjustment lever

Lever cap

Depth adjustment knob

Knob

Chip breaker

Handle or "tote"

Toe

Mouth

Frog

Frog adjustment screw

Heel

Sole

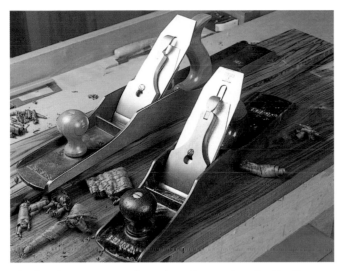

The big boys. A No. 6 fore plane (bottom) and a No. 7 jointer plane (top) are used for truing long surfaces on the face and edges of work.

Flattening on a diagonal. A bigger jointer plane has the needed length for flattening large surfaces by hitting only the high spots and skipping over the valleys, or dips. You start by planing on the diagonal.

Smooth finish. After planing the surface roughly flat, smooth it by taking light shavings with the grain of the board.

More mass means less work. Smoothing large surfaces is easier with a bigger plane, since the increased heft helps to carry the plane through the cut.

Even if you use a longer plane only on occasion to true surfaces, it still pays to own a heavier fore or jointer plane since the extra heft helps when surfacing large work. For example, when you're faced with smoothing a particularly large expanse of wood, such as a tabletop, the extra mass of a big plane helps power the cut once you give it the necessary momentum. The theory is similar to powering up a large boat, like an oceanliner. Once you get it going, its own weight and mass carry it along with minimal energy. The result is that using a large plane lets you tackle large work with less effort. (See photo, above.)

Another use for bigger planes, including jack planes, is when shaving end grain. Here again, the sheer mass of the plane helps immensely when cutting through harder material. (See photo, right.)

End-grain cut. A bigger plane, such as this No. 5, makes working end grain easier.

169

The ultimate tool for shaving end grain is a **low-angle jack plane**, sometimes called a **miter plane**. The low-angle jack has an iron that's bedded at a lower angle, typically 20 degrees. However, the iron is placed bevel-side up. To achieve a low-angle cut, I grind the bevel to 20 degrees, which provides a combined cutting angle of 40 degrees—5 degrees less than a standard bench plane. This lower cutting angle makes shaving end grain easier and cleaner. (See photo, right.)

One of the most useful planes in any woodshop is a **block plane**. Small enough to use with one hand, a block plane is near my work all the time. Block planes come in many styles, old and new, but all are about 6 inches long and vary in width by a few sixteenths of an inch. (See middle photo, right.) You'll find standard block planes with 20-degree bed angles, and low-angle block planes that have irons bedded at a lower angle, typically 12 degrees. (See bottom photo, right.)

Higher cutting angles on block planes are good for face work, such as planing the edge of a board or leveling the face of a frame. Low-angle block planes are better for

tackling end grain, but will handle face work respectably if you take a light cut. Keep in mind that the actual cutting angles of both types of planes, like low-angle jack planes, are in fact higher than their respective bed angles since the iron's bevel faces up, effectively altering its cutting angle. (See fig. 3.)

Big and low. A low-angle jack plane has the necessary heft for tackling large end-grain surfaces or miters along with a low-angle iron for cleaner cuts.

Small and sweet. Small enough to fit in one hand, block planes are a delight for small work such as trimming edges, chamfers, and other detail cuts.

High and low. There are two styles of block planes: Standard-angle planes (left) for face-grain work; low-angle planes (right) have lower cutting angles better suited for shaving end grain.

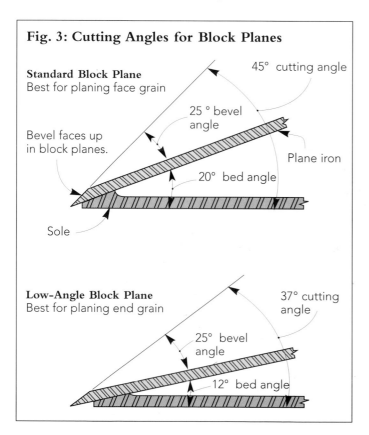

Fig. 3: Cutting Angles for Block Planes

Standard Block Plane
Best for planing face grain

45° cutting angle

25° bevel angle

Bevel faces up in block planes.

Plane iron

20° bed angle

Sole

Low-Angle Block Plane
Best for planing end grain

37° cutting angle

25° bevel angle

12° bed angle

Quick chamfer. Holding a block plane at roughly 45 degrees, you can plane a distinctive chamfer on the edge of your work.

Rolling a roundover. To plane a roundover, start with a chamfer, then roll the plane over until it's almost parallel with each face.

One of the most useful jobs a block plane can perform is to ease over the sharp edges of your work. A few swipes on a corner with the plane held at roughly 45 degrees, followed by some light sanding, is enough to relieve an edge. Heavier cuts produce small chamfers, which is often faster than setting up a router bit. With practice you'll get used to holding the plane at the necessary angle. (See photo, above.) For really small chamfers, I usually count the number of passes—three or four usually does it—so that the chamfer is even on all edges. For larger chamfers, I use the same planing technique, except I check the edge frequently by eye. The resulting chamfer will be somewhat uneven from edge to edge, but it's this very inconsistency that sets your work apart from the mass-produced stuff churned out in factories. I think it speaks to the handmade aspect of furnituremaking.

Another effective use for a block plane is to round over an edge, again not having to set up a router and a bit. Start by planing a chamfer as described above, then continue making passes over the edge with the plane rolled over. Finish with the plane almost parallel with each face of the work. (See photo, above.)

GET A GOOD BLADE

Many old planes and spokeshaves are missing blades or have cutters too rusty or bent to use. And the irons on new edge tools are often thin in cross section and poorly made. You can buy a better aftermarket blade from many woodworking suppliers. Good aftermarket irons are thicker and heftier than standard blades, which reduces chatter for a smoother cut. And initial conditioning, such as lapping the back and polishing the bevel, usually takes less time because surfaces are more accurately ground.

New steel for old tools. Aftermarket blades are available for most bench planes, including block planes, as well as metal-bodied spokeshaves. Good blades can better the performance of many old or new edge tools.

Making a Bench Plane Perform

Most metal-bodied planes need tuning before you can use them, a procedure often described as *fettling*. Old planes can be refurbished to better-than-new condition, and most of these techniques can also be applied to a new plane.

First assess the plane's condition. Some problems can be fixed with a tune-up. You *can't* fix the following:

- **Cracked or chipped castings.** Look for hairline cracks or chips, especially around the mouth.

- **Deep rust pitting on the sole.**

- **Rust pitting on the back of the blade.** Pits on the blade will prevent you from producing a sharp, continuous cutting edge.

- **Bent blade.** A bent blade will chatter in use.

- **2 inches or less of blade length from the long slot.** Repeated sharpening may have removed the hardest steel, and the blade won't hold an edge.

The following to-do list will have your plane performing beautifully with very little effort:

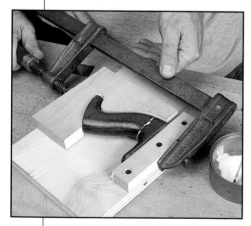

Handle jig. Glue a broken handle back together by clamping it in a simple homemade jig.

Repair broken handles and knobs. If the break is clean, you can easily fix a cracked handle using a clamping jig and glue. (See photo, left.) Splintered handles are more difficult to repair; consider buying a "junker" plane and scavenging the handle, buying a replacement handle, or making one yourself from scrap. (*See* Acquiring a New Handle, page 177.)

Key points of contact. You can mark these areas on the sole before flattening. Once the marks are gone, the sole is flat enough for precision work.

Flatten the sole. Small bumps or hollows prevent the cutting edge from making full contact with the workpiece, and any overall curvature makes it impossible to plane flat surfaces. New planes are culprits, too. For a plane to work, the entire sole does not need to be flat—only a few key areas do: around the mouth, along the edges, and at the heel and toe, as shown in the photo, above. Leave the lever cap in position, but back off the blade. Work the sole on a fresh sheet of 320-grit wet/dry sandpaper taped to a flat surface, such as the top of your table saw or a sheet of melamine-coated particleboard. Use a light machine oil as a lubricant, and keep changing the paper when it dulls. (See photo, right.) Rub with even, downward pressure, using the same motion as when hand planing. When you see dull, abraded spots at the key areas, you're done.

Flattening with paper and plastic. True the sole by rubbing it over a sheet of 320-grit wet-dry sandpaper taped to a dead-flat sheet of melamine, a particleboard panel coated with plastic. A liberal spray of oil lubricates the work and makes the paper cut faster.

Fit the chip breaker to the blade. A properly set chip breaker forces shavings up and out of the plane. The leading edge of the breaker must be in full contact with the blade, or it will jam with shavings and make the plane hard to push.

Check the fit of the breaker to the blade by screwing the parts together with the chip breaker screw. *Don't* simply hold the parts together. If you see light between the breaker and the iron, you'll need to work the bevel on the back of the breaker. Note that the angle of the bevel should be more acute to take into account the flex of the breaker when it's screwed tight to the blade. (See fig. 4.)

If the angle of the bevel on the breaker isn't correct, use a fine file across the bevel to alter its slope, then hone the bevel dead flat on a medium stone. (See photo, right.) Check the fit again by screwing the parts together, and repeat the honing procedure until you don't see any gaps.

Keep your blade sharp. If the cutting edge has nicks or gouges, first dress the edge on a grinding wheel. After grinding, hone the back of the blade and the bevel on waterstones or oil stones. (See Sharpening a Plane Iron, page 176.)

Flatten the bevel. Dress the angled back of the chip breaker on a medium-grit stone. To maintain the correct angle, lower the opposite end of the breaker about ⅛ inch below the stone.

Adjust the frog. Most planes won't need this procedure, but it's worth checking your frog to see that it's in good condition and is adjusted properly. The iron must sit evenly on the frog, or it will chatter during planing. Look for bumps or rough spots on the surface and remove them with a mill file.

On most metal-bodied planes, the frog can be adjusted to decrease or increase the mouth opening. Loosen the screws that anchor the frog to the plane body, then turn the adjusting screw (if there is one) or slide the frog manually to move it forward or backward. It's usually best to position the frog even with the back of the mouth opening. You can check this arrangement by inserting the plane iron and checking the mouth. When the frog is properly adjusted you should see a gap of about ¹⁄₁₆ inch between the blade and the front of the mouth. You can close up the mouth even more if you wish, which in theory helps reduce tearout. But in practice I find it's usually not worth the extra fuss; I simply set the depth of the iron for an extra-fine cut in difficult woods. *(continued next page)*

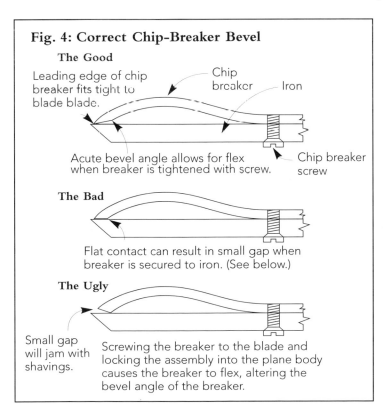

Fig. 4: Correct Chip-Breaker Bevel

The Good

Leading edge of chip breaker fits tight to blade blade.

Chip breaker

Iron

Acute bevel angle allows for flex when breaker is tightened with screw.

Chip breaker screw

The Bad

Flat contact can result in small gap when breaker is secured to iron. (See below.)

The Ugly

Small gap will jam with shavings.

Screwing the breaker to the blade and locking the assembly into the plane body causes the breaker to flex, altering the bevel angle of the breaker.

Breaker back a hair. Screw the chip breaker to the back of the iron so its leading edge is parallel with the blade and back about 1/32 inch.

Assemble the plane parts. Screw the chip breaker to the back of the blade, using a screwdriver—never the lever cap, or you risk nicking the edge of the cap. Adjust the breaker about 1/32 inch or less back from the cutting edge, making sure its leading edge is parallel with the iron. (See photo, above.) With the breaker in position, place the blade assembly bevel-side down on the frog and secure it with the lever cap.

The next step is to set the plane iron for the correct depth of cut. Many woodworkers do this by sighting along the sole to inspect the speck of blade that projects. My eyes are (luckily) in great shape, and while this technique works fine, I've discovered how to set a plane iron without relying on 20/20 vision. In the long run, I feel it's a better approach. When my eyesight eventually goes south, I'll still be able to adjust my plane. Here's how to do it:

Adjust the depth of cut by turning the depth adjustment knob. The idea is to project the blade just enough to take the appropriate shaving thickness, while keeping the blade square to the mouth of the plane. Start by turning the knob and feeling the projecting tip of the blade with your fingers by rubbing them backward over the cutting edge. Yes—*backward*, which can slice your fingers if done carelessly. So do it slowly and lightly, just enough to feel the metal on your fingertips. You'll easily feel how far the blade is projecting, and which side it favors.

Now take a cut. As you plane, look into the mouth to see if the shavings favor one side or the other. Once you know which side to correct, pivot the lateral adjustment lever to square up the blade. Then take another cut. If the plane shaves smoothly through the work, and the shaving is of even thickness across its width, you're set. But chances are you won't get any shavings at all, or the plane will cut too thick a shaving and stall. The trick is to modify the depth of cut with the adjustment knob and take another shaving. Keep shaving and looking in the mouth at your shavings, adjusting the depth of cut until the plane moves easily over the surface and takes a full-width shaving in stride. (See photo, below.)

Lubricate the sole. A well-lubed sole reduces friction and makes planing nearly effortless. Paste wax is my lubricant of choice, although any light oil will work fine. Rub the sole lightly with the lubricant, then buff it vigorously with a clean rag. Be sure to rub from the heel to the toe to avoid sagging the blade's cutting edge. If you have a lot of planing to do, you'll want to stop often and re-lubricate to keep the plane sailing smoothly though the wood.

Ready to go. Look in the mouth to see if your plane is prepared for action. A properly set up plane takes a thin, full-width shaving.

Joinery Planes

The bulk of what are sometimes called specialty planes are hand planes designed to fashion and fit joints: the rabbet, the shoulder, the bullnose, the chisel, and the router plane.

For fitting and truing joints, cleaning up sawn rabbets, and making other inside cuts, a **rabbet plane** is the tool of choice. There are many styles of rabbet planes, but they all share one characteristic: the iron extends out to at least one side of the body. (See photo, below.) Tuned up and sharpened, a rabbet plane can perform some pretty tricky maneuvers. With the blade set flush with one side, you can work this specialized plane inside a corner—against the shoulder of a tenon, a rabbet, or any type of adjacent surface—to create a perfect 90-degree shoulder, or rabbet. (See photo, below.)

Another characteristic that some rabbet planes share is a nicker, or small knife-like cutter, located on one side of the body and just ahead of the cutter. The knife is designed to score wood fibers cleanly when cutting across the grain, preventing tearout. (See bottom photo, right.)

The iron on a rabbet plane is bedded at about 20 degrees, with the bevel placed up like a block plane. The resulting 45-degree cutting angle makes these planes suitable for trimming face grain. Generally, a rabbet plane is best suited for light trimming cuts in long grain,

Cutting a corner. With the blade set flush to one side, a rabbet plane makes a perfect 90-degree shoulder.

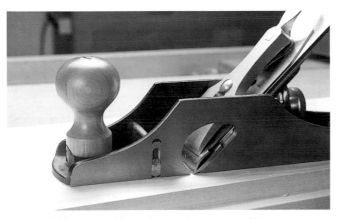

Exposed blade. A rabbet plane is distinguished by its cutter, which extends to one or more sides of the body.

Scoring prevents tearout. The small nicker on this rabbet plane cuts a small groove ahead of the blade, an especially useful feature when planing across the grain.

Modern–Day Planemakers

Ask Bill Clark and Larry Williams, of Clark & Williams, what their favorite hand tool is and you can bet they'll point to a hand plane. That's because these woodworkers-turned-planemakers make wood-bodied planes in a variety of models and styles, including molding planes, smoothers, panel-raisers, and other specialty planes. The surprising part of their business is the fact that modern plane-making is still very much a hands-on operation, since they rely on hand tools for many of the important cuts—just as their predecessors did over 200 years ago.

A typical coffin smoother (so-named because of the familiar box-shaped body) starts out as a solid chunk of select beech. Critical angles are first laid out on the blank for the opening that accepts the iron and wedge. Then careful chopping by hand with a chisel shapes the angled bed for the iron, or escapement. (See bottom photo, left.)

To flatten and refine key surfaces, Clark and Williams use specialty plane-making tools called *floats*, making these file-like tools themselves. (See photo, below.) Once the body has been shaped and finished, the plane is set up with a freshly sharpened iron and a wedge, and a test shaving is taken. When Clark and Williams are satisfied that the plane is in good working order, it's shipped out the door. The customer receives the new plane in a box, ready to go—with the test-shaving intact.

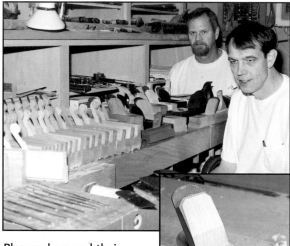

Planemakers and their wares. Bill Clark (left) and Larry Williams (right) of Clark & Williams show off a few of their wooden planes. The coffin smoother, made from select beech (inset) is one of their specialties.

Chopping by hand. A keen eye and a razor-sharp chisel are two key ingredients for cutting the escapement on a smooth-plane blank.

Filing with floats. To shape and flatten the abutment where the wooden wedge fits, Clark uses homemade, file-like tools called planemaker's floats.

such as when making lapped joints in as series of boards, say, for a cabinet back.

There are many styles of rabbet planes, including some with skewed cutters for cleaner cuts in difficult grain. However, you can get by very well with one rabbet plane for almost all your work. For years I've used a Record No. 778, and it continues to be a favorite

Edge control. Record's model No. 778 rabbetting plane comes with a fence for more control. This is a useful feature for starting a rabbet on the edge of a board, or for truing an edge square to its face.

ACQUIRING A NEW HANDLE

If your plane handle or knob is missing or splintered beyond repair, you have a couple of options for fixing the situation. You can buy brand-new wood or plastic handles and knobs, or you can make them yourself. New knobs, called totes, and handles are available from common mail-order woodworking catalogs. If you decide to make your own handle, choose a durable wood such as rosewood, cherry, or walnut. Totes are easily turned on the lathe, then secured with the plane's existing bolt and nut. You can rough-shape a handle on the band saw by copying an existing handle, then refine the curves with rasps and files.

because of its versatility. The No. 778 makes a great tool for cleaning up tenons, squaring edges, or even shooting narrow edges. And this relatively inexpensive rabbet plane can be converted to a bullnose plane (see page 179) by repositioning the cutter at the front, or toe. In addition, the No. 778 comes with an adjustable metal fence that's handy for stabilizing the body at 90 degrees to the work, such as when starting a rabbet or for truing edges. (See photo, above.) For more control, it's a good idea to add a strip of dense wood such as rosewood to the metal fence. (See photo, right.)

Make 'em or buy 'em. You can fashion your own handles from rosewood or other hardwoods such as walnut or cherry (left), or buy new handles, knobs, and bolts to fit your old planes (right).

Wood is good. Adding a wooden auxiliary fence to the plane's standard metal fence enhances control of the plane. Use epoxy to adhere a thin strip of dense wood such as rosewood to the metal surface.

Done correctly, sharpening a plane blade is fast and lets you get back to planing without fuss. The same idea holds true for a chisel. Curiously, it's often not the act of sharpening itself that prevents us from keeping our blades true, but the thought of stopping in the middle of our work to sharpen a dull edge. But using a fresh blade is always worth the trouble. To minimize my downtime, I keep extra blades for each of my planes. When all my blades are dull, I schedule a massive sharpening session, so I always have fresh blades when I need them most.

If your iron is dull, but is otherwise in good shape, you can move straight to the honing process. But if there are any nicks or chips on the cutting edge, you'll have to re-grind the bevel. (See Grinding, page 27.) On a new blade, you may want to alter the bevel angle to suit your work. (See drawing, Bevel Angles, page 27.)

One note: Some woodworkers grind a very slight crown, or curve, on the edge of their blades. The theory is to prevent track marks when planing wide work, due the corners of the blade digging in. In my view this isn't necessary. In practice, if you aim for a dead-straight edge off the grinder, your hand-honing procedure will naturally produce an imperceptible crowning of the cutting edge. In addition, the last step in the honing process is to ease the corners, which virtually eliminates tracks, as I'll describe.

Once the bevel is ground, the honing procedure for a new blade starts with flattening the back of the blade. For the most part, this is a one-time affair. You'll use the same procedure outlined below to sharpen a dull blade, but the process will go more swiftly since you won't need to work the back nearly as much.

Begin honing by positioning about one-third of the back of the blade on a medium-grit (800 to 1,200

grit) stone. Unlike a chisel, a plane iron doesn't need its entire back flattened because the clamping pressure from the lever cap and the chip breaker compensates for any small dips or bellies. Rub the blade back and forth or in a circular motion for about 5 to 10 seconds, then check the back. You'll immediately notice abraded areas, which appear as dull spots. These are the

Rubbing the back flat. A stout block of wood helps place even pressure on the blade to quickly bring it to flat.

high areas that need leveling. Keep working the iron on the stone until the entire lower third shows an even, dull sheen, right up to the cutting edge. New blades can take a fair amount of work to lap flat. To speed up the process, I press a notched block of wood over the blade as I rub, which exerts heavy but even pressure. Grooves across the underside of the block help grip the blade. (See photo, above.)

Once the blade is flat, move to your fine stone (4,000 to 8,000 grit) to polish the back. Continue rubbing in the same manner, again using the block, and bring the surface up to a bright, mirror polish.

Here, you only need to concentrate on the lower ½ inch of the blade. A properly flattened back should reflect light evenly across this lower portion. (See photo, right.)

Shiny and smooth. A well-prepared back should be mirror-bright near its cutting edge and reflect light evenly.

Next, turn your attention to the bevel. You have three choices at this point: You can smooth the entire bevel (whew! it takes some work), or you can smooth the leading edge and the back edge of the bevel. The third option is to hone a secondary bevel, or *microbevel*, which is a narrow bevel at the very tip of the iron. (See fig. 5.) After working my blades all three ways, I've come to the conclusion that a microbevel gives me the best performance with the least amount of headaches.

To use this technique, get out your medium stone and position the blade bevel-side down on the surface. Rock the bevel back and forth until it feels fully seated on the stone. Now, without letting the cutting edge move from the stone, lift the back of the iron a smidgen, roughly 3 degrees. The exact angle isn't critical. Just make sure the back of the bevel isn't contacting the stone. Holding this new angle, rub the blade five or six times over the length of the stone. Eyeball the new bevel; it should be 1/16 inch or less in width. Then feel the back of the iron at the cutting edge. It should have a slight hook, or wire edge.

Once you feel the hook, move to your fine stone and gently lap the back until you can't feel the wire edge. Then flip the blade over and repeat the same honing technique as before, rocking the bevel until it's seated, then lifting slightly and honing the microbevel with a few strokes. Finish by lapping the back to remove what should be a whis-

Small, bright, and sharp. The finished edge of a microbevel should reveal a narrow, glinting surface on the bevel side at the very edge of the iron.

per-thin wire edge. The finished bevel should be a narrow, bright gleam along the cutting edge. (See photo, left.)

The beauty of using a microbevel is the speed with which you can sharpen it. Best of all, subsequent sharpening is super-fast, requiring only a light honing on the bevel and a quick swipe or two on the back to remove the wire edge. One caution: You can't re-sharpen a microbevel indefinitely. Once the bevel gets wider than 1/4 inch or so, it's wise to re-grind or you'll be effectively honing the entire face, making far more work than is necessary. But you can re-sharpen many times before having to go to the grinder.

The last step is to ease the corners of the blade to minimize track marks during planing. Do this by taking four to five passes on each corner over your hardest stone, cocking the blade at 45 degrees and pulling it toward you. Don't use *any* pressure at all or you'll cut a nasty groove in your stone; let the weight of the blade itself do the work. (See photo, below.)

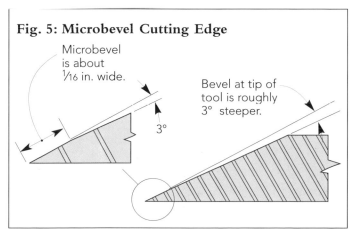

Fig. 5: Microbevel Cutting Edge

Microbevel is about 1/16 in. wide.

Bevel at tip of tool is roughly 3° steeper.

3°

Chamfer the corners. Pull the sharp corners of the blade lightly over your hardest stone, rounding the edges to reduce track marks in your work.

Rabbet on the run. A large jack rabbet plane has enough beef for big cuts, letting you tackle large shoulder cuts such as cleaning up wide rabbets. A lateral adjustment lever makes it a snap to square the blade.

If you need the mass, a large **jack rabbet plane** is about 14 inches long, and has enough heft for really big rabbet and shoulder cuts. You can use this style of plane for cutting rabbets in really large work, such as cutting half-laps in a series of back pieces for a big cabinet. (See photo, above.)

As its name suggests, a **shoulder plane** is a specialized type of rabbet plane used for trimming square shoulders on tenons and rabbets, or wherever you need to make very fine adjustments to shouldered parts. Cuts made with this type of rabbet plane are typically very thin, especially when planing across the grain. But when correctly set up and adjusted, the wonderful heft and feel of a precision-made shoulder plane has no equal. (See photo, left.)

More mass means more control. The solid body of a shoulder plane has the necessary mass for planing shoulders or tenon faces, when accuracy counts, making it the most precise of all rabbet planes.

Like any rabbet plane, one rule is constant on a shoulder plane: The sides must be accurately machined at 90 degrees to the sole so you can plane shoulders dead square. It pays to check the sides with a small square. (See photo, below.)

There are various sizes of shoulder planes available, for small or large work. (See bottom photo, right.) Smaller, narrower shoulder planes are easier to control for very fine cuts, and allow you to get into tight spaces. Larger and heavier versions have the needed mass for planing bigger stuff, such as trimming the faces of wide and long tenons. One of the

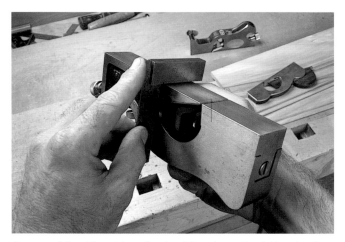

Square sides. The sides of a shoulder plane should be dead square to the sole. Check them with a small square.

Thick or thin. Narrower shoulder planes work best for light work, such as when taking lights cuts on a shoulder or when working in tight spaces. Wider and heftier planes can tackle bigger work, such as trimming the face of a long tenon.

handiest styles of shoulder plane is the Stanley No. 92, which has a removable front sole. With the front piece taken off, you can use the tool as a chisel plane for working right up to a corner, as shown in the photo, below.

Two planes in one. The Stanley No. 92 shoulder plane quickly converts to a chisel plane with the removal of the toe piece.

Close quarters. Cleaning up near a corner is easy and accurate with a bullnose plane, such as this Stanley No. 90.

As close as it gets. A dedicated chisel plane can work right into a corner and is far more accurate than chiseling by hand.

With all rabbet planes—especially with shoulder planes, where accuracy is paramount—sharpening and set-up must be done with care. The process is a little fussy, but once you get the hang of it you'll be planing perfectly square shoulders and rabbets in no time. (See Tuning a Rabbet Plane, page 182.)

The **bullnose plane** is a small rabbet plane with the cutter located very close to the toe of the body for working in tight spaces, such as a stopped rabbet. (See middle photo, left.) Some bullnose planes, such as the Stanley No. 90, can be converted to a **chisel plane** by removing the toe, letting you plane right up to a inside edge. A chisel plane is far more accurate than trying to make the cut with a hand-held chisel, since the sole of the plane guides the cut. (See bottom photo, left.)

Although the electric router has found its way into most modern woodshops, a **router plane** is a helpful hand tool for odd jobs, for example, cutting a groove or dado. (See photo, below.) With its chisel-like cutter, this specialized plane can cut a small groove or recess in the time it takes to set up a noisy router and bit. Plus you can add custom curved wooden soles to some of these planes for routing convex or concave grooves, something a mechanical router would be hard-pressed to do.

Routing by hand. Cutting grooves and dadoes is easy with a router plane, and is often faster than using the electric equivalent.

There are several styles of router planes available, including both modern metal versions and older antique routers, often made from wood. The modern metal variety comes in two flavors: a small plane with a relatively narrow cutter and a diminutive sole, and a larger version that sports a bigger sole with a pair of handles and accepts wider cutters, adjustable via a threaded rod and nut. (See photo, right.)

The small router plane, such as the Stanley No. 271, is great for light-duty cleanup work, cutting small grooves or dadoes, and routing and smoothing narrow recesses like those needed for inlay work. And its small size lets you get into tight spaces. Its larger cousin, the Stanley No. 71, can do most of the work performed by the No. 271, but accepts wider cutters, allowing you to cut wider grooves more efficiently. The No. 71

has two holes in the sole for attaching a homemade wooden sole, which can be made in a variety of

Big and small routers. A small router plane (left) is great for inlay work and cutting other small grooves; its bigger cousin (right) accepts bigger cutters for routing wider grooves and dadoes.

TUNING A RABBET PLANE

The key to tuning any rabbet plane is to align the iron both with the sole and with the side (or sides) of the plane. The object is to have the cutting edge parallel with the sole and parallel with, and just barely peeking out, on the side, depending on the cuts being made. (See fig. 6.)

Once you've aligned the iron with the side, check that it's parallel with the sole. The only way to remedy any misalignment is to grind and rehone the edge. In theory, the blade should have a perfectly square edge, but it pays to check the blade while it's in the plane. With the iron properly ground and honed, careful honing in the future should keep everything in alignment.

The outside of the nicker or spur (if there is one) should be flat and in line with the cutting edge, and it should be honed razor sharp. Hone

the nicker only on the inside edge, and if necessary, bend it slightly with light taps from a small hammer to bring it into alignment with the iron.

Fig. 6: Setting a Rabbet-Plane Iron

90° Shoulder Cuts

Adjust iron flush with side of plane.

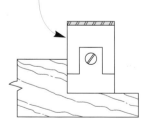

For cleaning up tenons and other square-shouldered work, align blade flush with side of plane to prevent blade from digging into shoulder.

Cuts at Angles Greater than 90°

Extend blade a hair beyond side of plane.

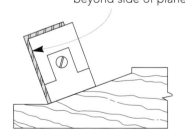

When planing surfaces that intersect beyond 90°, such as where a tongue meets the bevel on a raised panel, extend the iron slightly beyond the side of the plane.

Bent assortment. Cutting irons for router planes come in wide and narrow versions. V-shaped tips work best when planing with the grain; square chisel-like cutters are best used across the grain.

shapes, including a concave curve to follow a curved recess in the workpiece. Both varieties have two iron positions, either normal or bullnose, allowing you to get into tight spots such as stopped dadoes.

The distinctive bent cutters made for router planes are available in different widths for cutting narrow or wide grooves. You'll find two shapes on the business end of the cutters: V shaped and square. (See photo, above.) The V-shaped, or pointed, tip is best for cutting grooves with the grain since the planing action slices instead of plows for less tearout. Plus the tip is great for working into tight corners. The square or chisel-shaped cutter is better for plow cuts across the grain, such as when cutting dadoes.

Using a router plane is simple. Adjust the blade for a shallow, $\frac{1}{16}$-inch cut, and knife a shoulder line for the cutter to follow. Once you've established the groove, cut in $\frac{1}{16}$-inch increments until you reach the desired depth, whereby the plane's sole stops the depth of cut perfectly. The Stanley No. 71 comes with a fence, which is useful if you're grooving near the edge of a workpiece, and it also accepts an auxiliary sole piece for extra stability. (See bottom photo, left.)

While using a router plane is straightforward, sharpening the bent cutters is a challenge. You can hone the back of an iron on bench stones as you would a chisel or bench-plane iron, but you'll need to hone the front, or bevel, with a slipstone. Once you've sharpened and polished the cutter, set the iron for a medium cut since any light tearout will most likely be hidden in the bottom of the groove in the finished piece.

One of the handiest uses for a big or small router plane is cleaning up an existing groove. Because the sole of either style of plane is relatively small, it will follow the contours of the workpiece and allow you to clean up routed or tablesawn grooves to a consistent depth. This feature alone makes owning one of these planes worthwhile. (See photo, below.)

Guided by a fence. The Stanley No. 71 has a fence that helps guide the cut, a useful feature when grooving near the edge of a board. An adjustable sole piece locks into the front of the plane for added stability.

Consistent clean-up. Small inconsistencies in a sawn or routed groove can quickly be addressed by setting the cutter to the full depth of the groove, then taking light passes until no more shavings appear.

Shaping Planes

There are some wonderful planes you can get your hands on for shaping wood to all sorts of profiles, including a variety of moldings, convex or concave curves, and wide chamfers. Molding planes make up the bulk of what are called shaping planes and can be found in a wide assortment of patterns for shaping an endless array of molding profiles. More specialized

Metal molder. The Stanley No. 45 combination plane is a wonder of versatility, sporting numerous cutters for plowing grooves, rabbets, dadoes, and beads. But with all its parts and adjustments, setting one up can be tedious.

It's in the sole. Old and new molding planes are available for planing everything from grooves, fillets, and roundovers to a wide assortment of moldings. Look at the sole to determine the particular profile the plane will cut.

planes such as the compass plane and the chamfer plane can cut curves and chamfers quickly and cleanly.

A variety of **metal molding planes** were made by Stanley and other manufacturers in the eighteenth and early nineteenth centuries. The most versatile of these types of planes are the combination planes, and the most well-known in this genre are the Stanley No. 45 and the more sophisticated No. 55. Both of these planes came with an assortment of cutting irons in different profiles. The No. 45 will groove, rabbet, dado, match (tongue and groove), and bead. (See photo, below.) The more complex No. 55 can tackle these cuts as well as make an almost infinite variety of moldings. It's ironic that the drawback to combination planes is their very adaptability. Setting up one of these planes can test your patience, since there are numerous parts to adjust and align. And you'll get acceptable results if you use mild, even-grained stock such as clear pine. The cutters tend to cause tearout in hardwoods, especially in figured grain. But if you want maximum capacity for all types of moldings in a single tool, look for a combination plane. Keep in mind that these planes are considered collectible, so expect to pay accordingly.

In contrast to the metal variety, **wooden molding planes** are overlooked powerhouses of versatility, ease of use, and just plain fun when it comes to making

First cuts. Begin cutting a molding by guiding the plane against a straightedge, such as when using this round plane, which cuts a hollow. Only the deepest part of the iron cuts at this point.

Planing by hand. Follow your previous cuts by hand. When the molding reaches full depth, the plane stops taking shavings.

grooves, fillets, roundovers, and a host of moldings. And unlike the concentric cut of router bits, the linear motion of a molding plane allows the cutters to be shaped in elliptical curves instead of arcs of a circle, giving your moldings added vibrancy. Although only a handful of companies are making wooden molding planes today (see Modern-Day Planemakers, page 176), you can still pick up all sorts of serviceable molding planes at flea markets, tool auctions, and old-tool dealers. Each style of molding plane is distinguished by the shape of its sole, which is a reverse image of the molding or pattern it cuts. (See top right photo, opposite page.)

If you're just starting out, it's best to choose a simple molding plane over one with a complex cutter and heavily shaped sole. Bead cutters or hollows and rounds are a good choice for the beginner, and they're relatively easy to find. Once you've mastered the setup and feel of the simpler planes, you can move on to more elaborate profiles such as ogees, ovolos, coves, thumbnails, and the heavily contoured cornice or crown-molding planes. When shopping for an old plane, check that the stock is sound. Reject bodies that have severe checks, dry rot, or extensive bug damage. Always sight down the plane from toe to heel: If the stock is warped, the plane won't track properly and will be impossible to use. Check that the iron is in good shape, with a profile that matches the sole precisely, and with no heavy pitting or rust near the cutting edge.

The easiest types of molding planes to master are hollows and rounds. The hollow plane, with its concave sole, cuts a rounded shape. The round plane has a convex sole and cuts a hollow in the workpiece. Paired hollows and rounds should have matching radii. Using these planes is straightforward. You'll have the best luck if you start by practicing on a piece of pine or other mild and straight-grained wood. While some molding planes have fences that ride against the edge of the work, you'll need to begin the cut with a hollow or round plane by guiding the plane against a straightedge. (See top photo, left.) Make each pass with a firm, steady stroke, taking a full shaving. If the plane is hard to push, try retracting the iron for a lighter cut.

Once you've made a few passes and deepened the cut about ¼ inch, you can remove the guide fence and let the plane follow the hollow. Try rolling the plane to one side or the other as necessary to widen the hollow to the desired profile. When the cutter reaches full depth, the plane will stop cutting. (See middle photo, left.) For a more elaborate profile, work the molding further by using a combination of different molding planes, as well as a rabbet plane for smoothing any flat areas, as shown in the photo, below.

Add rounds and flats. A hollow plane cuts the round profile. Clean up flats with a rabbet plane.

Fig. 7: Relief Angles on a Molding Iron

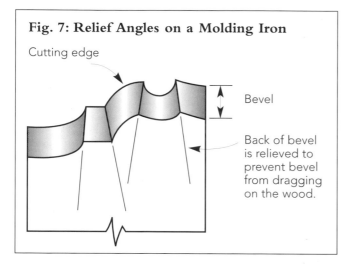

Cutting edge

Bevel

Back of bevel is relieved to prevent bevel from dragging on the wood.

such as when trying to mate two curves exactly or wherever you need a consistent curve. The trick for using a compass is to set the iron for a very fine cut, and to creep up on the final curve by adjusting the sole to a tighter radius. On the final cuts, adjust the sole to match the finished radius, keeping the cut light. (See top photo, opposite page.)

One final shaping plane I find useful in the shop is a **chamfer plane**. Cutting chamfers on your furniture will soften hard edges, making your work more comfortable to touch and producing longer-lasting edges that wear well and won't chip. While a block plane or

Sharpening irons for wooden molding planes can be complicated, but there are a few tricks that will help you achieve success. The real key is to follow the existing profile. Any small alterations in the shape of the cutting edge will cause misalignment with the shaped sole, and the plane won't cut. Be sure to follow the relief angles on the iron's bevel or the plane will stop cutting as it rubs the back of the bevel during deep cuts. (See fig. 7.)

Good tools for sharpening include small round and triangular files, or dowels and custom-shaped pieces of wood wrapped in fine sandpaper, which are useful for rough shaping of the edge. Once you've abraded the overall shape, follow up by honing the profiles with medium- and fine-grit slipstones. (See middle photo, right.)

For smoothing arcs of a circle, a **compass plane** can afford more control than a spokeshave. You can find old wooden or metal compass planes, or buy a brand-new metal version much like the ones made over 100 years ago. The metal variety has a flexible metal sole. A large screw allows you to change the curvature of the sole to an exact convex or concave shape for cutting outside or inside curves. (See photo, right.)

Compass planes are notoriously difficult to work with, and for good reason. Their tendency is to stop and start abruptly, and jam with shavings. But with patience you can get good results. A compass plane works best when you're shaping a true arc of a circle,

Honing a profile. Use slipstones to hone the bevel of a molding iron, moving the stone over the tool instead of the other way around.

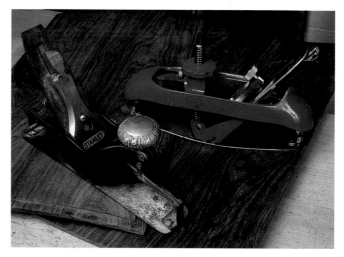

Curved soles. You can shape both convex and concave curves with a compass plane by flexing the sole via a large screw. Shown are an antique Stanley No. 113 (left) and a new Record No. 20 (right).

True arc. A compass plane works well for fairing the outside of a curved tabletop. You'll get good results if you take a light cut and if the curve is a true arc of a circle.

a router bit can cut a chamfer quite efficiently, I find a chamfer plane very useful when I need a consistent bevel, or for smoothing a machined chamfer to remove tool marks. Chamfer planes are distinguished by their soles, which are shaped in a deep right-angled V. This V-shaped sole guides the plane along a square edge, and you adjust the iron or the body of the plane, depending on the model, to cut wide or narrow chamfers. (See photo, left.)

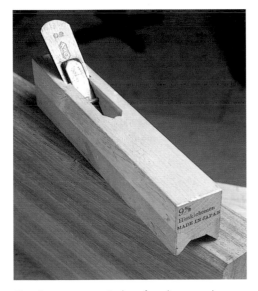

Cutting corners. A chamfer plane, such as this Japanese version, is guided by its V-shaped sole along the square edge of a workpiece.

Older metal chamfer planes can be found at old-tool dealers, as well as antique wood-bodied planes. The most common new variety of chamfer plane is made in Japan; you can choose between planes with adjustable-width soles (for cutting wide or narrow chamfers) or dedicated chamfer planes designed to produce specific sizes of chamfers. One of the best uses for a chamfer plane is when cleaning up sawn or routed chamfers. Rather than sanding by hand, which can produce uneven results, a quick swipe or two with the iron set for a fine cut will smooth a chamfered surface while keeping the shape crisp and true. (See photo, right.) By planing to full depth, the same plane can be used to add a distinctive detail of small fillets, or flats, along the edges of a chamfer, as shown in the photo, below.

Quick clean-up. Chamfer planes work well for smoothing previously cut chamfers. Set the blade for a light cut, and take thin shavings to produce a polished and finished surface.

Chamfer and fillet. Cutting to full depth with this chamfer plane leaves small flats for a decorative detail.

Hand Saws

One of the oldest hand tools used by humans, hand saws offer a delightful balance between quick, rough work and ultra-precise cuts. With the right collection of saws, you can tackle everything from sawing rough stock to size and cutting large panels into bite-size chunks, to crafting precision joints, such as tenons and dovetails. No other tool can claim such a wide range of versatility.

Hand saws can be divided into four groups: panel saws, backsaws, frame saws, and specialty saws, including flush-cutting saws, veneer saws, keyhole saws, and miter saws. Once you become familiar with these tools, you can begin to build up a decent saw collection that will help you broaden and refine your woodworking skills.

Panel Saws

Panel saws are probably the oldest types of saws, and fall neatly into two categories: rip and crosscut. Although they don't get a lot of use in my shop (an electric circular saw is often my preferred tool), these saws are handy when electricity is scarce, such as on a jobsite, or when you need to cut material that's deeper or thicker than a power saw can handle.

Collectors of antique tools know that there are still many old saws available, and some saw lovers have amassed extensive collections. Part of the appeal of panel saws, as well as other hand saws, is their inherent beauty and stone-simple design. A bit of wood for a handle, and a length of thin yet pliable and tough steel combine to make one of the simplest tools in woodworking.

With its blade joined at one end to a wooden enclosed grip, a panel saw can make very deep or wide cuts since there's no framework or back to obstruct the blade. This feature makes panels saws a good choice for dividing large stock into smaller portions, or for splitting boards in half. Typical panel saws measure about 30 inches long. Shorter saws, usually found

in the crosscut style, are useful for getting into tight spots and are a better choice for making precise cuts, such as when cutting a board to final length.

A **ripsaw** is distinguished by its tooth pattern, which is designed for ripping or cutting with the grain. (See fig. 1.) Chisel-like teeth allow a ripsaw to plow through wood fibers, and large and deep gullets between teeth provide clearance for dust and chips, which are generated in bountiful quantities when ripping wood. (See top photo, opposite page.)

A **crosscut saw** has more teeth per inch than a ripsaw, with a tooth pattern that more closely resembles the cutting action of a knife, cleanly slicing wood

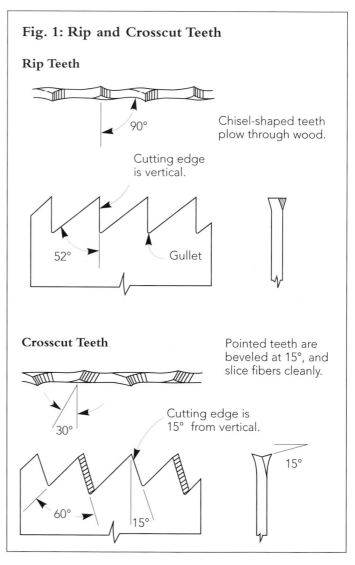

Fig. 1: Rip and Crosscut Teeth

Rip Teeth

90°

Cutting edge is vertical.

52°

Gullet

Chisel-shaped teeth plow through wood.

Crosscut Teeth

30°

60°

15°

Cutting edge is 15° from vertical.

15°

Pointed teeth are beveled at 15°, and slice fibers cleanly.

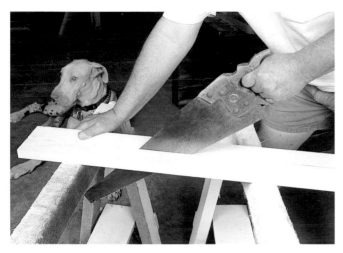

Big rip. A rip saw isn't hampered by a back or spine, allowing you to quickly rip through stock of practically any length.

fibers without tearing them. (See fig. 1.) As its name implies, it's designed for crosscutting material across the grain. Occasionally I reach for my bigger crosscut saws for breaking down panels and other large work to rough size. But more often I find a shorter saw much handier for more precise cuts; for example, cutting rough boards to length, making cutouts such as notches, and other short cuts. (See photo, below.)

The art of sawing is deceptively simple and can be applied to any type of saw. There are a few key techniques to keep in mind for accurate cuts. First, always mark your work with a layout line, then place the saw on the line, using your thumb or forefinger as a guide. To start the cut, pull the saw back, or against the direction of the cut. Use very light pressure forward to establish the kerf. (See photo, right.) Once the teeth have entered the wood and are surrounded by a kerf, you can remove your thumb. At this point, concentrate on sawing straight and square to the work (or at the correct angle, if you're making an angled cut, such as a dovetail), and continue using light pressure. Look at the handle and blade to make sure they're in line with the kerf. When about 1 inch of the blade is in the kerf, increase the sawing pressure and move the full length of the blade through the work. If you started the cut correctly, the saw will practically guide itself through the cut. (See photo, below.)

It's all in the thumb. Starting a cut accurately is much easier if you pull backwards and ease into the cut, using your index finger or thumb on the side of the blade as a guide.

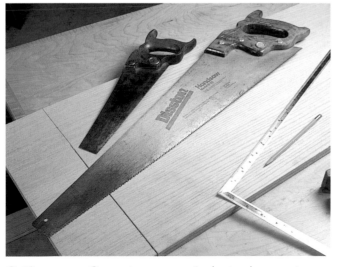

Cutting across. Crosscut saws come in short or long versions, and are handy for big or small crosscuts.

Keep it straight. Once the saw is in the kerf, increase the sawing pressure and guide the blade in line with the cut. As you saw deeper, the kerf helps to guide the blade.

Japanese Saws

Like the pull planes made primarily in Japan (see Wood Planes, page 166), all Japanese saws cut on the pull stroke. This pulling action allows the maker to fashion blades from much thinner stock, since the blade is always in tension during the cut. I favor Japanese saws for their thin blades and specially sharpened teeth that slice through wood fibers like butter. (See fig. 2 and photo, below.)

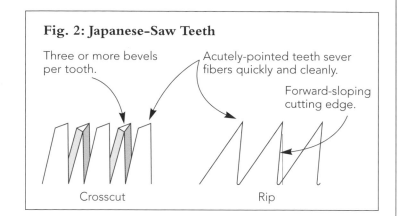

Fig. 2: Japanese-Saw Teeth

Three or more bevels per tooth.

Acutely-pointed teeth sever fibers quickly and cleanly.

Forward-sloping cutting edge.

Crosscut   Rip

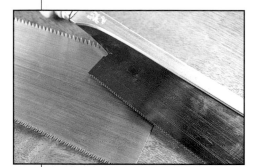

Razor-sharp teeth. The pointed teeth on Japanese saws are faceted with multiple acute bevels, allowing them to cut very fast through the toughest of woods.

Japanese saws cut incredibly fast and produce a very thin kerf, which allows you to cut to a marked line more easily. (See left photo, below.) A pull saw does, however, take some practice to use correctly. Cuts must be swift and deliberate, yet light and without much pressure. You should concentrate on keeping the handle straight, with the blade and the entire saw aligned with the kerf. Mistreating a Japanese saw by overpowering the cut, or failing to follow these simple guidelines risks chipped teeth or a severely kinked blade, which destroys the accuracy of this tool. (See center photo, below.)

Like any saw, a Japanese saw won't cut well when the teeth are dull. The good news is the steel is so hard in these saws that it takes a long time before the teeth need attention. But I rarely attempt to sharpen a Japanese saw. The process involves special **feather files**, which are quite slim in cross section in order to fit the deep gullets and narrow teeth on this style of saw. (See right photo, below.) You use the same sharpening process as you would an ordinary saw, filing across the existing bevels (see Sharpening Hand Saws, page 194), except there are more bevels to deal with, and you must be extremely careful not to break the delicate, brittle teeth as you file. I usually buy another saw, or I start with a Japanese saw that has a replaceable blade (see Japanese Blade-Change, page 196), and install a new blade when the old one goes south.

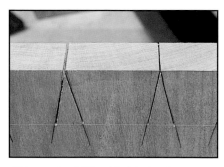

Thinner kerf. The thin blade of a Japanese saw produces a very fine kerf, making it easier to cut to a marked line (right). By comparison, the kerf left by a Western saw is wider (left).

Bad teeth. A sorely mistreated Japanese saw often shows missing teeth, excessive rust, and a kinked blade.

Special files. Small and large feather files are necessary for accurately sharpening the fine teeth on Japanese saws.

It's vital to keep your saws sharp. A sharp saw is much easier to control, and cuts more quickly and efficiently. You can send your saws out to a sharpening service, but sharpening them yourself is not particularly difficult and requires only simple tools. (See Sharpening Hand Saws, next page.)

My favorite panel saw is a Japanese **ryoba saw**,

which sports a combination of rip and crosscut teeth on opposite edges. With this one saw, you can make deep rip cuts or wide crosscuts. Like any Japanese saw, a ryoba cuts on the pull stroke. (See Japanese Saws, opposite page.) The long bamboo-wrapped handle is comfortable to hold and permits you to make very powerful cuts in deep or wide stock. (See photo, left.)

Two saws in one. A Japanese ryoba has two teeth patterns, one side for ripping and one for crosscutting.

Backsaws

Backsaws are my most-used saws in the shop. This is the style of saw I reach for when I need to make extremely precise cuts to a line, such as the cheek or shoulder of a tenon, or the sloping angle of a dove-tail. Handles and grips can be enclosed or open, with the former more suited to saws that make more powerful cuts like rip cuts. Distinguished by its back, or spine, which is made from a heavy strip of brass or steel folded over the top edge of the blade, a backsaw will make very straight cuts because the rigid spine keeps the relatively thin blade from buckling in the cut.

A **tenon saw** will make short but accurate work of cutting tenon cheeks. Since cheek cuts are primarily rip cuts, a good tenon saw should be sharpened in the rip style and have a wide, somewhat thick blade with a massive spine. Tenon saws have a relatively large amount of set, or the degree to which alternating teeth are bent in opposite directions. The set keeps the blade from binding during cutting, and a

(continued page 196)

Jointing the teeth. The first step to sharpening a saw is to level the tips of the teeth with a mill file.

Sharpening a hand saw is a simple job and adds to your skills in the shop. All Western-style saws can be sharpened with a few simple tools. Japanese saws take more skill, and require special files to tackle the job (see page 192).

The first step in sharpening is to joint the saw so all the teeth are level. Use a 10-inch mill file for the job, and clamp the saw between a pair of straight boards to help guide the file. Hold the file square to the blade, and file only until all the tips of the teeth are level, as shown in the photo, above. After jointing, use a **saw set** to set the teeth so they have a consistent degree of bend, with every other tooth bent in the same direction. A saw set is a pliers-like device that you adjust to the amount of set needed for a particular saw. (See middle photo, right.) Start at the toe of the blade, working every other tooth. When you reach the heel, turn the blade around and set the alternate teeth. A general rule of thumb is to set the teeth a maximum of one-third the thickness of the blade, or slightly less for ripsaws. Keep in mind that the finer the set, the finer the cut. But too fine a set will make the saw bind in the cut. Conversely, too coarse a set and the saw will wobble in the kerf and leave a rougher finish. Experimenting with the amount of set for a particular saw pays off in the long run.

Once you've set the teeth, you're ready to file them sharp. First, you need to clamp the blade securely. Small saws can be clamped between straight boards. Larger panel saws are best held in a **saw vise**, which grips the blade firmly very near the teeth. You can buy modern saw vises, or hunt flea markets and tool dealers for older, cast iron versions. (See bottom photo.)

Saw files are key to sharpening saws. These small triangular files come in many sizes and taper along their length. You'll need to match the right size of file to the amount of points-per-inch (the tips of the teeth) of your saw, as shown in the chart, opposite page.

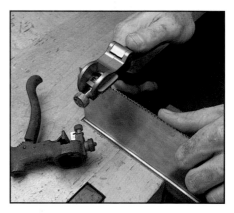

Producing the set. Use a saw set to bend alternate teeth in a uniform manner.

Blade holders. New and antique saw vises will securely grasp a saw blade close to the teeth, preventing the blade from chattering as you file the teeth.

Filing a rip-style saw is straightforward: Simply file straight across the teeth, holding the file at 90 degrees to the blade and oriented so you file a vertical cutting edge and a flat, chisel-shaped top edge (see fig. 1, page 190). Use long, deliberate strokes until all the teeth look sharp. (See photo, below.)

Crosscut saws require a more deft approach. You'll need to tackle the job in two steps. Begin at the blade's toe and file every other tooth, starting with the first tooth that is set away from you. You'll need to angle the file to follow the existing tooth pattern, which usually involves tilting the file 15 degrees from horizontal and angled 30 degrees so the handle points back toward the heel of the saw. Orient two adjacent faces of the file so they contact the leading edge of one tooth and the back of the adjacent tooth. (See bottom left photo.) Use the same number of strokes per

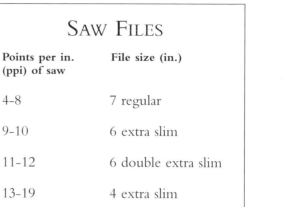

SAW FILES

Points per in. (ppi) of saw	File size (in.)
4–8	7 regular
9–10	6 extra slim
11–12	6 double extra slim
13–19	4 extra slim
20–22	4 double extra slim

tooth and carefully file the cutting edge just shy of a sharp point.

Now turn the saw around in the vise, go back to the toe, and repeat the same process of filing on the alternate teeth. On this second step, bring all the teeth up to a sharp point.

Before putting your newly sharpened rip or cross cut saw to use, it's always best to take a test cut. Chances are you'll notice a somewhat rough surface on the cut faces, or the saw won't track dead straight. If you see scarring on the wood, or if the saw is difficult to track, the last step is to pass a mill file lightly over both sides of the teeth to make them perfectly uniform and remove any burrs on their edges. (See photo, below.)

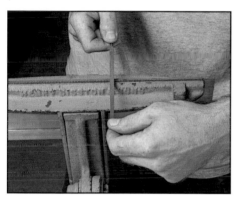

Rip filing. Use a saw file to sharpen a ripsaw, holding the file square to the blade and filing straight across the teeth.

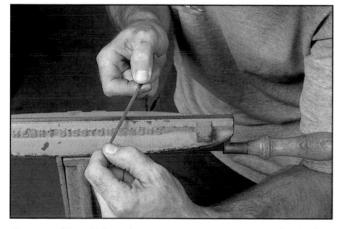

Crosscut filing. When sharpening a crosscut saw, angle the file down 15° and back 30°, making sure the two faces of the file make contact with the cutting tooth and with the tooth in front.

Finish filing. Pass an unhandled mill file lightly over the sharpened teeth to remove any wayward set.

195

Swift dovetails. A Japanese dozuki, or backsaw, cuts on the pull stroke and leaves a very fine kerf, making it a good choice for dovetails and other precision cuts. To steer the cut, grasp the handle near the blade and keep the long handle in line with the kerf.

heavier set is needed for ripping. (See photo, left.) Tenon saws are typically 10 to 14 inches long, with up to 20 teeth per inch (tpi). Generally, the more teeth per inch, the finer the cut.

With as much as 26 tpi and a fine set, a **dovetail saw** will make much finer cuts than a tenon saw. The tooth pattern on dovetail saws is designed for crosscuts. With such a fine cut, dovetail saws are the best choice for cutting dovetails, crosscutting shoulders, or anytime you need an ultra-precise but relatively shallow cut. The blade on a dovetail saw is quite narrow and about 8 inches long. Handles can be fashioned straight behind the blade or in a pistol-grip style for more powerful cutting. (See photo, below.)

The **dozuki saw** is a Japanese backsaw with very fine teeth in the crosscut style. Like all Japanese saws, it cuts on the pull stroke. (See Japanese Saws, page 192.) Because of this pulling action, the blade on a Japanese

Powerful rip. A tenon saw, with its stiff spine, wide blade, and heavy set, will power its way through heavy rip cuts such as cutting the cheeks on tenons.

saw (and its kerf) can be much thinner than Western saws, allowing it to cut more swiftly and with less force through the hardest of woods. I favor the long, straight handle on this type of saw, but grasping the tool correctly takes practice. Swift cuts can be made by holding the handle near its end. For slower, more controllable cuts, keep your hand close to the blade for accuracy, and let the handle extend under your forearm. (See photo, above.)

JAPANESE BLADE-CHANGE

While Japanese saws can be a challenge to sharpen and require special files for the job (see page 192), many dozuki saws and other Japanese saws come with replaceable blades. You can avoid the sharpening dilemma if you keep spare blades on hand, including blades in a range from fine to coarse (still plenty fine) teeth.

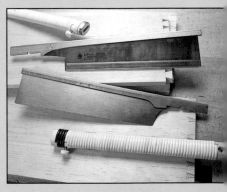

Quick change. You can buy dozuki and other Japanese saws with replaceable blades, letting you discard old blades and install new ones for less than the price of a new saw.

Small and precise. Dovetail saws have very fine teeth for very fine cuts, such as when cutting dovetails or small shoulders. Open handles vary between turned varieties and pistol-grip styles.

metal frame. With such a small blade and fine teeth, it's easy to make very accurate, tight curving cuts, such as coping small or large moldings to radii as minute as ¼ inch or less. The depth of cut on a coping saw is determined by the distance between the frame and the blade, typically from 5 inches up to about 8 inches. Saws with larger frames let you take deep cuts in thick stock. (See bottom photo, left.)

One of the great attributes of coping saws, and practically all other frame saws, is that you can easily remove and re-fit the blades. On coping saws, the blades are usually pinned at the ends. The pins slip over notches in the frame, making blade changing a snap. A removable blade is useful for *inside cuts,* letting you remove the blade and pass it through a previously drilled hole, which allows you to cut enclosed curves. (See photo, below.)

Frame Saws

Frame saws all have blades held rigid in frames of metal or wood, and generally are used for straight cuts as well as curves. The exception is the metal-cutting hacksaw, which is designed for straight cuts in a variety of metals.

There are two very small frame saws that are capable of quite delicate cuts. The first, a **coping saw**, has multiple teeth on a short, narrow blade (usually about 7 inches long) held between a stiff but lightweight

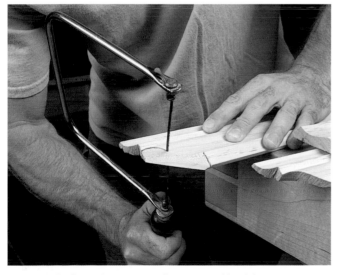

Cope with this. A coping saw lets you tackle delicate curves and coped cuts in moldings and trim. A stiff frame keeps the narrow blade rigid during sawing.

A smaller-bladed nephew to the coping saw is a **fret saw**, sometimes mistakenly called a jeweler's saw. The fret saw has a frame size that's the same or larger than a coping saw but accepts a much narrower blade. With its tiny but exceptionally smooth-cutting blade, this saw is designed to cut only thin work, such as veneer or other delicate

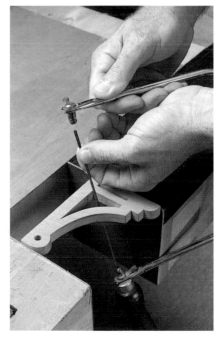

Inside and out. The easily removable pin-style blade on a coping saw lets you position the saw inside a workpiece for pierced cuts.

Small and delicate. Fret saws can have deep or shallow frames, and they accept tiny blades for delicate cuts in fragile materials such as veneer.

natural materials. Fret saws are available with deep throats for making cuts far into a workpiece, such as into the center of a wide piece of veneer. (See photo, above.)

Since much of the work done with a fret saw involves inside cuts, blade changing should be positive and swift. The easiest type of blade-holding mechanism involves separate blocks that hold the blade itself. Once you've locked the blade to the holders, the blocks slip over the frame and a tensioning device on the frame pulls the blade taut. (See photo, below.)

To use a fret saw successfully, you can buy or make a **bird's mouth vise,** which really isn't a vise at all but a tiny workbench that supports the work. If you have a hard time locating a bird's mouth vise at your regular woodworking suppliers, check a jewelry

Easy blade change. Separate blade holders let you install the blade between metal blocks. The blocks slip over the frame and a tensioning nut pulls the blade taut.

supplier, since jewelers use this vise when sawing metals and other precious materials. The device works by supporting the cut when you're sawing very thin or delicate stock. A V-shaped opening in the vise allows you to support the work as closely as possible to the blade, reducing the chance for tearout or breakage. (See photo, right.)

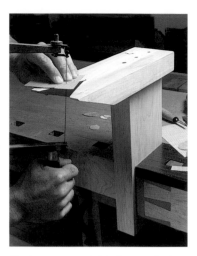

Beak support. A bird's mouth vise supports delicate materials when sawing with a fret saw. You can make one in a matter of minutes from scrap hardwood.

Erroneously looked upon by many woodworkers as a relic of the past, the traditional **bowsaw** is a tool that has saved me time and again in my modern woodshop when no other saw could handle a certain job. (See photo, below.) Originally designed as a timbering tool, this incredibly powerful saw can dance between heavy-duty rough cuts, such as ripping large slabs into planks or resawing boards into thinner sections, and fine joinery work, such as cutting dovetails. A bowsaw is especially useful for large-scale joinery work in which

Master of straights and curves. Bowsaws have large wooden frames and can be fitted with wide or narrow blades. Smaller blades are best for cutting curves; wide blades excel at joinery work.

you need to cut large tenons or massive dovetails, since it cuts through thick work with ease while maintaining accuracy. Yet the same saw can make short work of smaller cuts with the same precision, such as a standard set of dovetails. As a frame saw, the bowsaw's curve-cutting facility is unsurpassed when fitted with a narrow blade. Saws with wide blades are great for cutting large joints, since a wider blade tracks better in the cut.

Using a bowsaw is simple. All cutting is done on the push stroke, with the teeth facing away from you. Instead of aligning the blade vertically with the arms of the frame, angle it 10 to 30 degrees. This allows the stretcher to clear the work and gives you a clear view of the cutline. Although you can clamp the work in your bench vise for sawing, it's often more convenient to saw on a low pair of sawhorses, especially when making heavy rip cuts. In this position, you can use your hand as well as a foot to clamp the work. (See photo, below.)

Making delicate joinery cuts, such as sawing dove-

Precision cuts for joints. Sawing dovetails and other precise joints is easy if you align the blade with the waste side of the layout line.

tails, involves aligning the blade to your layout lines and using your thumb or index finger as a guide to start the cut. For accurate cuts, keep the blade on the waste side of the line, and sight down the length of the blade as you saw. (See top photo, right.)

Heavy cuts down low. You can achieve more powerful strokes and better control by sawing on a low pair of saw-horses, using your hand as well as your leg as a clamp.

Strictly for cutting metals such as steel, aluminum, and brass, a **hacksaw** is an important tool in the wood-shop. Fitted with a metal-cutting blade, a hacksaw will cut all sorts of metal parts, such as bolts, rods, heavy sheet stock, and other common shop hardware. Because of the force involved when sawing metal, it's always wise to clamp the work in a metal vise. (See photo, below.) The secret in getting a hacksaw to cut well is to tension the blade as tightly as possible, and to keep it well-lubricated. Any wobble or flex in the blade results in swerving cuts. Look for a hacksaw frame that has a cam-operated lever for setting the blade tension; this arrangement is far superior to the standard wing-nut and bolt mechanism for tightening the blade in the frame. To keep the teeth sharp and make sawing easier, wipe a light oil directly on the blade to reduce friction and heat.

Cutting metal. A hacksaw fitted with a metal-cutting blade makes short work of trimming bolts and other hardware to size.

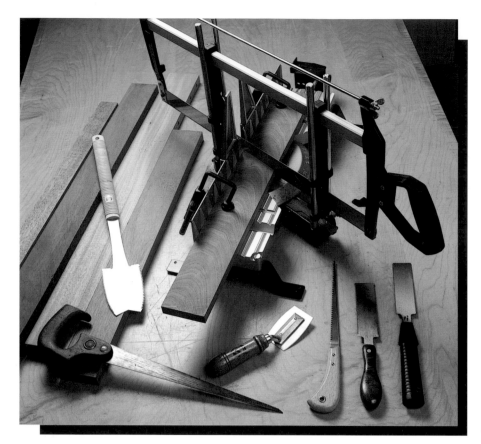

A **flush-cutting saw** has the unique ability to cut right to the surface of your work without scarring it. This is a great aid when you need to trim parts, such as protruding dowels, flush to your work. (See photos, below.) These types of saws have teeth set on one side only. The unset side is placed down on the work so you won't scratch the workpiece as you saw.

When making a flush cut, bend the blade so the cutting area is pressed flat to the work. To keep the thin blade in tension, a flush-cut saw has teeth that cut on the pull stroke, allowing you to make precise cuts without kinking the blade. (See right photo, below.)

Specialty Saws

There are a few specialty saws that make life easier in the shop, and they're worth seeking out. These include a flush-cutting saw, a veneer saw, a piercing saw, a key-hole saw, and a hand miter box.

If you do any veneer work, you'll want to get your hands on a **veneer saw**. While a sharp knife does a fine job for many types of veneer cuts, only a veneer saw can make dead-straight crosscuts and, more importantly, perfectly straight rip cuts without tear-

Flush trimmers. Flush-cutting saws have thin, flexible blades with the teeth set on one side only so they won't mark your work. Double-edged saws are handier for sawing either side of a tight spot.

Bend and saw. By bending the flexible blade to the work, you can trim parts precisely flush with the surrounding surface. Cutting on the pull stroke prevents kinking the thin blade.

Fine saw. A veneer saw has a curved blade and a flat back for accurate straight cuts in veneer and other delicate materials.

Guided cut. Use a straightedge to guide the saw, taking multiple light cuts until you've sawn through the veneer.

ing out delicate wood fibers or wandering along grain lines. Since the edge of the saw is curved, only a few teeth are engaged in the work at one time to produce very fine cuts. (See photo, above.)

Cutting with a veneer saw involves using a guide fence, which can be a simple piece of wood that's been milled dead straight. Place the veneer on a piece of flat scrap (so you don't saw into your workbench) and clamp the fence to the work. Then hold the saw square to the edge of the fence to saw. Instead of sawing in one fell pass, take several light, scoring cuts until you've sawn through the sheet. (See top photo, right.)

The sharpening technique for a veneer saw is similar to most hand saws (see Sharpening Hand Saws, page 194), and you can use triangular saw files to reshape the teeth when necessary. But to bring the teeth to a point, use a fine file on the bevel side of the blade. First place the blade on the edge of a flat surface and angle the file until it makes full contact with the bevel. Then file in a series of sweeping movements, following the blade's curvature. (See middle photo, right.)

Similar in some ways to a veneer saw is a **piercing saw**, which is available as a Japanese saw known as a *noko giri*. With its curved-edge blade, a noko giri can be used as a veneer saw for trimming work against a straightedge. And its slim profile makes it a good choice for working in restricted areas without dam-

aging adjacent surfaces. But the real purpose of a piercing saw is to start cuts in the middle of work, such as when making mortises or cutouts in panels. (See photo, below.)

Sharpening on a curve. Use a fine file on the bevel side of a veneer saw to sharpen the teeth, sweeping the file around the blade's curved edge.

In the middle. A noko giri, or Japanese piercing saw, lets you start cuts in the middle of work.

MAKING TOOL HANDLES

Custom grips. All sorts of hand tools—and types of wood—are fair game when it comes to making your own tool handles and knobs. Some of the author's favorites are shown here.

Replacing damaged or missing wooden handles with new shop-made grips is one way to keep your woodworking tools in top shape. New handles are suspect, too, since today's tools are more likely to come with blister-inducing handles made from slippery plastic or less expensive beech or birch (stained to imitate rosewood, walnut, or cherry), and left with hard edges and sharp corners. Replacing a factory handle with a custom grip made from the wood of your choice will result in a tool that fits your hand like a glove, looks great, and improves your woodworking. Practically any tool is fair game, from axes, chisels, knives, and other carving tools to files, saws, and planes.

Round handles are the easiest to make and can be quickly turned on the lathe. For socket-type chisels, taper one end of the handle and test-fit the blank until it seats firmly into the tool's socket. Handles for tanged chisels and other tang-type tools need to be drilled to fit the tang after turning, and then fitted with a metal ferrule to keep the stock from splitting. A few

woodworking suppliers sell brass or mild-steel ferrules, or you can scavenge them from old tools. I usually make my own ferrules from brass tubing or copper plumbing pipe. To avoid distorting the ferrules, cut them to length with a **pipe cutter**, available from a plumbing supplier. (See photo, above.)

Making ferrules. You can make your own ferrule from brass tubing or copper pipe. Don't use a hacksaw for cutting the pipe or it will distort. Instead, use a pipe or tube cutter to make a clean cut around the pipe.

For saw and plane handles, I usually find the pattern I like from a favorite handle or from an old tool catalog, then trace the profile onto a blank. Saw the rough profile on the band saw, then refine it with roundover bits in the router table, planes, a carving chisel or knife, rasps, files, and some hand sanding. The idea is to refine the shape, easing over any sharp edges, until the handle pleases your eye and hand. (See photo, left.)

Finishing touches. A few deft cuts with a block plane, a rasp, some sandpaper, and a sharp knife can create an eye-pleasing saw handle that fits your hands like well-worn gloves.

Recess the tang. For flat-tanged tools such as this flush-cutting blade, chisel a shallow recess in one half of a sawn-apart blank to the thickness of the tang.

Shaped to your hands. Use rasps, files, and sandpaper to shape the handle until it feels comfortable in your hands.

Put it all together. Assemble the blanks and the blade using epoxy and clamps. Marks on the edges help you match the grain.

Some tools require a little finesse when it comes to attaching the handle. While many saws can be inserted into a kerf cut into the handle and secured with bolts and nuts, flat-tanged blades often require two blanks glued on each side of the tang. Start with a solid blank ripped in half. Trace the outline of the tang on the inside face of one blank, then rout or chisel a shallow recess. (See top photo, left.)

Next, use epoxy to glue the blanks together with the blade between them. (See photo, above.) Once the epoxy has cured (it's best to leave it overnight), you can shape the blank however you wish. I make a few initial cuts with a chisel, then shape and contour the handle using a combination of rasps, files, and sandpaper until the handle feels good in my hands. (See photo, above.)

Be sure to give your new handle a few coats of shellac, oil, or lacquer. Regular maintenance with paste wax will keep your grips glowing through the years, and your hands will appreciate the feel of a custom-made handle.

From rough to fine. The finished walnut handle on this flush-trim saw has an inlaid button of contrasting woods to mark the correct side for flush-sawing work.

Keyed cuts. Keyhole saws will cut small curves, and they can reach inside a cutout to shape keyholes and other inside cuts. Western-style keyhole saws cut on the push stroke (bottom); Japanese versions have more flexible blades and cut on the pull stroke (top).

For delicate curved cuts and inside cuts, a **keyhole saw** does the job with aplomb. The long, pointed blade can be used in very tight spots, and by first drilling a hole through the workpiece, you can make inside cuts like the finely shaped hole for a key in a drawer front or door. Western-style keyhole saws have stiffer blades and cut on the push stroke. The Japanese version, with its thin, flexible blade, has very sharp teeth and cuts on the pull stroke. (See photo, above.)

For those of us without a power miter saw, a hand **miter box** is an affordable alternative for cutting miters of practically any angle. Miter boxes come with fine-toothed saws that are held between posts, and an L-shaped "box" against which the work is positioned. You adjust the blade to the angle you want to cut, then clamp or hold the workpiece

against the fence for sawing. Older antique miter boxes have backsaw-type saws, with stiff brass or steel spines to help keep the blade rigid. Newer miter boxes rely on a frame-type saw with tensioning rods that do a great job of keeping the blade straight and true. Better-quality miter boxes also come equipped with hold-down clamps and extension tables for handling large work, such as long moldings. (See photo, below.) Look for sturdy bases that can be clamped or bolted in place for more solid sawing. Really fancy boxes have pivoting heads that angle the frame of the blade, allowing for compound-angled cuts, such as when fitting moldings to angled walls or cabinets.

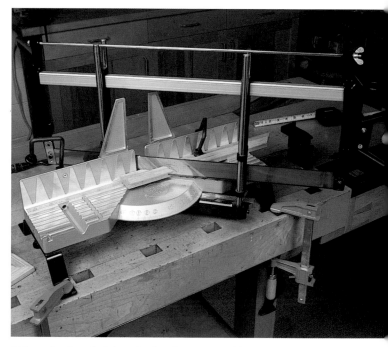

Miters by hand. A hand miter box can tackle miter cuts up to 45° or more, plus make square cuts at 90°. Look for hold-downs and extension devices for supporting long work.

METRIC CONVERSION TABLE

Inches	Centimeters
1/8	3 mm
1/4	6 mm
3/8	9 mm
1/2	1.3
5/8	1.6
3/4	1.9
7/8	2.2
1	2.5
1 1/4	3.1
1 1/2	3.8
1 3/4	4.4
2	5
2 1/2	6.25
3	7.5
3 1/2	8.8
4	10
4 1/2	11.3
5	12.5
5 1/2	13.8
6	15
7	17.5
8	20
9	22.5
10	25
11	27.5

Inches	Centimeters
12	30
13	32.5
14	35
15	37.5
16	40
17	42.5
18	45
19	47.5
20	50
21	52.5
22	55
23	57.5
24	60
25	62.5
26	65
27	67.5
28	70
29	72.5
30	75
31	77.5
32	80
33	82.5
34	85
35	87.5
36	90

SOURCES

Tools and Suppliers

Woodworking tools and supplies are available at local woodworking stores, hardware stores, and home centers, as well as on the Internet or through mail-order woodworking tool catalogs. For a complete list of woodworking suppliers online, check the craft supply sources at Lark Books (www.larkbooks.com).

Antique Tool Associations

For used or antique tools, contact the following tool associations or visit their Web sites. Most clubs offer memberships for a small fee, which gets you a regular newsletter and notifications of tool meets and swaps.

Early American Industries Association (EAIA)
167 Bakerville Road
South Dartmouth, MA 02748
(Web site: www.eaiainfo.org)

Hand Tool Preservation Society of Australia (HTPAA)
Box 1163
Carlton, Victoria, Australia 3053

Midwest Tools Collectors Association (MWTCA)
Rt. 2, Box 152
Wartrace, TN 37183
(Web site: www.mwtca.org)

Potomac Antique Tools and Industries Association (PATINA)
6802 Nesbitt Place
McLean, VA 22101
(Web site: www.patinatools.org)

The Tool and Trades History Society (TATHS)
60 Swanley Lane
Swanley, Kent, England BRB 7JG

The Tool Group of Canada
7 Tottenham Road
Don Mills, Ontario, Canada L0G 1M0

Woodworking Web Sites

Here are a few of my favorite woodworking Web sites from the thousands of hand tool enthusiasts who keep Web pages on the Internet.

Badger Pond (www.wwforum.com): Articles and forums on woodworking

Patrick's Blood and Gore (www.supertool.com): Straight-shooting information about old tools, especially older Stanley hand planes

The Electronic Neanderthal (www.cs.cmu.edu/afs/cs.cmu.edu/Web/People/alf/en/en.html): Information on hand tools, with extensive links to other hand tool-related pages

The Fine Tool Journal **(www.FineToolJ.com)**: Learn about and buy antique tools, or subscribe to the magazine for more in-depth information about old tools

The Oak Factory (www.theoak.com): Articles on woodworking, tool trades, and an energetic woodworking mailing list

Wood Central (www.woodcentral.com): Lively, informative message boards and woodworking articles